MEXICAN AMERICAN COLONIZATION DURING
THE NINETEENTH CENTURY

This study is a reinterpretation of nineteenth-century Mexican American history that examines Mexico's struggle to secure its northern border with repatriates from the United States in the aftermath of a war resulting in the loss of half its territory. Responding to past interpretations, José Angel Hernández suggests that these resettlement schemes centered on the developments of the frontier region, the modernization of the country with loyal Mexican American settlers, and blocking the tide of migrations to the United States to prevent the depopulation of Mexico's fractured northern border. Through an examination of Mexico's immigration and colonization policies as they developed throughout the nineteenth century, the book focuses primarily on the population of Mexican citizens who were "lost" after the end of the Mexican American War of 1846–1848 until the end of the century.

José Angel Hernández is assistant professor of history at the University of Massachusetts, Amherst. He is currently a faculty Fellow at the Center for Latin American, Caribbean, and Latino Studies. He has received fellowships from the Andrew W. Mellon Foundation, the Fulbright-Hays Dissertation Research Fellowship, and the Center for Mexican American Studies Fellowship at the University of Houston. Professor Hernández has had articles published in *Aztlán: A Journal of Chicano Studies*; *Landscapes of Violence: An Interdisciplinary Journal Devoted to the Study of Violence, Conflict, and Trauma*; and *Mexican Studies/Estudios Mexicanos*.

MEXICAN AMERICAN COLONIZATION DURING THE NINETEENTH CENTURY

A HISTORY OF THE U.S.-MEXICO BORDERLANDS

JOSÉ ANGEL HERNÁNDEZ

University of Massachusetts, Amherst

CAMBRIDGE UNIVERSITY PRESS

CAMBRIDGE UNIVERSITY PRESS
Cambridge, New York, Melbourne, Madrid, Cape Town,
Singapore, São Paulo, Delhi, Mexico City

Cambridge University Press
32 Avenue of the Americas, New York, NY 10013-2473, USA

www.cambridge.org
Information on this title: www.cambridge.org/9781107666245

First published 2012

Printed in the United States of America

A catalog record for this publication is available from the British Library.

Library of Congress Cataloging in Publication data
Hernández, José Angel, 1969–
Mexican American colonization during the nineteenth century : a history of the U.S.-
Mexico Borderlands / José Angel Hernández.
p.   cm.
Includes bibliographical references and index.
ISBN 978-1-107-01239-4 (hardback) – ISBN 978-1-107-66624-5 (pbk.)
1. Mexican-American Border Region – History – 19th century.   2. Mexico, North –
History – 19th century.   3. Mexicans – Mexican-American Border Region –
History – 19th century.   4. Return migration – Mexico – History – 19th
century.   5. Mexico – Emigration and immigration – Government policy – History –
19th century.   I. Title.
F786.H446   2012
972'.1–dc23   2012002707

ISBN 978-1-107-01239-4 Hardback
ISBN 978-1-107-66624-5 Paperback

Dedicado a mis padres,

Martha C. Hernández
&
José G. Hernández

Contents

Figures

ACKNOWLEDGMENTS

Like most historical monographs, this inquiry shares a narrative that has many entrances, interpretations, exits, contradictions, and shortcomings. These acknowledgments are likely to share a similar fate. Given that the book came about as an academic journey of sorts, involving many institutions, individuals, and ideas, I will focus on that particular perspective. To start, a special thanks to my editor, Eric Crahan, and the staff at Cambridge University Press, especially Abigail Zorbaugh and Bhavani Ganesh. In particular, I would like to express my gratitude to the two outside readers for their advice and recommendations. I've made an effort to include all of their great suggestions and critiques, but in the end all oversights and errors are my own.

The ideas and interests that started this particular journey began somewhat at San Antonio College (SAC) and at the University of Texas at San Antonio (UTSA), where I met a stellar group of professors that first introduced me to the field. A number of them also asked interesting questions about the intraethnic phenomena of diasporic communities, which in part informs some of my ongoing academic concerns. Among those professors who shaped my interest are Juan "El Profe" Rodríguez, Félix D. Almaráz, Norma Cruz-González, Roberto Calderon, María García, Yolanda Leyva, Ben Olguín, José Macías, John Igo, Stephen Casanova, Rodolfo Rosales, Frank Pino, Ellen Riojas Clark, Jacinto Quirarte, Andrés Tijerina, and especially Juan Mora-Torres. Indeed, it was my friendship with Juan at UTSA that not only stoked my interest in Mexican history, but also influenced my decision to pursue graduate studies. Nothing I write in these few words can relay the significant role he played in teaching, supporting, and mentoring this kid from the south side of San Antonio.

Other friends and acquaintances at UTSA were equally important in providing friendship, encouragement, and support. Marisol Pérez, Carlos Hernández, Jennifer Mata, Oscar Valdéz, Anita Revilla, Mariano "Mono" Aguilar, Marcos Valdéz, Kevin López, Raquel Favela, John David Naranjo, Saul Levario, Frank Abel Cantú, Lisa D. Anaya, José A. Macías Jr., Chico Mendez, Cecilia Perfecto, Nelly Casas, Raul Eduardo Ruíz, Jerry Portillo, Semilla Mestiza Rivera, Camerino Salazar, Davíd Armendariz, Michelle Alvarado, Michael De León, Brenda Mauricio Peña, Lisa Suárez, Roxanne Guerra, Barbara Peña, Raquel Aguilar, Belinda Ramirez, Regina Cantú, and Selena Tamez are all part of an amazing group of friends whom I met during this time, and I adore their friendship and comradery. Special *abrazos* for Mari, Carlos, Mono, Anita, Brenda, and Jennifer.

When I returned to Texas during the 2003–4 academic year in order to continue my dissertation research, Josephine Méndez-Negrete was kind enough to support me as a research affiliate with the Mexican American Studies Program for the semester. There, I also met Marie "Keta" Miranda and Elizabeth De La Portilla, who were very kind, warm, and welcoming. Rubén Martinez provided office space and other privileges during my tenure as a visiting research scholar with The Culture & Policy Institute during that spring, and I would like to acknowledge his support and that of the institute. Dennis Bixler Márquez was kind enough to host me at the University of Texas at El Paso as a visiting research scholar with the Chicano Studies Program for the 2004–5 academic year.

At the University of Houston, I was fortunate to have received a graduate fellowship with The Center for Mexican American Studies for two years, starting in 1998. This fellowship provided me with the time, space, and liberty to work solely on my graduate studies in Latin American history, but it also forced me to constantly consider the transnational perspective of the borderlands when thinking of my thesis. My thesis adviser, John Mason Hart, suggested the topic of Mexican colonies during the Porfiriato and I was immediately drawn to the multiple possibilities of the topic and to the transnational approach that such a study would entail. Aside from being supportive, John was an excellent teacher and encouraging adviser. Classes with Bob Buzzanco, Susan Kellogg, Thomas O'Brien, and Emilio Zamora rounded out an intense (historiographically speaking) and productive graduate experience, and I also made many friends along the way. Scott

Murray, Irving Levinson, Brian Behnken, Courtney Forsloff Shah, Chris Danielson, Christos Frentzos, David Urbano, Julia Sloan, Roy Vu, Theresa Rae Jach, Ron Milam, Russell Contreras, Scott Parkin, James Carter, and Ellen Fout were cheerful and intelligent friends in many seminars and class discussions. Thank you to Guadalupe San Miguel, Néstor P. Rodríguez, Tatcho Mindiola, Angela Valenzuela, and Lorenzo Cano for their support and help with the thesis. While living in Houston, I also became fast friends with Abhilash Sivaraman, Carlos Romero Malpica, Madanmohan Catti Nandagopal, Trinidad Gonzalez, and Siddharth Poonja. Abhi and Madan: I'm looking forward to a serious game of dominoes or billiards as soon as humanly possible!

At the University of Chicago (UC) I met a cadre of scholars and academics who forever altered the way I thought about the production of history. Friedrich Katz (1927–2010) read through my master's thesis and encouraged me to pursue the topic further, and his inquisitive nature during classes, workshops, and while I served as his research assistant still informs the way in which I ask historical questions. The guidance and mentorship that I received from Claudio Lomnitz is immeasurable. Claudio forced me to think critically about questions of nationalism and Mexican history more broadly. Emilio Kourí arrived a few years later and was an amazing adviser and mentor during my time in Hyde Park, and his support, advice, and guidance are greatly appreciated. Aside from being a provocative thinker, Dipesh Chakrabarty is an excellent teacher. He patiently taught me to think critically through his classes and office hours, and as a member of my dissertation committee. By this time, Juan Mora-Torres was back in Chicago at DePaul University, where he helped get my first real teaching job and then continued to mentor me, only now as part of my dissertation committee.

Friends and *colegas* at UC were central to my survival, and I would like to thank them here: Jaime Pensado and Jennifer Morales Pensado, Mihwa Choi, Marcy Jane Barrientes, Rocío Magaña, Romina Robles Ruvalcaba, Quincy T. Mills, Nilda Barraza, Luis Barrón, Allyson Hobbs, Dwaipayan Sen, Michael Mantak, Jessica Graham, John H. Flores, Sarah Osten, Kittiya M. Lee, Robin Bates, Dora Sánchez Hidalgo, Carlos Bravo Regidor, Muhannad Salhi and Ruma Niyogi Salhi, David Jacobson, Matt Clark, Julia Grace Darling Young, Ana Serna, Paul Liffman, Omar Acha, Beth Cooper, Todd Paul Prudencio Romero,

Benjamin Johnson, Nicole Mottier, Brendan Swagerty, Amanda Hartzmark, Daniel Cohn, Eduardo Moralez, Elise LaRose, Laurencio Sanguino, Jovita R. Baber, Ann Schneider, Antonio Sotomayor, Ariana Hernandez Reguant, John Eason, Mike Czaplicki, Illya Davis, José Luis Razo, Josh Beck, Colby Ristow, Susan Gzesh, Shane Green, Toussaint Lossier, Ev Meade, William Leslie Balan-Gaubert, Paul Ross, Maru Balandran, Patrick Iber, Mikael Wolfe, Steven Platzer, Pushpam Jain, Gregory Malandrucco, and especially Pablo Ben – who was my roommate in Ciudad Juárez, Chicago, and Mexico City. I would especially like to acknowledge the various writing and workshop groups with Julia Young and John H. Flores, and especially those with my dearest friends, Pablo Ben and Jaime Pensado. Jaime and I lived parallel lives of sorts, and I will always cherish the intellectual exchange and friendship that developed during those years in Hyde Park and beyond.

Funding from various agencies and institutions throughout the past decade were also key in the completion of this latest outline, and I would like to acknowledge the support of the Fulbright Hayes Dissertation Fellowship; the Center for Mexican American Studies Fellowship at the University of Houston; various grants from the Department of History at the University of Chicago; Tinker and Mellon Foundation grants from the Center for Latin American Studies at UC; research and travel money from the Center for the Study of Race, Politics and Culture at UC; the University of Chicago Human Rights Program; and the Hispanic Scholarship Fund. Since my arrival at the University of Massachusetts, Amherst, I have also received support for my research from the Department of History; as a Center for Public Policy and Administration workshop Fellow; a Lilly Teaching Fellowship; as Center for Latin American, Caribbean and Latina/o Studies Faculty Fellow; and with the support of a Research Intensive Semester grant at UMass.

A number of librarians and archivists were instrumental in obtaining and sharing information that is well documented in this inquiry, and here I would especially like to mention Fernando Blando Baeza and all of the staff of the Archivo Histórico de Terrenos Nacionales in Mexico City; Felipe Talavera García of the Biblioteca Arturo Tolentino, which also houses the Archivo Municipal of Ciudad Juárez; Juan Sandoval, Samuel Sisneros, Claudia Rivers, and all of the staff of Special Collections at the University of Texas at El Paso; Margo

Gutiérrez and the helpful staff at the Nettie Benson Latin American Collection at the University of Texas at Austin; the wonderful and pleasant staff at the Archivo Histórico Genaro Estrada, Secretaría de Relaciones Exteriores in Mexico City; all of the librarians, friends, and staff of the Regenstein Library at the University of Chicago; the staff at the Archivo Colección Porfirio Díaz at the Universidad Iberoamericana; the helpful folks at the Archivo Histórico Militar Mexicano, Secretaría de la Defensa Nacional in Mexico City; and to all the staff at one of my favorite hangouts in Mexico City, Bibiloteca Miguel Lerdo de Tejada. And a special thank you to the librarians and staff of the W.E.B. Dubois Library at the University of Massachusetts, Amherst, especially my good friend Peter Stern.

Friends and colleagues in Mexico City and throughout the state of Chihuahua helped me with research, with housing, with direction, and, most important, with friendship. Early on I was lucky to have met Beatriz Carrillo González, formerly of the Archivo Histórico de Relaciones Exteriores, who was kind enough to orient me to the many archival holdings of the city. Martha Loyo of the Universidad Nacional Autónoma de México wrote me a letter of support during my year as a Fulbright Fellow. In La Ascensión, Chihuahua, the help, assistance, and comradery of Ramón Ramírez Tafoya were invaluable, and I am very appreciative of our collaboration since we met in 2004. Lilia Esthela Bayardo Rodríguez helped me with transcribing hundreds, if not thousands, of documents during the course of my research. Although limited information was located for my research at the time, I think it is important to thank the directors and their staff at the following local archives in the state of Chihuahua: Municipio de La Ascensión, Municipio de Guadalupe, Municipio de Janos, Municipio de Práxedis Guerrero, and the Archivo Municipal de Ciudad Chihuahua. I would also like to say thank you to Professors Victor Orozco and Jorge Chávez Chávez of the Universidad Autónoma de Ciudad Juárez for their help and assistance during my residence in Ciudad Juárez, Chihuahua.

Friends and colleagues at the University of Massachusetts, Amherst, have also provided feedback, support, encouragement, suggestions, discussions, and criticism, and I would especially like to acknowledge Joel Wolfe, Joye Bowman, John Higginson, Brian W. Ogilvie, Audrey L. Altstadt, Jennifer N. Heuer, Anna Taylor, Jon Olsen, Heather Cox Richardson, Daniel Gordon, Heidi V. Scott, Richard T. Chu, Laura

L. Lovett, Anne Broadbridge, Richard Minear, Larry Owens, David Glassberg, Stephen Platt, Barry Levy, Charles Rearick, Bruce Laurie, Andrew Donson, Brian Bunk, Joyce Avrech Berkman, Christian Appy, Jane M. Rausch, Carlin Barton, Bob Potash, Jennifer Fronc, Rachel Martin, Barbara Krauthamer, Marla Miller, Alice Nash, Sigrid Schmalzer, Mary Christina Wilson, Suzanne Bell, Mary Lashway, and Jean Ball. Friends and colleagues in the greater New England area whom I would like to thank include Mari Castañeda, Davíd Carrasco, Joya Misra, María Soledad Barbón, Mathew L. Oullett, Melissa Madera, Douglas S. Massey, Kym Morrison, Wilson Valentín-Escobar, Nina Siulc, Renato Rosaldo, Flavia Montenegro-Menezes, Brian Baldi, Joselyn Almeida-Beveridge, Amilcar Shabbaz, Diana Coryat, Rick Lopez, Micaela Jamaica Díaz-Sánchez, Isaac Peter Campos Costero, Whitney Battle-Baptiste, Mark Overmyer-Velasquez, Toby Barnes, Angelica Bernal, Patricia Gubitosi, José N. Ornelas, Sonia E. Alvarez, Mario Ontiveros, Gloria Bernabe-Ramos, Mike Funk, Rani Varghese, Ata Moharreri, Jonathan Rosa, Laura Briggs, Luis Marentes, Cruz Caridad Bueno, Harry Franqui Rivera, Patricia Medina Ferrer, Agustín Lao Montes, Joseph Krupczynski, Alberto Ameal Pérez, and especially my dear friend Diana Yoon. A special thank you to my friend Ramón Solórzano for all his help with editing and doing some of the translations in the manuscript.

Last, but surely not least, I would like to acknowledge the incredible support, encouragement, love, kindness, and warmth my family has provided through this and many other life journeys. I'm not sure how much I can say about each of my brothers and sisters, nephews and nieces, cousins or aunts, but they have all shaped and influenced me in many ways. First of all, I would like to say *muchísimas gracias* to my daughter, Jessi Ylaní Hernández, for enduring this long trip with me … I love you *mija*. My sisters, María Guadalupe Hernández Tovar and Lucía Gabriela Hernández, have always shared their homes, advice, love, ideas, and great cooking. *Hermanas*, I love you very much. When in San Antonio, Texas, I love spending time with my nieces and nephews, Zolt Hernández, Luciano Tovar Hernández, Caesar Alexander Mendez Hernández, Susanna Tovar Hernández, and Zsofia Hernández. I would also like to acknowledge the help, kindness, and support of my *cuñados*, Lucio Tovar and Bobby Mendez, and also my *cuñada*, Zsuzsanna Sterl Hernández. My brother, César Daniel Hernández, has been my closest and dearest friend since childhood and a real "partner in crime." *Carnal*, know that I love you very much and that I appreciate all that you have done for me, *Papi*. There are no words, and not enough pages in the world, to express the love and gratitude that I have for my parents Martha C. Hernández and José Gabriel Hernández. They were my first teachers, and I dedicate this inquiry to them.

To criticize Caesar is not to criticize Rome.
To criticize a government is not to criticize a country.

Carlos Fuentes, to Excelsior
reporter Guillermo Ochoa, March 4, 1969

Introduction

On September 6, 2001 – five days prior to the tragic events of 9/11 – Vicente Fox Quesada, then president of Mexico, addressed the United States Congress regarding the changing diplomatic relationship between Mexico and the United States. In that speech, which discussed the need for immigration reform and more trust between the two nations, President Fox Quesada made a call for Mexicans in the United States to return to Mexico and help "modernize" the country with the experiences and technology that they had learned during their tenure abroad. He stated: "And let me also salute the Mexican migrants living in this country and say to them, Mexico needs you. We need your talent and your entrepreneurship. We need you to come home one day and play a part in building a strong Mexico."[1] This statement, which was followed by thunderous applause from the U.S. Congress, continued with the following remarks: "When you return and when you retire, we need you to come back and help us convince other Mexicans that the future lays in a prosperous and democratic Mexico. My dear countrymen, Mexico will not forget you and will support you. We will not fail you."[2]

Fox Quesada would take these and other subsequent comments even further in the months and years to come, going as far as apologizing to Mexican migrants for years of neglect and rejection. During his first public ceremony at the presidential palace in Mexico City, for example, the incoming president was quoted in 2000 as saying: "The times are gone when Mexico viewed the emigrant and the emigrant's children

---

[1]   "Mexican President Vicente Fox Addresses a Joint Meeting of Congress," Aired 6 September 2001; 11:13, ET http://transcripts.cnn.com/TRANSCRIPTS/0109/06/se.02.html.
[2]   Ibid.

with resentment."[3] In fact, this particular president turned the tables in an even more direct manner when he referred to Mexican migrants as heroes and not as "sellouts," "*pochos*," or "traitors" to the nation.[4] Clearly, these and other statements by Fox Quesada and other politicians are indicative of a long-standing relationship between the state of Mexico and its growing diaspora abroad – a relationship that has a long history, that has changed over time, and that is contingent on the economic and political influence of this particular community disproportionately situated within the territorial confines of the United States.

These statements and the benevolent notions of returning to Mexico, however, need to be examined critically and they ultimately require us to historicize this rapport in order to get at the contemporary significance of this particular discourse. The first observation that we can make from these public statements is that there is apparently an extended relationship between the nation of Mexico and its diaspora in the United States – a migratory process that now spans a century and a half and that has developed in some areas a certain "rite of passage" status because of its longevity. Second, the idea of returning to Mexico to help build a more "democratic and modern" Mexico is also not without precedent. And finally, these phrases echoed by the then president of Mexico are also misleading if we were to examine the social history of those Mexicans and Mexican Americans who actually did return to Mexico, particularly those who returned under government-sponsored repatriation and resettlement programs during the mid- to late nineteenth century.

One representative example of this discourse comes from noted Mexican anthropologist Manuel Gamio, which I believe will suffice for our purposes. He pointed out in a 1929 lecture on Mexican migrants in the United States, that "these individuals, who ethnologically are generally Indian or mestizo, have reached in our neighboring country a cultural level which is more advanced than that which characterized them in Mexico and *superior* to that of millions of their compatriots of the same social class who have never left their native soil."[5]

3   Richard Rodríguez, "Prodigal Father – Mexico's Change of Heart Towards Mexican Americans," *Pacific News Service*, December 6, 2000, http://www.pacificnews.org/content/pns/2000/dec/1206prodigal.html.
4   Jorge Durand, "From Traitors to Heroes: 100 Years of Mexican Migration Policy," *Migration Policy Institute*, (March 2004). http://www.migrationinformation.org/Feature/display.cfm?ID=203.
5   Manuel Gamio, "The Influence of Migrations in Mexican Life," (Unpublished Paper, circa 1931), University of Texas-Austin, Benson Latin American Collection, Rare Books (hereafter cited as BLAC).

In the eyes of Mexico's most famous anthropologist, these potential repatriates "could form an ideal group" to return and settle in Mexico. We know from secondary research that the repatriates who returned to government-sponsored colonies in the years following Professor Gamio's lecture did no better (at least economically) than their counterparts in Mexico who had never left. Historians Franciso E. Balderrama and Raymond Rodríguez note about the repatriate colonies formed in post-revolutionary Mexico: "virtually all of the colonizing endeavors ended in dismal failure."[6]

The belief that migrants in the United States are somehow different than their compatriots who never left is a narrative trope that spans centuries. In the Mexican case, the United States was seen as "exceptional" and "modern," so the thinking went, and these characteristics and ideas could be "learned" or acculturated via less than exceptional and "premodern" Mexican peasants. Such ideas unwittingly reinscribe the idea that the United States is not just different, but exceptional.

Mexican migrants in the United States do not have a "higher cultural level" nor are they "superior" because of their residence in the United States, but because of their experiences as migrants. Algerian sociologist Abdelmalek Sayad notes about the changing political demeanor of Algerian migrants to France:

> He lives in a cosmos that is very different from his own, a world which consists of a mode of relations, a mode of existence, a system of exchanges, an economy, a way of being, etc – in short, a culture and the comparisons to which the investigation gives rise provide an effective introduction to two differentiated social existences and to differences between them.... Emigration provides an experience of a social, economic, cultural and, in a word, political world that is different from the familiar world.[7]

Migrants and travelers throughout the world, judging at least from what we can cull from the literature, are transformed during their tenures abroad and now have a larger world to compare, can analyze different political systems, and are familiar with different ways of being in the world. A similar observation is made by historian Mark Wyman's study

6 Franciso E. Balderrama and Raymond Rodríguez, *Decade of Betrayal: Mexican Repatriation in the 1930s* (Albuquerque: University of New Mexico Press, 2006 [Revised Edition]), 202.

7 Abdelmalek Sayad, *The Suffering of the Immigrant* (Cambridge: Polity Press, 1999), 90–1.

that examines the many facets of return migration to Europe during a period of intense global immigration. Wyman notes that "One visible result of the immigrants' immersion to the American environment was that remigrants seemed independent."[8] When it comes to the changes that take place during migration and return, the change that migrants undergo in the United States is not the exception but the universal rule.

In this context, therefore, I would like to pose the following questions in order to elaborate an explanation as to why I think these questions and polemics are important. Thus, what is the history of this relationship between Mexico and its diaspora? In other words, what has been the evolving relationship between the Mexican-origin population in the United States and the state of Mexico and how could we historicize this relationship with archival and empirical evidence? With respect to Mexicans returning home one day and "play[ing] a part in building a strong Mexico": How did migrants fare under the Mexican system of governance once they returned to their country with their "entrepreneurship" and "talent"? Did they in fact help to modernize the country, or were calls to return to the homeland simply nationalist discourse intended to solidify and ultimately project the nation's own sense of nationalism by extending its imagined boundaries beyond the international border? Have the recent enunciations of Mexican presidents Fox Quesada, Calderón Hinojosa, Salinas de Gortari, or Zedillo translated into cogent policies for migrants or to other social programs intended to assist the diaspora?

This monograph, therefore, is concerned with a number of these questions and themes and examines Mexico's immigration and colonization policies as they developed throughout the nineteenth century by focusing primarily on that population of Mexican citizens that was "lost" after the end of the Mexican American War of 1846–1848 up to the close of the century.[9] Under these programs and policies, various

[8] Mark Wyman, *Round-Trip to America: The Immigrants Return to Europe, 1880–1930* (Ithaca and London: Cornell University Press, 1993), 172.

[9] I focus on this period due in part to the existing historiography on the return migration of ethnic Mexicans from the United States, which completely overlooks the period of the nineteenth century. Historian Robert McKay notes that the "most neglected era of Mexican repatriation from the United States is before 1930." See "Mexican Americans and Repatriation," in *The Handbook of Texas Online*. Texas State Historical Association. http://www.tshaonline.org/handbook/online/articles/MM/pqmyk.html. Some key texts for repatriation

governments in Mexico enticed potential migrants to "return to the homeland." The aftermath of the Mexican American War and Mexico's evolving immigration and colonization policies serve as the empirical basis of this research and as the source that attempts to answer a number of these questions.

The practice and process of repatriating Mexicans from the ceded territories after the Mexican American War, and the various colonies established thereafter, form the case studies that I examine in order to elucidate and answer a number of these concerns via a historiographical articulation of heretofore unexamined primary documents.[10] These sources were gathered over the course of a decade and situated in over three dozen archives and libraries spread across the United States, Chihuahua, and Mexico City. Many of them have never been examined by historians, cited, or even considered as part of Mexican history,

after the 1930s are, Mercedes Carreras de Velasco, *Los mexicanos que devolvió la crisis, 1929–1932* (Tlatelolco, México: Secretaría de Relaciones Exteriores, 1974); Fernando Saúl Alanis Encino, "El gobierno de México y la repatriación de mexicanos en Estados Unidos, 1934–1940," (Ph.D. Dissertation, El Colegio de México, 2000); R. Reynolds McKay, "Texas Mexican Repatriation during the Great Depression," (Ph.D. Dissertation, University of Oklahoma, 1982); Juan Ramon Garcia, *Operation Wetback: The Mass Deportation of Mexican Undocumented Workers in 1954* (Westport, Connecticut: Greenwood Press, 1980); Abraham Hoffman, *Unwanted Mexican Americans in the Great Depression: Repatriation Pressures, 1929–1939* (Tucson: University of Arizona Press, 1974); Francisco E. Balderrama and Raymond Rodríguez, *Decade of Betrayal: Mexican Repatriation in the 1930s* (Albuquerque: University of New Mexico Press, 1995); Francisco E. Balderrama, *In Defense of La Raza: The Los Angeles Consulate and the Mexican Community, 1929–1936* (Tucson: University of Arizona Press, 1982). Other texts examine repatriation within their own studies and illustrate the impact of these processes in particular Mexican American communities. See, for instance, George J. Sánchez, *Becoming Mexican American: Ethnicity, Culture, and Identity in Chicano Los Angeles, 1900–1945* (New York: Oxford University Press, 1995); Camille Guerin-Gonzales, *Mexican Workers and the American Dreams: Immigration, Repatriation, and California Farm Labor, 1900–1939* (New Jersey: Rutgers University Press, 1994).

10 When using the term *historiography* I employ Aviezer Tucker's definition: "Historiography is the study of the way history is and has been written. In a broad sense, history refers to the methodology and practices of writing history. In a more specific sense, it can refer to writing about rather than of history. As a meta-level analysis of descriptions of the past, this latter conception can relate to the former in that the analysis usually focuses on the narrative, interpretations, worldview, use of evidence, or method of presentation of other historians." See Aviezer Tucker, *Our Knowledge of the Past: A Philosophy of Historiography*, (Cambridge: Cambridge University Press, 2004).

the history of the U.S. borderlands, or Mexican American studies. Indeed the historiography has scarcely mentioned this episode of repatriate colonies after the war.

After the end of hostilities, the inhabitants of several settlements in southern New Mexico, Texas, and California who wanted to remain within Mexican territory founded or resettled various towns along the northern frontiers of the fractured republic. In New Mexico Territory, for instance, individuals from San Elizario, Isleta, Doña Ana, and Socorro – communities that had found themselves on the U.S. side of the border after the war – established La Mesilla in the 1850s with the aid of a Mexican commission sent to the region after the war in a skirmish to try and settle Mexican-origin peoples on the newly established "Mexican" side of the international boundary. Throughout the rest of the nineteenth century other important towns would be founded and repopulated right across the new international boundary like Nuevo Monterrey, Piedras Negras, San Diego, San Juan, Palo Blanco, Agua Dulce, La Ascensión, Santo Tomás, El Sauz, Los Olmos, San Luis, Pansacola, Zapata, San Ignacio, and Los Saenz, El Remolino, to name only a few.[11] These resettlements were backed legally by a decree signed on August 19, 1848 by the José Joaquín de Herrera administration (in office June 3, 1848 to January 15, 1851), which sought to repatriate and resettle Mexicans who wanted to return to the republic and remain citizens of Mexico. Article One of that decree read, "All of the Mexicans found in the territory during the celebration of peace that, because of the Treaty of Guadalupe Hidalgo, remained in the power of the United States of [the] North, and want to come and establish themselves in that of the Republic, will be transferred to this one [Mexico] on account of the treasury and in the form established in the following articles."[12]

[11] Arnoldo De León, "Life for Mexicans in Texas After the 1836 Revolution," in *Major Problems in Mexican American History: Documents and Essays*, edited by Zaragosa Vargas (Boston and New York: Houghton Mifflin Company, 1999), 167–75.

[12] "Decreto de 19 de Agosto de 1848; para que familias mexicanas que se encuentren en los Estados Unidos puedan emigrar a su patria," en *Código de Colonización y Terrenos Baldíos de la República Mexicana, formado por Francisco F. De La Maza y Publicado Según el Acuerdo del Presidente de la República, Por Conducta de la Secretaría de Estado y del Despacho de Fomento, Años de 1451 a 1892*, (México: Oficina Tipográfica de la Secretaria de Fomento, 1893): 407–12; original: "Todos los mexicanos que a la celebración de la paz se encontraban en el territorio que por el Tratado de Guadalupe Hidalgo quedó en el poder de los Estados Unidos

By looking at a number of colonies that were founded and how they fared under a Mexican system of governance once they were resettled, this study seeks in part to question Fox Quesada's call for Mexicans to return to Mexico by highlighting several cases of citizens who in fact returned to Mexico during the middle of the nineteenth century. After going over numerous examples of repatriate colonies founded after the end of hostilities, I conclude that these cases of repatriation illustrate that the discourse of nationalism enveloped in the language of "returning to the homeland" did not translate into practice. In effect, Mexico's nineteenth-century colonization policies were "determined by practical, rather than moral or ideological considerations."[13]

In fact, this study illustrates a more *longue durée* approach to many of the conclusions reached by other scholars of twentieth-century repatriation to Mexico. These conclusions, to a very large degree, add to our understanding of Mexico's historic relationship with this "lost population" via the growing, but temporally limiting literature on issues affecting U.S.–Mexican diplomatic relations. By examining these case studies historically, this burgeoning literature is further complicated by outlining the longer relationship between the state and its diaspora, thus contributing to ongoing debates situated disproportionately within the fields of political science, diplomatic history, and sociology. In short, I seek to historicize that literature by calculating into the equation examples of repatriate colonies.

Relationship between Mexico and Its Diaspora

The literature dealing with the relationship between states and their diasporas has seen an increase in production due largely to the economic, political, and social impact of the immigrants who have left their homelands for other places of residence. Due in large measure to their own economic and political influence in the countries where they reside, immigrant lobbies and the billions of dollars in remittances that contribute to the fledgling economies from whence they originated, are directly tied to this growing literature. In the case of Mexico, which shares a longer history with its diaspora, at least since 1848, this evolving rapport has occurred in both directions. The following

---

de Norte, y quieren venir á establecerse en el de la República, serán trasladados á ésta de cuenta del erario y en la forma que se establece en los artículos siguientes" (hereafter *Código de Colonización*).

[13] See *Oxford English Dictionary Online* (Oxford: Oxford University Press, 2007).

historiography traces this evolution by examining a number of recent studies before going into a general overview of the same set of questions on the American side of this equation.

Hence, literature on the relation between Mexico and its diaspora emerged in a dialectical link that had much to do with the country's neglect of its citizens abroad, not to mention the historic disdain that it openly expressed for Mexicans who had opted to reside in the United States – the very nation deemed responsible for the loss of much of Mexico's claimed northern territories just prior to the Mexican American War. This disdain was initially articulated by military officials in Mexico that employed the term "Bad Mexicans" to describe those individuals who often threatened to secede from the splintered nation or who on their own accord convinced others that joining the United States would be more to their advantage than if they opted to remain citizens of the republic of Mexico.[14] The term "Bad Mexicans" was employed during the war and signified those who encouraged "Good Mexicans" (read loyal) to secede from Mexico and therefore served as the antithesis of Mexican identity during a period of "changing national identities."[15]

This continued disparagement of ethnic Mexicans in the United States also has a very long literary history in Mexico proper, and today one can still read such sentiments in the writings of several authors, most notably by intellectual and novelist Elena Poniatowska. In a speech presenting her new novel in Caracas, Venezuela in early July 2001, this prominent Mexican author referred to Mexican migrants as "cockroaches" and "lice ridden" individuals who were in the process of reclaiming the southwest for Mexico. According to her speech, which was carried by the Venezuelan magazine El Imparcial, "the common people – the poor, the dirty, the lice ridden, the cockroaches are advancing on the United States, a country that needs to speak Spanish because it has 33.5 million Hispanics who are imposing their culture."[16]

[14] See, for instance, "Circulares para la formación de una policía orgánica en cada Comandancia General, a efecto de perseguir a los malos mexicanos que excitan al pueblo a anexarse a los Estados Unidos. Año de 1853," in Archivo Histórico Militar Mexicano, (hereafter AHMM), XI/481.3/3534.

[15] My use of the term Changing National Identities is in reference to the work of Andrés Reséndez's excellent study of the first half of the nineteenth century. See Changing National Identities at the Frontier: Texas and New Mexico, 1800–1850 (Cambridge: Cambridge University Press, 2004).

[16] El Imparcial, "Elena Poniatowska dice que México va recuperando tierras en EU," 3 Julio 2001.

This disdain has a longer history than one might care to resuscitate, but one that would ultimately require an extended study of its own.[17] To cite just one nineteenth-century example as background for Poniatowska's chauvinism: Guillermo Prieto noted this derision for the diaspora during his exile to the United States when describing the Mexican populace of California in 1877. According to his memoirs, written as he traveled throughout the United States, this intellectual and statesman commented on Californios (Mexicans from California) in the following manner:

> He uses strong boots, wields a stupendous knife, with which he polishes and sharpens his nails, he whittles sticks and then cleans his teeth, he speaks little and then always in English, almost always goes to bed face up and then fixes his feet upon a table, or a bar, or the wall, drinks whiskey, chews tobacco, gives a hard squeeze of the hand to the first individual that speaks to him and then sprinkles his conversation after the greeting with shamelessness, calling attention to his battered and disheveled hat.[18]

For Poniatowska these "cockroaches" are imposing their language on the United States; for Prieto U.S. influence has "contaminated" the Californios. Prieto and Poniatowska apparently shared the notion that Mexicans who leave, those who live outside of the national territory, somehow *lack* the culture of those from the center of the republic, namely Mexico City.

Prieto's description of a California Mexican cowpoke is reminiscent of Octavio Paz's understanding of "duality" and the "extremes" at which the Mexican in the United States can arrive due to continued contact with American culture and modernity. In his illustration of the infamous *pachuco*, for example, this 1990 Nobel Laureate and Mexico's most celebrated intellectual noted that this individual was an "impassive and

[17] An excellent starting point would be Richard Griswold del Castillo's "Mexican Intellectuals' Perceptions of Mexican Americans and Chicanos, 1920–present," *Aztlán: A Journal of Chicano Studies* 27;2 (Fall 2002): 33–74.
[18] Guillermo Prieto, *Viaje á los Estados Unidos, 3 vols.* (México: Imprenta de Dublán y Chávez, 1877–1878), I; 394; Original: "Usa bota fuerte, esgrime estupenda navaja, con la que pule y aguza sus uñas, labra palos y se limpia los dientes, habla poco y siempre en ingles, casi se acuesta boca arriba y fija los pies en una mesa, o un barrote, o la pared, bebe whiskey, masca tabaco, da sendos apretones de mano al primero que le habla y salpica con desvergüenzas desde el saludo, llamándose a los ojos su machucado y desgobernado sombrero."

sinister clown whose purpose is to cause terror instead of laughter."[19] His "will-not-to-be" converted the *pachuco* into a "symbol of love and joy or of horror and loathing, an embodiment of liberty, of disorder, of the forbidden." In short, "he is someone who ought to be destroyed." Much like Prieto's and Poniatowska's description of diasporic Mexicans, the *pachuco* is "also someone with whom any contact must be made in secret, in the darkness." For these intellectuals, all "common people" outside the center are "the poor, the dirty, and the lice ridden, the cockroaches [that] are advancing on the United States...."[20]

Recalling these "cockroaches" that Poniatowska described, it seems that the discourse of "darkness," the fear of "cockroaches" and "lice," and the loss of the Spanish language share a number of common characteristics that have subsequently been appropriated by the very individuals demeaned in these literary productions.[21] For all these particular critiques, however, it is patently clear that the diaspora in the United States not only played a significant role in the formation of nineteenth-century Mexican national identity, but historically has begun to occupy (slowly) the center of this imaginary since the end of the Mexican American War.

After seeing such a disdain for the very people who merely seek to better their lot, it comes as no surprise to learn that some of the first studies to examine this relationship between Mexico and the United States emerged among the very population that bore the brunt of this disparagement: the Mexican American community situated in the United States. A 1976 publication of Juan Gómez-Quiñones, titled "Piedras Contra La Luna, México en Aztlán y Aztlán en México," serves as the ideal point of departure.[22] One of the first articles to examine the relationship between

[19] Octavio Paz, *The Labyrinth of Solitude and Other Essays* (New York: Grove Press, 1985), 16.

[20] *El Imparcial*, "Elena Poniatowska dice que México va recuperando tierras en EU," 3 Julio 2001.

[21] The term *cockroaches* was a term of derision appropriated by the Chicano movement of the 1960s and then reinverted by one of its most famous activists and attorneys, Oscar Zeta Acosta. See *The Revolt of the Cockroach People* (San Francisco: Straight Arrow Books, 1973); the fear of losing Spanish is now celebrated with the invention of a "new language" and what are often referred to as *pochismos*. See, for instance, Rosaura Sánchez, *Chicano Discourse: Socio-Historical Perspectives* (Houston: Arte Público Press, University of Houston, 1994 co. 1983).

[22] Juan Gómez-Quiñones, "Piedras Contra La Luna, México en Aztlán y Aztlán en México: Chicano-Mexican Relations and the Mexican Consulates, 1900–1920,"

Mexico and its diaspora during the twentieth century, the appearance of "Piedras Contra la Luna" marks a turning point in the field of Mexican American studies. Examining the role of the Mexican consulates situated within the territorial confines of the United States, Gómez-Quiñones opens his article with a loaded title indeed. The "moon of Anahuac has been a loadstar for the peoples of Aztlán," he states, yet the Mexican intelligentsia shares a "disdain for the Chicano." Although some exceptions to this disdain do exist, like the Flores-Magón brothers who were exiled to the United States at the turn of the twentieth century, the overall effort to protect Mexican citizens in the United States was not the Mexican consulates' primary duty. By approaching his article as one that is "casting rocks against the moon [of Mexico]" Gómez-Quiñones maintains quite explicitly that the relationship between the state of Mexico and its diaspora "has not been equal or felicitous."

Four years after the publication of Gómez-Quiñones's article, political scientist Rodolfo O. De La Garza published "Chicanos and U.S. Foreign Policy: The Future of Chicano-Mexican Relations." De La Garza followed this 1980 publication with several others throughout the next two decades, making him, in my estimation, the leading scholar in the area of Chicano–Mexican relations.[23] Given the numerous articles

chapter 26 in *Contemporary Mexico: Papers of the IV International Congress of Mexican History*, edited by James W. Wilkie, Michael C. Meyer, and Edna Monzón de Wilkie (Berkeley: The University of California Press, 1976): 494–527.

[23] Rodolfo O. De La Garza has published numerous articles in this area, thus I will list only a number of these. Please see "Chicanos and U.S. Foreign Policy: The Future of Chicano-Mexican Relations," *The Western Political Quarterly* 33;4, (December 1980): 571–82; "Demythologizing Chicano-Mexican Relations," *Proceedings of the Academy of Political Science 34;1*, "Mexico-United States Relations," (1980): 88–96; "Texas Land Grants and Chicano-Mexican Relations: A Case Study," *Latin American Research Review 21;1*, (1986): 123–38; *Mexican Immigrants and Mexican Americans: An Evolving Relation* (Austin: CMAS Publications, Center for Mexican American Studies, University of Texas at Austin, 1986); "Mexico, Mexicans, and Mexican-Americans in U.S.-Mexican Relations," (Austin: Institute of Latin American Studies, University of Texas at Austin, 1989); *Bridging the Border: Transforming Mexico-US Relations*, (New York: Rowman & Littlefied Publishers, 1997); "Interests Not Passions: Mexican-American Attitudes toward Mexico, Immigration from Mexico, and Other Issues Shaping US-Mexico Relations," *International Migration Review* 32;2, (Summer 1998): 401–22; "Latinos and U.S. Foreign Policy: Representing the 'Homeland'?" (Lanham: Rowman & Littlefield Publishers, 2000); "Looking Backward Moving Forward: Mexican Organizations in the US as Agents of Incorporation and Association," (Claremont, CA: Tomas Rivera Policy Institute, 2003).

that this author has published since the early 1980s, I will only touch
on the main themes of his arguments and then segue into my final historiographical contribution before discussing these questions among
intellectuals in North America.

In De La Garza's first publication, he posed the question of a potential lobby by Mexicans in the United States and what this *acercamiento*
could mean for the Chicano community and the Mexican government.[24]
In other words, his 1980 study examined the "foundation on which
such a relationship might be built, what Chicanos might gain and lose
from it, and, if it were established, what impact Chicanos might have
if they became a lobby for the Mexican government." Mexico's recent
oil finds, its rise in international stature, and the increased migration of
undocumented workers to the United States, according to De La Garza,
"have led to the speculation that conditions are now propitious for creating a close relationship between Chicanos and the Mexican government." What effects could such a relationship have on U.S. domestic
and foreign policy? Diasporic lobbies, as some literature demonstrates
thus far, are often the source of conspiracy theories and of homegrown
suspicions regarding ethnic loyalties.

De La Garza ultimately concluded that "it is unlikely that a Chicano
lobby would be very successful."[25] Neither the United States nor
Mexico, it seems, is willing to aid the Mexican American community
and the author believes that it would be "naïve" for Chicanos to believe
otherwise. In this particular context, De La Garza ended his study with
a telling and critical position reminiscent of the cultural and linguistic
position of Chicanos during this period: that they are neither Mexican
nor American but something in between and a little of both. Or, to follow the author:

> Neither government has a history of being concerned about
> Chicanos, and there is no reason to expect that either will change
> its policies for altruistic reasons. If a strong Chicano-Mexican
> relationship is to develop, therefore, it would behoove Chicano
> leaders to pursue it with a clear understanding of the gains and
> risks involved, and it would be presumptuous to assume either
> that such a relationship will necessarily serve Chicanos better
> than would involvement with the American political process,

[24] The idea of *acercamiento* literally means a policy of the state and the diaspora
"coming together" or "coming closer together."
[25] De La Garza, "Chicanos and U.S. Foreign Policy," 579.

or that it will be built easily and automatically on cultural foundations.[26]

Thus, although the "moon of Anahuac has been a loadstar for the peoples of Aztlán" in the past – and one could make the argument it still is for many Chicanos today – the evidence presented by De La Garza in this and other articles contradicts this potential *acercamiento* via contemporary surveys and studies.[27] In fact, the author goes further in subsequent journal pieces by pointing out historical instances when the Mexican government manipulated Mexicans in the United States for their own ends, as in the case of the 1915–1916 Tejano uprisings in south Texas. Although some may debate the veracity of this claim, De La Garza's more contemporary examples are not as debatable, like the fact that the "unofficial policy" of Mexico was to not accept a "Chicano ambassador from the United States until 1979."[28] If we are to discuss the relationship between the state (Mexico) and its diaspora (Mexicans in the United States), then these latter examples are part of that historical narrative, and as such, merit a historical analysis.

The literature on Mexican–Chicano relations, though, has lacked a more concrete historiography that would lend more weight to some of the assessments shared by De La Garza and other political scientists and sociologists.[29] To his credit, De La Garza's historical analysis in his "Texas Land Grants and Chicano-Mexican Relations: A Case Study" is one of the only pieces that examines this relationship during the nineteenth century.[30] Where I would disagree is his assessment that Mexico showed "great concern" for citizens left in the ceded territories after the end of hostilities. According to his own wording, "After their disastrous defeat and huge territorial losses in the US-Mexican War, Mexican officials showed great concern for the well-being of those Mexican citizens who chose to remain in the lands annexed by the United States."[31] In the author's defense, nonetheless, De La

[26] Ibid., 582.
[27] Ibid.
[28] De La Garza, "Demythologizing Chicano-Mexican Relations," 89.
[29] Another example of these concerns can be seen in collection of essays edited by Tatcho Mindiola Jr. and Max Martínez, *Chicano-Mexicano Relations* (Houston: Center for Mexican American Studies, The University of Houston Press, 1986, 1992).
[30] De La Garza and Schmitt, "Texas Land Grants and Chicano-Mexican Relations," 135.
[31] Ibid., 124.

Garza is not a historian and all of the research required to examine this question empirically are located in Mexico proper. In other words, research in Mexico would be required to accurately determine whether or not "Mexican officials showed great concern for the well-being" of those individuals who opted to remain in the lands now ceded to the United States. Given the postwar environment, foreign intervention, the Wars of Reform, a depleted treasury, and the continued war against "Indios Bárbaros," perhaps more pressing concerns impeded such altruistic policies.

Much like the various historical cases in which a large number of immigrants provoked fears and stirred nativist hysteria, today's increase in Mexican migration contributes to some of the questions raised by De La Garza, and this structural shift also influences related xenophobic writings in the U.S. academy. If contemporary studies of the period are any indication of this "social phenomenon," contact between Mexican American and Mexican migrants has now given rise to accusations of disloyalty, potential secession, and a fear that radical *reconquista* nationalists will foment discord in the community in order to "take back" the lands lost by Mexico. In the middle of June 1979, the same year Julian Nava was appointed as Ambassador to Mexico, former CIA director William Colby was quoted in the *Los Angeles Times* asserting that Mexican migration – and the rise of a "Spanish-speaking Quebec in the US Southwest" – represented a greater future threat to the United States than did the Soviet Union.[32] A generation later, North American academics like Samuel P. Huntington added to this discourse of disloyalty and subversion, lending academic credence to unfounded fears of a reconquest, and by extension, disloyalty.

THE "CLASH OF CIVILIZATIONS" COMES HOME

In May 2004, noted Harvard political scientist Samuel P. Huntington wrote an article titled "The Hispanic Challenge" in *Foreign Policy*, a journal of international affairs he had founded. In that article, Huntington argued that Mexican migration to the United States was different from past immigrations (read "European"). If this migration continued, he added, it could undermine the United States's cultural hegemony and also parts of its territory, most notably the southwestern sectors that

---

[32] Quoted in James D. Cockcroft, *Outlaws in the Promised Land: Mexican Immigrant Workers and America's Future* (New York: Grove Press, 1986), 39.

were "lost" during the Mexican American War over 150 years earlier. His main thesis is summarized in the following manner:

> The persistent inflow of Hispanic immigrants threatens to divide the United States into two peoples, two cultures, and two languages. Unlike past immigrant groups, Mexicans and other Latinos have not assimilated into mainstream U.S. culture, forming instead their own political and linguistic enclaves – from Los Angeles to Miami – and rejecting the Anglo-Protestant values that built the American dream. The United States ignores this challenge at its peril.[33]

In short, Mexican migration threatens to create a society that is bicultural and bilingual lest the United States either assimilate or thwart this mass migration to those areas already thoroughly under "Latino control."

This fear of Mexican migration had led Pat Buchanan, the well-known conservative commentator and three-time presidential candidate, to publish his own theories a few years earlier, but his and Huntington's theses are almost identical. In *The Death of the West: How Dying Populations and Immigrant Invasions Imperil Our Country and Civilization*, Buchanan dedicates a chapter to the problem of Mexican migration titled "La Reconquista." Mexicans, he believes, have a legitimate historic grievance with the United States, and his five-point outline regarding this question is identical to Huntington's: (1) The numbers are greater than those of past migrations and they are mostly from one country and concentrated in specific areas; (2) Mexicans come not only from another culture, "but millions are from another race" (read Indian); (3) Millions are here illegally and have already broken the law; (4) Unlike past immigrants who were separated by the seas from their homelands, Mexicans enjoy the proximity of their homeland and feel no need to learn English; and (5) current Mexican immigrants are *different* from past immigrants because they come with the idea of racial rights and ethnic entitlements, an attitude "encouraged by cultural elites who denigrate the melting pot and preach the glories of multiculturalism."[34]

[33] Samuel P. Huntington, "The Hispanic Challenge," *Foreign Policy*, (March/April 2004): 30–45.
[34] Patrick J. Buchanan, *The Death of the West: How Dying Populations and Immigrant Invasions Imperil Our Country and Civilization* (New York: St. Martin's Press, 2002), 123–46.

Huntington's chapter on immigration is similar to Patrick Buchanan's outline in "La Reconquista." According to Huntington, "Mexican immigration is leading toward the demographic *reconquista* of areas Americans took from Mexico by force in the 1830s and 1840s, Mexicanizing them in a manner comparable to, although different from, the Cubanization that has occurred in Southern Florida."[35] Furthermore, Mexican immigration is "different" from past immigrations because of (1) its continuity, (2) its numbers, (3) its illegality, (4) its regional concentration, (5) its persistence, and (6) a historical claim to lands lost in 1848. With respect to the last reason outlined by the author, Huntington believes that Mexican Americans enjoy a sense of "being on their own turf that is not shared by other immigrants" and this concept of "turf" takes "human form in the some twenty-five Mexican communities that have existed continuously since before the American conquest." These two paragraphs sum up the content and contention of *Who Are We?* and *Death of the West*.[36] Beyond some well-known demographic data on Mexican migration, neither of these authors explains how the *reconquista* will evolve, and neither has provided any concrete piece of evidence of any such movement – in the past or in the present.

Recently, other monographs have surfaced, most notably by U.S. politicians hoping to stir anti-Mexican fears. Congressman J. D. Hayworth – who recently lost against Senator John McCain during the Republican primaries in Arizona in 2010 – and Tom Tancredo of the U.S. Republican Party have published their own tirades against undocumented Mexican workers in the United States and heavily employ the framework and discourse of Buchanan and Huntington in their works.[37] *In Mortal Danger* and *Whatever it Takes* appeal to the law, security, and terrorism, but ultimately conclude with the idea that if Mexican migration continues, the territorial, political, and social hegemony of the United States will be threatened.

Given the long history of nativism in the United States, it is unfortunate to witness the increase in deportation raids targeting mostly Mexican migrants and their families and the justification of these

[35] Huntington, *Who Are We?: The Challenges to America's National Identity* (New York: Simon & Schuster, 2004), 221.
[36] Ibid., 230.
[37] John D. Hayworth, *Whatever It Takes: Illegal Immigration, Border Security, and the War on Terror* (Washington, DC: Regnery Pub, 2006); Tom Tancredo, *In Mortal Danger: The Battle for America's Border and Security* (Nashville: WND Books, 2006).

policies by U.S. politicians and the media.³⁸ Some media outlets have gone as far as calling for the reimplementation of the notorious 1952 deportation campaign known as "Operation Wetback," while others have actually called for the annexation and forced assimilation of the entire country of Mexico!³⁹

What is interesting about these latter works and their Mexican counterparts which I mentioned earlier (by Paz, Prieto, and Poniatowska) is not only their lack of sensitivity for Mexicans in the United States, but their collective participation in a set of culture wars that continues to use the Mexican American War as a site of postwar trauma, or the location for staking out the culture battles of a particular "collective memory." I use the terms *trauma* and *collective memory* as they were first introduced by French sociologist Maurice Halbwachs and later adopted by the historian of the Jewish experience in the United States, Peter Novick. As Novick explains, "Instead of viewing collective memory as the past working its will on the present, Halbwachs explored the ways in which present concerns determine what of the past we remember and how we remember it."⁴⁰ The Mexican American War – and the collective memories generated about it – are not immune to such an analysis. Indeed, they provide fertile ground for examining how demographic shifts generate and regenerate continued postwar historical traumas 150 years after the event. Dreams and fears of Mexican migrants reconquering those territories "sold" in the aftermath of a war that ended over a century and a half ago are contemporary manifestations of such trauma by American and Mexican thinkers alike.

Even noted Mexican novelist Carlos Fuentes is guilty of this particular form of historical trauma when he was quoted as saying to an audience at the University of Texas at San Antonio that the United States would be bilingual this century.⁴¹ More disconcerting to U.S. nativists,

---

³⁸ Think here of numerous cable network shows that constantly aired anti-Mexican views and conspiracies, particularly recent programs like those of Bill O'Reilly on Fox News and CNN's Lou Dobbs (now off the air).

³⁹ John Dillin, "How Eisenhower Solved Illegal Border Crossings from Mexico," *The Christian Science Monitor*, 6 July 2006; see also Erik Rush, *Annexing Mexico: Solving the Border Problem Through Annexation and Assimilation*, (Jamul, CA: Level 4 Press, 2007), passim.

⁴⁰ Peter Novick, *The Holocaust in American Life* (Boston: Houghton Mifflin, 1999), 3.

⁴¹ Hector Saldaña, "Fuentes Sees Bilingual U.S. in This Century," *San Antonio Express*, 28 March 2002.

however, were his statements to the *Second Annual International Congress of the Spanish Language*:

> And now, in the face of the *silent reconquista* of the United States, we confront a new linguistic phenomenon: a continental mixture, the spanglish or *espanglés*, well it sometimes consumes the English expression, at times the Castilian, a fascinating border phenomenon, sometimes dangerous, always creative, necessary or fatal as were the old encounters between Spanish and Nahuatl....[42]

The discourse of *reconquista* certainly harkens back to the long, episodic battles Christians and Moors fought in medieval Spain, but here the term is being applied to a similar process in the U.S. Southwest. Just as Nahuatl and Spanish produced a particular form of contemporary Mexican speech which Fuentes so wonderfully demonstrated, so will the linguistic phenomenon of *espanglés* become the fate of the United States, according to Fuentes.

The site of these contemporary culture wars is situated around the "loss" of Mexico's territories and the role of Mexican migrants in that process. Missing from both sites (Mexico and the United States) of contestation is recognition that the lands in question were in fact inhabited, occupied, contested, and settled by numerous independent Indian groups that had successfully resisted the imposition of Mexican and U.S. hegemony. Mexican intellectuals suffer the perceived loss of stolen territories while academics and politicians in the United States are traumatized by a historical narrative that paints a picture of lands stolen. Conveniently overlooked in this battle between nations and nationalisms is that both were implicated in the pacification of the "barbarous Indians," and all were complicit in the structural and symbolic violence that the war engendered. Examining the problems and process of colonizing the newly established boundaries after the war with repatriates demonstrates the settling of the borderlands was accomplished by a variety of *fronterizos*, migrants, *Indios*, and repatriates – not

[42] Armando G. Tejeda, "El español, "esperanto" de la comunidades indígenas de América, señala Carlos Fuentes, *La Jornada,* 20 Octubre 2001; Original: "Y ahora, frente a la reconquista silenciosa de Estados Unidos, estamos ante un nuevo fenómeno lingüístico: el mixturado continental, el *spanglish* o *espanglés*, pues a veces priva la expresión inglesa, a veces la castellana, en un fenómeno fronterizo fascinante, peligroso a veces, creativo siempre, necesario o fatal como lo fueron los encuentros antiguos del castellano con el náhuatl, gracias al cual nuestra lengua y algunas más pueden hoy decir chocolate, tomate, aguacate."

nations. The consistent flow of Mexican migrants to the United States is simply a byproduct of this international conflict, and the continued debate about immigration reform in the United States is one example of the residual circumstances that emanated in the aftermath of the war.

Organization of the Book

Today the diaspora is called *Mexico de Afuera*, a term coined by José Vasconcelos – the noted intellectual and one time secretary of education – in the late 1920s when he earned yet another distinction as being the first presidential candidate in a Mexican election to campaign outside of the international boundary.[43] This idea of "Mexico beyond" marks a shift in how Mexicans in the United States have been imagined, but the underlying influence may well be the millions of dollars in remittances during the period.[44] Be that as it may, and as I will illustrate throughout this study of repatriation-cum-colonization, this name and sentiment was not always the case. At different times and in different contexts, this population has been termed "lost" or "forgotten" by various Mexican and American intellectuals describing this diaspora in the United States.[45] One could say that the relationship between the state and the diaspora has changed over time from "Mexico Perdido," to "Mexico Olvidado," to the contemporary "Mexico de Afuera." I seek to historicize this relationship between Mexico (the state) and the diaspora (the migrants) by empirically examining the process and practice of repatriating and colonizing Mexicans and Mexican Americans from the United States between 1831 and 1892.

---

[43] John Skirius, "Vasconcelos and México de Afuera (1928)," *Aztlán: A Journal of Chicano Studies 7;3*, (Fall 1976): 479–97.

[44] See Manuel Gamio, *Mexican Immigration to the United States: A Study of Human Migration and Adjustment*, with a new introduction by John H. Burma, (New York: Dover Books, 1971), 32.

[45] The examples of "lost" and "forgotten" are replete in the primary documentation; however, some more recent tertiary examples are worth noting here. See, for instance, Federico Allen Hinojosa, *El Mexico de Afuera*, (San Antonio: Artes Graficas, 1940); Agustín Cue Cánovas, *Los Estados Unidos y el México olvidado*, (México City: B. Costa-Amic, 1970); David J. Weber, ed., *El México perdido: ensayos sobre el antiguo norte de México, 1540–1821*, (México City: Secretaría de Educación Pública, 1976); David R. Maciel, *El México olvidado: la historia del pueblo Chicano, 2 tomos*, (Ciudad Juárez/El Paso: Universidad Autónoma de Ciudad Juárez & University of Texas at El Paso, 1996).

In order to convey this narrative, I've divided the book into three different sections, each with its corresponding chapters, in order to capture the global, national, and local particularities of this process. Thus, Part I begins with an international analysis of global immigrations and then moves to an analysis of the repatriation of Mexicans throughout the U.S. Southwest on a national level. I then track these repatriations in a comparative perspective before narrowing my focus to one repatriate colony that made its way back to Chihuahua in 1872. By employing this three-fold structure, we are better able to grasp the global, national, and local context of Mexico's evolving immigration policies as they came to include and exclude particular groups of people throughout the long nineteenth century.

The changes in Mexico's immigration, colonization, and repatriation policies after the Mexican American War and through the Porfiriato were shaped by the debates that took on an international perspective following independence. While previous scholars have emphasized Mexico's "failure" to settle the country with "energetic and ambitious Europeans," more important at the turn of the century was the double threat of "Indios Bárbaros" and "Anglo-Americans." These two entities threatened the territorial integrity of the nation. Immigrants, "people of color," repatriates, "civilized Indians," Europeans, and North Americans were all seen as potential settlers of the northern frontier regions of the republic. Mexican colonization and immigration policies, moreover, occurred at a moment in history that saw the migration of millions of Europeans to the Western Hemisphere. Mexico's policies were, at least in the case of Texas, "too successful" as Euro American settlers came to outnumber the local Mexican population, establishing the social and demographic conditions for an armed confrontation with the young nation only fifteen years later.

This broader perspective helps to illustrate how Mexico's immigration and colonization policies were informed and impacted by the global mass migrations taking place throughout the nineteenth century. Unlike its neighbors to the north and south, however, Mexico's population was predominantly indigenous. This demographic reality greatly influenced the development of Mexico's immigration and colonization policies, as the incorporation of the native peoples into the growing country was of the utmost national importance. The incorporation of the northern indigenes, in fact, was at the center of the first set of recommendations made to the new government after independence in 1821. These first proposals laid the foundation for immigration and colonization policies for the remainder of the nineteenth century.

Although this policy of Euro American inclusion was reversed after the 1830s, the Texas episode would forever alter Mexico's national immigration and colonization policies and set them off from those of Brazil, the United States, or Argentina. Unlike its southern neighbors, Mexico had to contend with an economically robust neighbor with a swelling population to the north that was expanding toward its territory. Likewise, growing populations and the accompanying competition for land also provided the structural conditions for the expulsion of ethnic Mexicans in the states of Texas and later California. As Mexico entered into war with the United States, the former's "failure" to populate the northern frontiers was seen as one of the primary causes of conflict with the latter. In a state of civil war after 1821, and in the wake of "the loss" of its northern territories to its expanding neighbor, Mexico sought to reinforce its immigration and colonization policies with laws favoring the return of Mexicans left in the ceded territories.

At the national level, the repatriation of thousands of Mexicans to the new states of Chihuahua, Sonora, Coahuila, and Tamaulipas from the mid-nineteenth century onward form the empirical centerpiece of the work. In chapters three and four I begin to detail a number of requests for repatriation and settlement in Mexico proper. Previous studies of Mexican repatriation have overlooked the latter half of the nineteenth century and have all but ignored what happened once these repatriates returned to the "homeland." The scattered writings on the topic, in fact, essentially regurgitate the nationalist emplott-ment of historian Lawrence Douglas Taylor Hansen, who argued that "the Mexican government has never forgotten the Mexican population that has lived on the other side of that dividing line and it has always been disposed to resettle them in the event they were left unhappy or without possibilities to continue residing abroad."[46] In contrast to this dominant interpretation in the literature, I argue that several repatri-ate colonies (in Sonora, Tamaulipas, Chihuahua, and Coahuila) were founded after the war for reasons of *realpolitik*, national security, con-venience, and territorial integrity, mixed with the gloss of national-ist rhetoric. The state desired to populate the northern frontiers with

[46] Lawrence Douglas Taylor Hansen, "La repatriación de Mexicanos de 1848 a 1980 y su papel en la colonización de la región fronteriza septentrional de México," *Relaciones 18, no. 69* (1997): 198–212.

repatriates from the United States because the latter were perceived as having the most suitable cultural, linguistic, religious, nationalistic, and martial characteristics for the challenging task of settlement along a colonial frontier.

The final chapters of this study narrow the field of focus from the national to the local and follow one repatriate colony as it made its way back to Mexico on three separate occasions: 1850, 1853, and 1872. My case study of La Ascensión, Chihuahua will illustrate how one repatriate colony fared first under a U.S. and later a Mexican system of governance. I devote more than one chapter to this particular colony because of the availability of documentation and its own biographical nature, an aspect quickly seen through the disproportionate amount of primary documents used to tell this history. A riot following an election in southern New Mexico prompted repatriates to leave in 1872 and a number of the participants were involved in yet another election riot twenty years later, this time in Chihuahua. These events are not only interesting in their own right, but they also provide an opportunity to bring in a transnational perspective requiring research beyond the nation–state. Through archival documents gleaned from La Ascensión, Ciudad Juárez, and Ciudad Chihuahua, Mexico City, Las Cruces, New Mexico and El Paso, Texas, I follow the trail of these repatriates as they made their way back to *la madre patria* in 1872.

The present study adds depth to our understanding of Mexico's historic relationship with this "lost population" in a way that can contribute to current immigration debates and U.S.–Mexican diplomatic relations. These case studies help to outline the long-term relationship between the state and the diaspora and serve to enrich the process of what historian Friedrich Katz called "the transformation of the northern frontier into *the border.*"[47] Methodologically, the task of following these communities as they made their way back toward the borderlands requires a transnational approach to archival research, which is to say that my analysis employs Mexican archives to articulate a more complex interpretation of nineteenth-century Mexican American life. I conclude the monograph with an overview of my findings and some final remarks concerning a number of important themes in the work.

---

[47] Friedrich Katz, *The Secret War in Mexico: Europe, the United States, and the Mexican Revolution*, (Chicago: The University of Chicago Press, 1981), 7, my italics.

PART I

MIGRATION TO MEXICO IN AN AGE OF GLOBAL IMMIGRATIONS

The best means for holding a newly acquired state is to establish colonies in one or two places that are as it were the keys to the country. Unless this is done, it will be necessary to keep a large force of men-at-arms and infantry there for its protection. Colonies are not very expensive to the Prince, they can be established and maintained at little, if any, cost to him; and only those of the inhabitants will be injured by him whom he deprives of their homes and fields, for the purpose of bestowing them upon the colonists; and this will be the case only with a very small minority of the original inhabitants. And as those who are thus injured by him become dispersed and poor, they can never do him any harm, while all the other inhabitants remain on the one hand uninjured, and therefore easily kept quiet, and on the other hand they are afraid to stir, lest they should be despoiled as the others have been. I conclude then that such colonies are inexpensive, and are more faithful to the prince and less injurious to the inhabitants generally; while those who are injured by their establishment become poor and dispersed, and therefore unable to do any harm, as I have already said. And here we must observe that men must either be cajoled or crushed; for they will revenge themselves for slight wrongs, while for grave ones they cannot. The injury therefore that you do to a man should be such that you need not fear his revenge.

Machiavelli, *The Prince*, 1532

CHAPTER ONE

FROM CONQUEST TO COLONIZATION

THE MAKING OF MEXICAN
COLONIZATION POLICY AFTER
INDEPENDENCE

This first chapter examines how the demographic and strategic position of Indios Bárbaros, immigrants, migrant Indians, and Mexicans north of the Rio Grande influenced the direction and ultimate implementation of immigration-cum-colonization policies after Mexican independence. Many intellectuals of the era argued that one of the primary reasons for dramatic U.S. economic growth and aggressive westward expansion was the arrival of European immigrants – a global phenomenon on which Mexico also sought to capitalize. But, unlike its neighbors, Mexico received few of these immigrants because of restrictive policies influenced by botched colonization schemes, lower wages, three Spanish expulsions, and religious intolerance against non-Catholics. Mexican colonization policy fluctuated between inclusion and exclusion, but ultimately these early trials and tribulations became the basis for a series of laws that would ultimately give preferential treatment to Mexicans willing to settle and colonize the frontiers of the Republic.

These conclusions contradict a view in the immigration and colonization historiography that suggests these policies were implemented solely to "whiten" the populations like those in the United States, Argentina, or Brazil. Aside from emerging in a period that witnessed the movement of millions of people across the globe, Mexico's immigration policies emerged in large part as a way to incorporate the majority of the indigenous populace into the larger "Mexican family," but also as a way to "Mexicanize" communities outside of state control like those residing on the frontiers of Tejas, Alta California, and Nuevo Mexico. The botched colonization project of Stephen F. Austin in Texas in the early 1820s – a project that set in motion the confrontation between Mexico and the United States in 1846 – forever altered not only the politics of colonization in Mexico, but the very way in which Mexican national identity was imagined.[1] Populations along the newly independent nation's frontiers, many of whom had been neglected for generations under the Spanish Empire, were now being courted to thwart European and Euro American immigrants making their way toward Texas and the frontiers of the two republics.

HISTORIOGRAPHY

In Dipesh Chakrabarty's pioneering study of postcolonialism and the writing of history, the author engages one of the central problematics of historical writing, which is the question of time and of temporality, and the pitfalls of a stagist history. Through his analysis of stagist history, Chakrabarty came to critique the founding statement and approach of the Subaltern Studies Collective he helped found when he noted:

> It is also with a similar reference to "absences" – the "failure" of history to keep an appointment with its destiny (once again an instance of the "lazy native" shall we say?) – that we announced our project of *Subaltern Studies*: "It is the study of this *historic failure of the nation to come to its own, a failure due to the inadequacy* of the bourgeoisie as well as of the working class to lead it into a decisive victory over colonialism and a bourgeois-democratic revolution of the classical nineteenth century type...or [of the] "new democracy" [type] – *it is the study of this failure which constitutes the central problematic of the historiography of colonial India.*[2]

Chakrabarty questions these earlier statements because "failure" here suggests that India failed to develop into a more European-style democracy instead of the kind of democracy currently in practice. It is with this critique in mind that I approach the subsequent historiography in the

[1] I am thinking here of Roger Bartra's observation that, "Without a doubt, confrontation with the northern Other has spurred the definition of Mexican identity." Part of that "other" is the border, which he notes "is a constant source of contamination and threats to Mexican nationality." Part of that "other," I would assume, includes the persons that reside along those borderlands. See *Blood, Ink, and Culture: Miseries and Splendors of the Post-Mexican Condition* (Durham: Duke University Press, 2002), 11–12.

[2] Dipesh Chakrabarty, *Provincializing Europe: Postcolonial Thought and Historical Difference* (Princeton: Princeton University Press, 2000), 31–2. My emphasis

growing literature on Mexican immigration and colonization policies, which collectively argue that Mexico's failure to attract Europeans signals a failure to become modern, a failure to become more like Europe and therefore less Mexican. The trope of failure, as I will demonstrate, is evident in much of this literature and has a long history that now goes back half a century.[3] As a result, subsequent narratives are tinged with a series of questions that do little to explain these policies on their own merits and in accordance with sensitivity to their historical temporality.[4] The failure of colonization in Mexico, for most historians, is a failure to whiten the populace.

Historiographically speaking, it could be argued that the works of Moisés González Navarro make up a significant portion of the colonization and immigration literature, and the approach taken by this particular author has greatly influenced subsequent studies.[5] It was he who first described colonization and immigration policies as "failures" in the historical literature. I would suggest that this tendency to read

[3] John A. Ochoa, *The Uses of Failure in Mexican Literature and Identity* (Austin: University of Texas Press, 2004), passim.

[4] On sensitivity to historical temporality, see William H. Sewell Jr. *Logics of History: Social Theory and Social Transformation* (Chicago: The University of Chicago Press, 2005), 15.

[5] In chronological order, these works include Moisés González Navarro, *La política Colonizadora del Porfiriato* (México: Separata de Estudios Históricos Americanos, 1953); Moisés González Navarro, *La colonización en México, 1877–1910* (México: 1960); Ignacio González-Polo, "Ensayo de una bibliografía de la colonización en México durante el siglo XIX," *Boletín del Instituto de Investigaciones Bibliográficas* 4, (1960): 179–91; George Dieter Berninger, *Mexican Attitudes Towards Immigration, 1821–1857* (Ph.D. Dissertation, Department of History, University of Wisconsin, 1972); Ignacio González-Polo y Acosta, "Colonización e inmigración extranjera durante las primeras décadas del siglo xix," *Boletín bibliográfico de la Secretaria de Hacienda y Crédito 412*, (1973): 4–7; Nancy N. Barker, "The French Colony in México, 1821–1861,: *French Historical Studies 9(4)*, (Fall 1976): 596–618; Dieter Berninger, "Immigration and Religious Toleration: A Mexican Dilemma, 1821–1860," *The Americas 32(4)*, (April 1976): 549–65; José B. Zilli Mánica, "Proyectos liberales de colonización en el siglo XIX," *La palabra y el hombre 52*, (Octubre-Diciembre 1984): 129–42; Moisés González Navarro, *Los extranjeros en México y los mexicanos en el extranjero, 1821–1970*, 3 Vols. (México: El Colegio de México, Centro de Estudios Históricos, 1993); Jurgen Buchenau, "Small Numbers, Great Impact: Mexico and Its Immigrants, 1821–1973," *Journal of American Ethnic History*, (Spring 2001): 23–49; David K. Burden, *La idea salvadora: Immigration and Colonization Politics in México, 1821–1857* (Ph.D. Dissertation, Department of History, University of California-Santa Barbara, 2005).

Mexican history in terms of failure, following the words of Chakrabarty, is to always see the figure of the Indian as a figure of lack. In the case of nineteenth-century Mexico, the Indian serves as the figure that holds back the progress of the nation. In this historiography, therefore, "there was always room in this story for characters who embodied, on behalf of the native, the theme of inadequacy or failure."[6] Ironically, it was precisely the Indian who influenced and shaped the formation of colonization policies previously read as failures, but for some reason not privileged in the historiographical record.[7]

González Navarro's first study of colonization policies during the Porfirian period appeared in an extended essay in 1953 and was followed by an expanded monograph in 1960, *La colonización en México, 1877–1910*. The inclusion and success of European and American immigrants in Mexico during the Porfiriato form the dominant narrative of these two works, as González Navarro paints a contradictory picture of immigration during the late nineteenth century. In these two early works, his trope of failure was taken up by later historians of all eras, including those who have studied Mexican colonization policies prior to his periodization. González Navarro himself came to view much of Mexican history through the lens of failure, as shown in his monumental three-volume study, *Los extranjeros en México, y los Mexicanos en el extranjero, 1821–1970*, published in 1993. In volume one of that trilogy, to point out just one example, he divides the book into five hefty sections, three of which are titled first, second, and third "falls" – or failures if you prefer.[8]

---

6 Chakrabarty, *Provincializing Europe*, 31–2.
7 An early ethnographic work describing the many "Indios Bárbaros" of the north can be read in José Cortés, *Views from the Apache Frontier: Report on the Northern Province of New Spain*, edited by Elizabeth A. H. John and Translated by John Wheat (Norman: University of Oklahoma Press, 1989).
8 The author has three sections in his book outlined in the following manner: chapter 2, "Primera caída y un tropezón"; chapter 3, "Segunda caída"; chapter 5, "Tercera caída." Although humorous and interesting to read the narrative of first, second, and third falls, one can clearly see the author's trope of a nation growing up. The first tripping is that of Texas and the "failed" project of Coatzoalcos in Veracruz. The second falling of the young nation is the expulsion of the Spaniards and the U.S.–Mexican War of 1848. The third fall signifies the external debt and the French invasion. Mexico, therefore, is not only emplotted within a narrative of a young nation trying to grow up but tripping up at the same time, but also one that fails to whiten its indigenous population. See González Navarro, *Los extranjeros en Mexico, vol. 1*.

From the beginning González Navarro laid out his reasons for characterizing Mexican immigration policy as a failure quite clearly. In the opening paragraph to *La política colonizadora del Porfiriato* (1953), González Navarro states:

> The colonies that had more success in their agricultural endeavors were precisely those (Mormons, Italians of Chipilo, Puebla, etc.) *that were less mexicanized*, and the colonies in which the foreigners mixed with the nationals were never prosperous enough to justify the great deal of resources expended in their creation.[9]

Note here that the author's correlation between success and failure is dependent on whether colonies were more or less Mexicanized, and not on whether the colonies survived and flourished or whether colonies continued to have "more success in their agricultural endeavours."[10] For the author, hence, Mexico's immigration policies are a failure because the state failed to whiten the population. Success here means those colonies that were less Mexicanized, thus the Mormons and Italians were more successful.[11]

[9] Moisés González Navarro, *La política Colonizadora del Porfiriato* (México: Separata de Estudios Históricos Americanos, 1953), 185; my emphasis on the terms *menos se mexicanizaron* original: "Las colonias que tuvieron más éxito en sus labores agrícolas, fueron precisamente aquellas (mormones, italianos de Chipilo, Puebla, etc.) que *menos se mexicanizaron*, y las colonias en que los extranjeros se mezclaron con los nacionales no tuvieron una prosperidad particularmente importante, que justificara los cuantiosos gastos que se emplearon en su instalación."

[10] Neither the Italian nor the Mormon colonies (save one) survive in contemporary Mexico. Most of the Mormon settlers that arrived in the late nineteenth century fled during the Mormon Exodus of 1912.

[11] It is interesting here to point out that in a number of Italian colonies in the state of Chihuahua, particularly Fernández Leal, the first Italian colonists actually had trouble with agriculture and required local knowledge to help them with the harvest. This only makes sense if you are accustomed to planting during a particular month in Italy versus the very difficult climate in Mexico. Thus, to provide one example, the inspector of the Colonia Fernández Leal pointed out that although this year's harvest was not too abundant, this year's would surely be. According to this individual "En este año se esperan mejores cosechas porque los Italianos se han dedicado a trabajar mejor, han abonado mas sus terrenos, han preparado las tierras con tiempo oportuno, según se les tiene prevenido." In México. Secretaria de Fomento, *Memoria Presentada al Congreso de la Unión por el Secretario de Estado y del Despacho de Fomento, Colonización, Industria y Comercio de la República Mexicana. General Carlos Pacheco Corresponde a los Años Trascurridos de Enero de 1883 a Junio de 1885, 5 vols.* (México: Oficina

González Navarro took up the theme of failure again in *La colonización en México, 1877–1910* (1960). This study, more detailed and rigorous than his first effort, likewise ends on a bitter note as failure is once again invoked and reinscribed into the historiography of immigration to Mexico. Here the author ends with a lament: "And this is how the grand illusion of an independent Mexico vanished until the Revolution: foreign colonization."[12] The "grand illusion" so cherished by González Navarro was that elusive prize Mexico could never possess: foreign colonization that would whiten the populace in the mind of this author. Indeed, González Navarro went on to say as much in *Los extranjeros en México, y los Mexicanos en el extranjero, 1821–1970*, when he noted that after the revolution, "one very important change is that the necessity to 'whiten' the Mexican populace disappears."[13] In other words, efforts to whiten the population no longer appeared in the record after the revolution of 1910. Though this may seem perplexing to some, policies to whiten the population were in fact never written into immigration or colonization laws, and one is left to wonder where the author obtained his information for these conclusions.[14]

On the U.S. side of this equation, two pieces will suffice to demonstrate how the continued trope of failure reemergence in this body of literature. The most recent piece is that of David K. Burden, in which the author employs the term "failure" four times throughout his essay, going as far as describing nineteenth-century Mexican liberals as politically immature when he posits that "the Liberals' faith in the benevolence of humankind seems amazingly näive."[15] In like fashion, Jurgen Buchenau echoes the thesis of Mexico's failure to whiten its population by titling an entire section of his article "The Elusive

Topográfica de la Secretaria de Fomento, 1887): I; 194 [hereafter cited as *Memoria de Secretaria de Fomento* with corresponding years].

[12] González Navarro, *La colonización en México*, 140; original: "Así terminó oficialmente la gran ilusión del México independiente hasta la Revolución: la colonización extranjera."

[13] González Navarro, *Los extranjeros en Mexico*, I:10; Original: "un cambio muy importante es que desaparece la necesidad de 'blanquear' a la población Mexicana."

[14] I've been unable to locate legislation or official decrees that use the term *blanquear*, at least for those laws having to do with colonization and/or immigration.

[15] David K. Burden, "Reform Before *La Reforma*: Liberals, Conservatives and the Debate Over Immigration, 1846–1855," *Mexican Studies/Estudios Mexicanos*, 23;2, (Summer 2007): 283–316.

Dream of a 'Whiter' Mexico." In that section, without citing any source concerning Mexican history in his footnotes, he notes that "Díaz joined his colleagues in Brazil and Argentina in viewing immigration as a way of 'whitening' a heavily miscegenated population."[16] In addition, he goes on to state erroneously that "what was curiously absent from all of these measures was a plan to assimilate foreign nationals, or at least make them into what one Porfirian thinker called the *new creoles*." As well, he errs in observing that there was no plan for assimilation, or what the Mexicans referred to as *Mexicanizar*. In fact, the vast majority of contracts for colonization under the Porfiriato had requirements to Mexicanize the population by incorporating Mexicans from within and without, and the genealogy of these policies can be read in the 1820s.[17] Interesting, Buchenau regurgitates the trope of failure but with a twist. Now, instead of Mexico simply failing to attract Europeans in the years 1821 through 1973, the "small numbers" of Europeans who did come had a "great impact" on Mexican history.[18]

Each of these studies has overlooked an examination of colonization policies over time in conjunction with a consideration for demography, but also larger questions having to do with national security, sovereignty, and the negative experiences of past colonization schemes. After living under a colonial caste system for generations, Mexico rejected race categories during the early phases of independence and such sentiments

[16] Bucheneau, "Small Numbers, Great Impact," 31; for his sources on this question of whitening in Mexico, Buchenau offers us Tom Holloway's *Immigrants on the Land: Coffee and Society in São Paulo, 1886–1934* (University of North Carolina Press, 1980) and José Moya's *Cousins and Strangers*, but with no page numbers. He offers no citation for an example of this "whitening" in Mexico during the Porfiriato.

[17] Most contracts awarded to survey companies and colonization companies stipulated that a certain percentage of the colonists had to be Mexicans. Luis Huller was awarded a contract to colonize Las Palomas, Chihuahua with a population that would have to be at least sixty percent Mexican, "preferably those Mexicans that reside in New Mexico, California, Arizona, and Colorado." See contract in México, Archivo del Senado, *Diario de los Debates de la Cámara de Senadores Decimocuarto Congreso Constitucional, Primero y Segundo Periodos* (México: Imprenta de Gobierno Federal, en el ex-Arzobispado, 1889), 72; 88–7 [hereafter cited as *Archivo del Senado*].

[18] Thus, Vicente Fox Quesada is Mexico's first president with immigrant parents and Carlos Slim is the wealthiest "immigrant" in Mexico. Or, to employ Buchenau's own compelling evidence when he cites how "immigrants and their descendants were well represented in the Diaz cabinet": José Y. Limantour was from a Barcelonette family and Ignacio Mariscal was "married to a woman from Baltimore." See Bucheneau, "Small Numbers, Great Impact," 32.

were inscribed into immigration and colonization policy, even if with some inconsistencies.

Nineteenth-Century Mexican Immigration Policies and Indios Bárbaros

In the years that followed independence from European rule and in the exuberance of defeating their one-time colonizers, the young nations of the Americas sought to throw off the yoke of colonialism while simultaneously inviting the migration and settlement of Europeans. This effort to attract European immigrants in the aftermath of American and Mexican independence coincided with a period of global mass migrations that lasted for about a century. Historian José Moya asserts that the movement of Europeans that began modestly after the end of the "Latin American wars of Independence gathered steam after mid-century, reached massive proportions after the 1870s, and lasted – with a pause during WWI – until the Great Depression" was unprecedented: "[N]othing resembling this massive movement had ever happened before anywhere on the planet," and nothing similar has happened since.[19]

Scholars of this particular period in world history, however, contend that most researchers who discuss world migrations often ignore the larger pattern of movements across the globe occurring at the exact same time. These critics argue that African and Asian migrations are ignored and "when mentioned, are usually described only as indentured migration subject to the needs of Europeans or as peasants fleeing over-population pressures." As such, historian Adam McKweon reminds us that along with the millions of Europeans coming to the Western hemisphere after several Latin American nations gained their independence, 48 million to 52 million Indians and southern Chinese migrated to southeast Asia, the Indian Ocean, and the South Pacific; while 46 million to 51 million Russians and northeastern Asians migrated to points in Manchuria, Siberia, Central Asia, and Japan. In short order, the period between 1846 and 1940 witnessed the global migration of 160 million individuals, and thus Latin America become one site of these multiple settlements.[20]

---

[19] José Moya, "A Continent of Immigrants: Postcolonial Shifts in the Western Hemisphere," *Hispanic American Historical Review* 86:1, (February 2006): 1–28.

[20] Adam McKeown, "Global Migration, 1846–1940," *Journal of World History*, 15; 2, (June 2004): 155–89.

There was also a direct correlation between the number of immigrants accepted by a particular nation and its economic production. Thus, to cite Moya once more, "It is no coincidence that the four most important receivers of European immigrants in the nineteenth century (the United States, Canada, Argentina and Brazil) also became the four most important recipients of British investment and the four fastest growing economies in the Western Hemisphere." The link between a booming economy and European immigrants was not lost on the Mexicans of the 1820s as they witnessed how a vast majority of those individuals would eventually settle in the United States, further spurring that nation to project an expansionist policy. Migrants and immigrants provided the demographic conditions for U.S. expansionist policy, which required more territory to settle the millions that were arriving. By the time of the global Great Depression of 1929, the United States had received the vast majority of these European immigrants whereas Mexico was only able to attract between one and three percent of the total.[21]

Why did Mexico receive so few immigrants while other locales became important sites for European settlements? What was problematic about Mexican immigration and colonization policies that prevented or impeded the migration of Europeans, particularly as compared to the policies of Brazil and Argentina? Did the ideology of Mexican colonization policy concern itself more with domestic issues to the detriment of those of an international nature? How did expulsions, low wages, a large indigenous population, unfertile and unsurveyed lands, and thwarted colonization schemes affect subsequent colonization policy? Why did Europeans prefer the United States, Canada, Argentina, and Brazil to Mexico, and how did the Mexican government respond?

The following chapter attempts to provide answers to these multiple questions by arguing that Mexico's colonization policies need to be evaluated not simply in terms of failure or success, but also as legal vehicles intended to encourage the incorporation of certain groups of people into the nation of Mexico and to discourage the incorporation of others.[22] Potential immigrants not only had to deal with lower wages, unsurveyed landscapes, "administrative disorder," and unclear

---

[21] Moya, "A Continent of Immigrants, 1–28; Magnus Mörner, *Adventurers and Proletarians: The Story of Migrants in Latin America* (Pittsburgh: University of Pittsburgh Press & UNESCO, 1985); Jürgen Bucheneau, "Small Numbers, Great Impact," 23–49.

[22] Bill Ong Hing, *Defining America Through Immigration Policy* (Philadelphia: Temple University Press, 2004), 2.

guidelines regarding colonization, but then had to contend with Mexican nativism surrounding the ambiguity of foreign colonization, especially after 1836 and 1848. Moreover, the official Mexican ideal of *mestizaje* that articulates a painful, if invented, community of miscegenation has conveniently overlooked the nation's violent practices of expulsions and exclusions that ultimately contributed to a hostile environment for European settlement. In this regard, although much of the historiography on Mexican immigration policy has made an argument for whitening analogous to Brazil or the United States, this sort of language was never codified into law. An examination of this historiography reveals that the origins of this argument date to the post-WWII period when scholars sought to solidify a critique of the *ancien régime* of Porfirio Díaz by painting it as despotic, pro-American, and thus anti-Mexican. In this regard, immigration and colonization policy in this early period seems more in line with the political thinking to which Claudio Lomnitz drew attention to in his study of Mexican national culture, in which he argued that writings on "Lo Mexicano" constitute a "racial ideology of Mexicaness [that] can be understood as a qualified (but not absolute) critique of Westernization and imperialism."[23]

Intellectuals at various times in the nation's history had called for the "whitening" of Mexico, but immigration policies that favored Europeans over Mexicans and Indians were never adopted.[24] On the contrary, Mexican immigration policy simultaneously permitted both the settlement of Euro Americans in Texas and the expulsion of Spaniards from Mexico. Following the Mexican American War, the 1848 decree that instituted the Department of Colonization specifically banned Euro American colonists from immigrating to Mexico. Otherwise, settlement in Mexico was open to the entire world.[25] By the time the 1883 Land and Colonization Law was passed, coupled with the experience

[23] Claudio Lomnitz, *Exits from the Labyrinth: Culture and Ideology in the Mexican National Space* (Berkeley: University of California Press, 1992), 2.

[24] For some examples of these varying discussions, please see Martin S. Stabb, "Indigenism and Racism in Mexican Thought: 1857–1911," *Journal of Inter-American Studies* 1, No. 4, (October 1959): 405–23; T. G. Powell, "Mexican Intellectuals and the Indian Question, 1876–1911," *The Hispanic American Historical Review* 48, No. 1, (February 1968): 19–36.

[25] F. de la Maza, *Código de colonización*, 386–406; Article 1, Chapter 3 of *Proyectos de iniciativa sobre colonización* stated: "[F]oreigners originating from any nation of the world will be admitted in the territory of the Republic, without the need of a passport."

of foreign invasions and repeated episodes of filibustering along the
northern frontiers, immigration policy favored Mexicans in the United
States over other potential immigrants to Mexico. Unlike more overt
attempts at whitening, – as in the examples of Cuba, the Dominican
Republic, Brazil, or the United States – Mexico's immigration policies
emerged in large part as a way to incorporate the indigenous populace
into the larger "Mexican family" but also as a way to Mexicanize communities outside of state control. Immigration policy was conceived
and contested in the context of a very substantial indigenous population, and then evolved to a policy that eventually placed Mexicans in
the United States at the top of the immigration pyramid.

Attorney and Asian American studies professor Bill Ong Hing provides a number of answers to the question of what immigration policies
can tell us about national identity in his 2004 study, *Defining America
Through Immigration Policy*. The inclusion or exclusion of particular peoples via immigration and colonization policies are "interactive
frames" by means of which intellectuals and politicians could shape
national identity in postcolonial Mexico.[26] Ong Hing points out that
"immigration policies are not simply reflections of whom we regard as
potential Americans, they are vehicles for keeping out those who do
not fit the image and welcoming those who do."[27] Mexican nationalism,
as it oscillated between exclusion and inclusion, "went from excluding Spaniards in the early Independence movement, to including them
at Independence, to excluding them again, all in a very short lapse of
time."[28] This is why immigration policies cannot be examined statically,
but as policies that change over time and in accordance with the social
and political context of the day. Such policies articulate a number of
facets regarding national identity when espoused, and they (immigration laws, decrees, and policies) deserve to be analyzed in their own
right as primary documents.

Certainly, political and economic concerns were of more interest to
post-independence politicians and military officials, whose main unease

[26] The term *interactive frames* is borrowed from Lomnitz, *Deep Mexico, Silent
Mexico*, 13–14.
[27] Ong Hing, *Defining America Through Immigration Policy*, 2.
[28] Lomnitz, *Deep México, Silent México*, 29. The same pattern, one could argue,
holds true for North Americans who were welcomed first as *empresarios*, then
excluded after the 1830s and 1848, only to be reinvited during the Porfiriato
(1876–1910) before again being excluded after 1911 (especially the Mormon
Exodus of 1912).

was the territorial integrity of the nation and the looming threat of U.S. and European expansion into its defined borders. Indios Bárbaros of the northern frontier regions, *fronterizos*, as well as migrant Indians, came into the purview of post-independence colonization policies that attempted through force and coercion to "amalgamate" independent Indian nations that had been resisting certain aspects of U.S. and Mexican westernization-cum-modernization for at least three centuries. Immigration and colonization policy in Mexico after independence, in contrast to the prevailing historiography, was not so much concerned with "whitening" as it was with incorporating independent Indians and subsequently creating a buffer zone against U.S. and European encroachments.

INDEPENDENCE AND THE PROMISE OF EMPIRE: INDIOS AND INTELLECTUALS

Independence in Mexico, as in most Latin American nations, was an historical watershed. When speaking of the transformation of Spanish American nationalism during this period, historian and anthropologist of Mexico Claudio Lomnitz argues that post-independence statehood in Spanish America "forced deep ideological changes, including a sharp change in who was considered a national and who a foreigner, a redefinition of the extension of fraternal bond through the idea of citizenship, and the relationship between religion and nationality and between race and nation."[29] Thus, all persons now born in Mexico were considered equal when Agustín de Iturbide's government "solved the so-called Indian problem by ending legal proscriptions for Indians and making them citizens."[30] With the issue of citizenship theoretically resolved, Mexicans imagined themselves as independent and on the way to full-fledged participation in the larger community of nations.

During the First Constituent Congress in 1821, those behind the first effort to implement a colonization policy believed that Mexico was in an "era that will change the face of the earth...putting commerce at the center of the nations among us in Anáhuac as the balancing point between Europe and Asia."[31] The authors of this document – among

[29] Ibid., 27.
[30] David J. Weber, *The Mexican Frontier, 1821–1846: The American Southwest Under Mexico* (Albuquerque: University of New Mexico Press, 1982), 103.
[31] José Gutiérrez de Lara, *Proyecto de Ley General de Colonización, 1822*; quoted in Burden, *La Idea Salvadora*, 54.

them some of the most important political and intellectual figures of the period – shared a vision of Mexico assuming a more prominent role in world history as the continent that would serve as the meeting point between the East and the West.[32]

Reinscribing their own historical trajectory back to the so-called discovery of the New World as the gateway to the East, these men now inverted that historical moment whereby Mexico–Anáhuac was to be the meeting point between two other civilizations. In his recommendations to the first independent government, Simón Tadeo Ortiz de Ayala made note of the fact that:

> The physical situation of the Mexican empire offers invaluable advantages, considered with regard to its communications and the remainder of the civilized world. Situated in an isthmus bathed by the Pacific and Atlantic oceans, the old empire of Anahuac seems destined to exercise a large influence on the political events that agitate the large nations. The government of the empire can communicate with Europe in five weeks, in six with Asia, and in three with both Americas (North and South America).[33]

This perception of Mexico as an equal partner and a middleman in world history rested in part on the belief that immigrants would help facilitate, but not control, this coming prosperity. European immigrants, aside from being conduits for commerce and trade, would also help to break down the "wasteful hacienda system" by increasing the population of the country and forcing the breakup of the large landholdings concentrated in the hands of the few, according to these same authors.[34]

---

[32] Some of these intellectuals included Manuel Mier y Terán, Antonio Cumplido, Refugio de la Garza, José Gutiérrez de Lara, Juan José Espinosa de Monteros, and Lorenzo de Zavala.

[33] Simón Tadeo Ortiz de Ayala, *Resumen de la estadística del imperio mexicano, 1822: estudio preliminar, revisión de texto, notas y anexos de Tarsicio García Díaz,* (México: Biblioteca Nacional, Universidad Autónoma de México, Reimprimido 1968), 53. Original: "La situación física del imperio mexicano ofrece ventajas inapreciables, considerada con respecto a sus comunicaciones con el resto del mundo civilizado. Situado en un istmo bañado por el Pacífico y Atlántico, el antiguo imperio de Anahuac parece estar destinado a ejercer un grande influjo en los acontecimientos políticos que agitan las grandes naciones. El gobierno del imperio puede comunicarse en cinco semanas con Europa, en seis con Asia y en tres con ambas Américas."

[34] Berninger's reading of Gutiérrez de Lara also makes this point. Please see "Mexican Attitudes Towards Immigration," 24–5.

The confidence of postcolonial Mexican intellectuals was further
fueled by the publication of Alexander Von Humboldt's (1769–1859)
studies of the continent, in which he too incorrectly declared that the
wealth of New Spain lay in its rich and abundant lands. His influence
on the intelligentsia is evident from an examination of Ortiz de Ayala's
Resumen de la estadística del imperio mexicano, 1822, which refers explicitly to the "wise baron."[35] According to Von Humboldt's observations,
"Those who know the interior of the Spanish colonies from the vague
and uncertain notions hitherto published will have some difficulty in
believing that the principal sources of the Mexican riches are by no
means the mines, but in agriculture which has been gradually ame-
liorating since the end of the last century."[36] The distinction that was
overlooked was not so much the largesse of the territory, but the lack of
arable land to irrigate and grow accordingly.

Much of Mexico's available lands in the post-independence period,
it would later be articulated, was not arable land, but land located either
in deserts along the northern frontiers or in extreme tropical locales
along the eastern and southern coasts of the Republic. More important,
and as Raymond Craib reminds us, much of the territory was not fully
surveyed.[37] True as this may have appeared to Humboldt, the bounty
and promise of Mexico's fertile lands were seen as the ideal incentives
for "energetic, industrious, and liberal-minded Europeans" to colonize in the country. Moreover, the intellectuals and politicians of post-
independence Mexico believed that the wealth derived from mining
during the colonial period would continue to increase.[38] Various expulsion orders against Spaniards, many of whom were middlemen and of
the commercial class, did little to ameliorate the dire economic situation after independence.

---

[35] Simón Tadeo Ortiz de Ayala, *Resumen de la estadística del imperio mexicano*, 14.
[36] Humboldt does mention earlier in his study that bullion also constituted a large
source of income for Europe when he pointed out that: "The quantity of gold
and silver annually sent by the New Continent into Europe amounts to more
than nine-tenths of the produce of the whole mines in the known world." See
Political Essay on the Kingdom of New Spain, trans. John Black (New York: I.
Riley, 1811), ci and 54.
[37] Raymond Craib, *Cartographic Mexico: A History of State Fixations and Fugitive
Landscapes* (Durham: Duke University Press, 2004).
[38] Javier Ocampo, "El entusiasmo, expresión espontánea ante el triunfo," Capitulo
I en *Las ideas de un día; el pueblo mexicano ante la consumación de su independencia*, (México: Colegio de México, 1969):13–45.

This optimism of the Mexican intelligentsia also had its roots in the colonial period, growing out of the conception of "New Spain" as the jewel of the Iberian world.[39] It had supplied the world with great riches in the form of bullion, crucial for the rise of the cash economy, and had also contributed the food staples that would eventually bring about the "demographic revolution" in Europe.[40] The large and ever-increasing shipments of silver to Europe and the myths of Mexico's untapped wealth, perpetuated by the writings of Von Humboldt, further bolstered the idea that Mexico would simply have to open its doors to Europe and the teeming millions would soon come rushing in.[41] Mexican intellectuals and politicians envisioned a republic composed of small yeoman farmers cultivating small plots of land; inevitably they would become part of the world economy and thus hasten the economic development of the nation as a whole. But unlike the United States, Argentina, or Brazil, much of Mexico's arable land was claimed in one form or another by the hacendado class. The "land-tenure system," as Victor Bulmer-Thomas argues, "revolving as it did around the plantation, the *hacienda*, the small farm, and communal Indian lands, was barely affected."[42] In the case of Mexico, a disproportionate amount of available land was not yet surveyed, difficult to work, or located along the frontiers of the republic that were still very much under the control of various independent indigenous groups, something worth discussing at length.

For most Mexican politicians and intellectuals, the model for parceling out lands to those willing to colonize frontier regions was based partly on their young and expanding neighbor to the north. Mexico,

---

[39] The optimism of Mexicans was something shared by many in independent Latin America. See Victor Bulmer-Thomas, *The Economic History of Latin America Since Independence*, 2nd Edition (Cambridge: Cambridge University Press, 2003), 2.

[40] Alfred W. Crosby, "The Demographic Effect of American Crops in Europe," chapter 9 in *Germs, Seeds and Animals: Studies in Ecological History* (Armonk, NY: M.E. Sharpe, 1994): 148–63. The term *demographic revolution* is also borrowed from Moya, *Cousins and Stranger*, 13–44.

[41] "Mexican industry experienced a boom in the first quarter of the century that was followed by successive spurts of growth that registered an output of between 1801 and 1810 to over 200 million pesos, more than four times the amount for 1701–1710. See Burkholder and Johnson, *Colonial Latin America*, 5th Edition (New York: Oxford University Press, 2004), 149–50; also John Lynch, *The Spanish American Revolutions, 1808–1826* (New York: W.W. Norton & Company, 1973), 295–6.

[42] Bulmer-Thomas, *The Economic History of Latin America*, 29.

however, developed a different policy toward the indigenes than that of the United States.[43] When discussing the sheer geographical challenge that the Mexican territories represented for these post-independence intellectuals, Ortiz de Ayala could only conclude after calculating the size of Mexico compared to its concentrated population that: "This proves the necessity of adopting the system of the United States, peopling the most depopulated areas with the surplus of inhabitants of some provinces."[44] Based on statements like this, many historians have concluded that Mexicans were quick to accept many aspects of the United States as a model for their own nation "[because] it was evident that the ease with which the United States altered and accepted immigrants had paid off handsomely," according to one view.[45] But the U.S. example would not be followed to the letter, since the formulation of and ideology behind Mexico's colonization policy ostensibly reflected Mexico's particular social and cultural milieu. Ortiz de Ayala qualifies his earlier praise of the U.S. system by stressing that Mexico should not "imitate in this part that of our neighbors."[46] And compared to that of the United States, Mexican demography enjoyed a larger indigenous population.

In the decades prior to the wars of independence, the population of Mexico – and several regions in Central and South America – was predominantly indigenous. These differing demographics are, in my estimation, important in analyzing why such different policies would be established. Take the estimates of New Spain's population in 1793 that two scholars of colonial Mexico offer the reader: of a population of 3.8 million, approximately 2.3 million were considered "Indian," or around sixty-one percent of the total.[47] Scholars examining the population statistics for the years between 1810 and 1821 differ with regard

---

[43] Historian David Weber posits that "Throughout the Spanish American mainland by the 1790s, numerous indigenous peoples had been incorporated rather than eliminated, and most of the Natives who still lived independently along the borders of New Spain's American empire had come to some form of accommodation with the Hispanic world, and it with them." See *Bárbaros: Spaniards and Their Savages in the Age of Enlightenment* (New Haven & London: Yale University Press, 2005), 2.

[44] Ibid., 19.

[45] Berninger, "Mexican Attitudes Towards Immigration," 18.

[46] Ortiz de Ayala, *Resumen de la estadística del imperio mexicano, 1822*, 85.

[47] Jaime E. Rodríguez O. and Colin M. MacLachlan, *Forging of the Cosmic Race: A Reinterpretation of Colonial México, Expanded Edition* (Los Angeles: University of California Press, 1990), 197.

to the total population but find essentially the same percentage for the indigenous population. Historian Eric Van Young states that during this period there were approximately 6.1 million inhabitants in New Spain, of which 3.7 million were Indian, or about sixty percent.[48] Thus the majority of the population was indigenous during this period and would remain the so until well into the nineteenth century. With a population composed primarily of indigenous peoples the demographic reality on the ground necessarily provided the reference point for most legislation dealing with the makeup of the population following the wars for independence. This legislation entailed, in some form or fashion, the acceptance of Mexican hegemony or the targeted extermination of indigenes by colonists and other allies of the state.[49]

These ideas shared a long trajectory going back to the colonial period and the rupture of the wars for independence provided another opportunity to settle unresolved issues. Other historians of Mexico have argued along these same lines, and noted historian William B. Taylor believes that "the Post Independence period brought massive impersonal changes to peasant life, comparable in scale to the sixteenth-century political revolutions, epidemics, resettlement programs, religious conversion, and labor and tax systems that resulted from Spanish colonization."[50] Laws enacted to eliminate the communal property holding of indigenous peoples "opened the way to the alienation of village lands." Moreover, "the process of dismemberment began in the late 1820s and reached its peak...when the Liberals attempted to integrate Indians into national society by dissolving their communal life."[51] Lomnitz expands on this observation in pointing out that "[t]he ideological, legal, and physical assault on communal village lands and other indigenous community institutions such as hospitals, public political offices, schools, and the management of community chests began in the first years of Independence."[52]

---

[48] Eric Van Young, *The Other Rebellion: Popular Violence, Ideology, and the Mexican Struggle for Independence, 1810–1821* (Stanford: Stanford University Press, 2001), pp. 46–7.

[49] Jorge Chávez Chávez, *Los indios en la formación de la identidad nacional* (Ciudad Juárez, Chih.: Universidad Autónoma de Ciudad Juárez, 2003).

[50] William B. Taylor, *Drinking, Homicide and Rebellion in Colonial Mexican Villages* (Stanford: Stanford University Press, 1976), 146.

[51] Ibid.

[52] Lomnitz, "Communitarian Ideologies and Nationalism," in *Deep Mexico, Silent Mexico*, 48.

The dissolution of communal life was a tactic of the state to incorporate those who had resisted the imposition of alternative modes of citizenship, like Indios Bárbaros and independent Indians. Among the laws that can be cited as instrumental in the process of incorporating the indigenous populations of Mexico into the larger "social organism" were those dealing with the question of colonization of and immigration to Mexico, to which we now turn.[53]

EUROPEAN IMMIGRATION, 1821–1900

At a more hemispheric level that follows our global approach, one scholar of Latin America argues that intercontinental immigration between 1824 and 1924 totaled "52 million individuals. Some 72% of these set out for the U.S., while 21% departed for Latin America and only 7% for Australia," according to Magnus Mörner. Of the 11 million immigrants who settled in Latin America, 5.5 million (fifty percent) settled in Argentina while thirty-six percent settled in Brazil, leaving the other Latin American nations only fourteen percent of all other European immigrants. By contrast, Mexico received a mere three percent of the Latin American total by Mörner's estimates.[54] José Moya's excellent study – which covers a period four years earlier and eight years later – offers us some different numbers worth considering. According to his research, Europeans who migrated to various

[53] It should also be pointed out that the role of the census plays a significant role in reorienting and therefore reclassifying indigenous populations as "Mestizo." See, for instance, Alexander S. Dawson, "From Models for the Nation to Model Citizens: Indigenismo and the 'Revindication' of the Mexican Indian, 1920–40," *Journal of Latin American Studies* 30, No. 2: 279–308; Anne Doremus, "Indigenism, Mestizaje, and National Identity in Mexico during the 1940s and the 1950s," *Mexican Studies/Estudios Mexicanos*, Vol. 17, No. 2 (Summer 2001): 375–402; for the reshifting of indigenous identities in Brazil see Muriel Nazzari, "Vanishing Indians: The Social Construction of Race in Colonial Sao Paulo," *The Americas* 57, No. 4, (April 2001): 497–524; for the case of Argentina see Gastón Gordillo, "Indigenous Struggles and Contested Identities in Argentina: Histories of Invisibilization and Reemergence," *Journal of Latin American Anthropology* v. 8 no 3 (2003): 4–30.

[54] Magnus Mörner. *Adventurers and Proletarians: The Story of Migrants in Latin America* (Pittsburgh: University of Pittsburgh Press, 1985); for studies of immigration in Chile and Argentina see Carl Solberg, *Immigration and Nationalism, Argentina and Chile, 1890–1914* (Austin: University of Texas Press, 1970); and José C. Moya, *Cousins and Strangers: Spanish Immigrants in Buenos Aires, 1850–1930* (Berkeley: University of California Press, 1998).

destinations between 1820 and 1932 totaled 56,183,000. In contrast to Mörner's total, Moya suggests that of the 56 million Europeans who emigrated, 13.4 million made their way to Latin America. In his calculations, the number of European immigrants to Mexico is half of one percent, just 270,000 by 1932.

Of the 13.4 million Europeans who immigrated to Latin America between the 1820s and the 1930s, estimates are that almost sixty percent eventually settled in Argentina. Moya's study of Spanish immigrants to Argentina has not only generated some new numbers and statistics, but has also revolutionized the manner in which historians approach the question of transnational migrations to and from the Americas.[55] Between 1820 and 1932, Moya estimates, Argentina received 6.5 million immigrants, coming in second to the United States, which took in 32.5 million immigrants, or five to one. Third was Canada with 5 million immigrants for the same period.

The larger percentage of immigrants to the United States was due to its geographical location, fertile lands, liberal land and immigration policies, higher wages, and a relatively low population density of indigenous peoples – a population that usually served to compete with incoming immigrants for wage labor. Argentina, too, offered higher wages than did Mexico during this period and did little to finance the travel costs of immigrants. Mexico would neither subsidize European immigrants to any significant degree nor raise wages for their sake.

The connection between a high concentration of land after independence and increased wages is something that previous economic historians have noted. Historian Victor Bulmer-Thomas argues, for instance, "the durability of the land-tenure system and the domestic capital markets implied that no drastic changes could be made in labor relations or in the operation of labor markets."[56] Countries more apt to adopt and adapt to global markets were also those that offered higher wages to potential immigrants seeking to earn better money abroad. Timothy J. Hatton and Jeffrey Williamson note in their *longue durée* analysis of global immigration during this period, "undoubtedly, the major incentive for emigration was the large difference between wages in the country of origin and those in the country of destination."[57]

55 Moya, *Cousins and Strangers*, 46–7.
56 Bulmer-Thomas, *The Economic History of Latin America*, 30.
57 Timothy J. Hatton and Jeffrey Williamson, "Migration during 1820–1920, the First Global Century," *World Economic and Social Survey* (2004), 10.

Wages in Mexico and "the Mexican economy stagnated throughout the first half of the nineteenth century…and it was not until the second half of the nineteenth century that the economy once again began to grow, slowly at first throughout the 1860's and 1870's, then accelerating during the final decades of the century," according to Enrique Cárdenas.[58]

And although legislation favoring some groups over others is perhaps not as important for some scholars, I would argue that it is crucial for understanding the question of national identity as it relates to the demographic composition of the country. Besides, what better way to analyze how a nation imagines itself if not by the very people who compose it? Legislation may not always be able to control who arrives in the country, but it certainly speaks volumes as to what kind of people are initially desired. Early ideas about immigration in Argentina favored North Americans and the English, but in the end, Argentina ended up with a population that was considered "least desirable" by the likes of Juan Bautista Alberdi – the intellectual author behind Argentina's immigration policies.[59] Brazil, on the other hand, sought to replace African slave labor with industrious and pliable European immigrants but ultimately ended up abandoning colonization projects for low-wage local laborers by the 1930s.[60]

Mexico's approach was multifaceted and shaped by a large population of indigenous groups along its northern frontiers. Fear of land loss shaped this colonization policy and forced the country to incorporate a population that could act decidedly in a battle for supremacy, and later as a "buffer zone" between the center and periphery of Mexico. The difference between the three countries is the presence of the United States and the new international boundary. As the quintessential

[58] Enrique Cárdenas, "A Macroeconomic Interpretation of Nineteenth Century Mexico," in *How Latin America Fell Behind*, Edited by Stephen Haber (Stanford: Stanford University Press, 1997), 65–92.

[59] Juan Bautista Alberdi, *Bases y puntos de partida para la organización política de la República Argentina* (Buenos Aires, 1852), 16; see also Sam Schulman, "Juan Bautista Alberdi and his Influence on Immigration Policy in the Argentine Constitution of 1853," *The Americas* 5;1, (July 1948): 3–17.

[60] George Reid Andrews has provided an interesting case study on the changing immigration policies of São Paolo, Brazil by pointing out this change over time. Whereas early European settlements had "failed" well into the 1880s, European immigration would be privileged for four decades, only to be replaced for native Afro-Brazilians by the 1930s. See especially his Chapter 3 "Immigration, 1890–1930" in *Blacks and Whites in São Paolo, Brazil*, 54–89.

preferred location of most immigrants coming from Europe, the higher wages and more intense labor demands pulled emigrants from Mexico at a time when places like Argentina, Brazil, and Cuba were enjoying the benefits of new immigrants.

What we can say from this brief overview of European immigration to Mexico is that by 1876, between twenty-five thousand and thirty-five thousand foreigners had taken up residence since the liberalization of immigration policies in 1823. The total number of immigrants (European and otherwise) to Mexico increased to 116,527 by the end of the Porfiriato in 1910. After the Great Depression this number more than doubled to 270,000 according to some scholars, though Mexico was in thirteenth place among the nations that received immigrants during this period, or about two percent of the Latin American total. By contrast Argentina received 6,501,000 immigrants, followed by Canada (5,073,000), Brazil (4,361,000), and Cuba (1,394,000).[61] In each of these countries, we can generally assume, laws were not passed that restricted immigration to those of the Catholic faith nor was legislation ambivalent about its treatment of foreign immigrants. There were no expulsion orders against Spaniards in any of these countries after independence comparable to those enacted by Mexico, nor did these countries share a border with the United States.[62] These countries, finally, offered better wages to potential immigrants.

These numbers stand in stark contrast to the numbers of Mexican laborers who migrated to the United States during the same period. For example, the 1930 U.S. Census states that there were 1,422,533 Mexicans residing in the U.S. Southwest while at the same time a mere 270,000 immigrants resided in Mexico, leaving a deficit in the population of 1,152,533.[63] Even during the period just prior to Porfirio Díaz taking

[61] Moya, *Cousins and Strangers*, 46–7.

[62] A recent study on Spanish expellees from Latin America during this period notes that the expulsions from the Mexican case "had a special reach and magnitude" due in large part to their numbers and to the fact that they had enjoyed privileged positions in the most key sectors of the administration, clergy, commerce, and military. See Jesús Ruiz de Gordejuela Urquijo, *La expulsion de los españoles de México y su destino incierto, 1821–1836* (Sevilla: Consejo Superior de Investigaciones Científicas; Escuela de Estudios Hispano Americanos, 2006), 227.

[63] See Mark Reisler, *By the Sweat of Their Brow: Mexican Immigrant Labor in the United States, 1900–1940.* (Westport, CT: Greenwood Press, 1976), 269; The numbers of Mexicans leaving the United States, however, does not take into account the longer history of migration to the United States since the

power, the foreign population numbered between twenty-five thousand and thirty-five thousand while the number of Mexican migrants to the United States totaled 68,399 by 1880. In other words, two Mexicans were leaving the country for every foreigner who arrived in Mexico between 1821 and 1876. After the 1870s this disparity would increase. By 1930, upwards of 5.2 Mexicans were leaving for the United States for every foreigner that arrived in Mexico. Put in another way, more Mexicans had migrated to the United States by the 1930s than Europeans had arrived in Cuba, which numbered 1,394,000 immigrants, and constituted the fifth most popular destination for immigrants to the Americas.

This paradox of inviting Europeans to colonize Mexican territory and then seeing its own population migrate northward did not occur in any other Latin American country during this period. Even Francisco I. Madero, Mexico's "apostle of democracy" and the first president of the revolution, lamented the situation in his country when he pointed out in 1910 that "Mexico is the only country in all of the Americas where its nationals migrate abroad."[64] Although the contrast between European immigration to Mexico and Mexican emigration to the United States is stark, it is important to keep in mind the historical context of this paradox. To begin with, while Mexico was one of the few countries to receive immigrants during this period, it shared a border with a northern neighbor (the preferred destination for 32.5 million immigrants) that also attracted Mexican laborers from the northern states of the republic – the very region that the country had struggled to settle and colonize prior to 1848. Thus, while Mexico sought to invite European settlers, if only on paper, its own laborers were migrating north in growing numbers, a trend which would escalate under the Porfirian regime and which continues almost without pause to this very day.

POST-INDEPENDENCE IDEOLOGIES OF MEXICO: INCLUSION AND EXCLUSION

The version of the Mexican nation championed by the government of Agustin de Iturbide – the failed constitutional emperor whose

---

establishment of the international boundary between the two countries. See M. Colette Standart, O.P., "The Sonoran Migration to California, 1848–1856: A Study in Prejudice," *Southern California Quarterly* LVIII, no. 3 (Fall 1976): 333–57.

[64] Francisco I. Madero, *La sucesión presidencial en 1910. El partido nacional democrático* (San Pedro, Coahuila, 1908), 238.

administration lasted less than a year after independence in 1821 – was considered the most likely to succeed in "modernizing" the country according to Western values and via symbols and rituals provided by the elite during the colonial period. Through various methods, the indigenous populations were obligated to "accept and assimilate the cultural values they [Iturbide's government] upheld and recognized as the only possible government and nationality for the state – the Mexican nation."[65] Noted intellectual José María Luis Mora summed up the postcolonial liberal stance when he pointed out that the Farías administration that ruled in the following decades ignored the distinctions "of past years that were proscribed in constitutional law, but he applied all his efforts towards forcing the fusion of the Aztec race with the general masses; thus he did not recognize the distinction between Indians and non-Indians in government acts, but instead he replaced it with one between the poor and the rich, extending to all the benefits of society."[66]

The goal was to *transform* the Indians who were the majority of the nation's population into Mexicans. The government's hope was that these new citizens would convert their property into private holdings and subsequently become part of the global economy; this would enable Mexico to join the larger community of modern nations. Here the inclusion of the indigenous population also entailed the loss of the institutional protections these communities had enjoyed during the colonial period. No longer able to rely on the large corporate holdings protected by the Spanish colonial system for 300 years, the indigenous peoples were expected to become private landowners who would be self-sustaining and therefore subject to state taxation and rationalization. For this reason, the immigration of Europeans – as individuals outside the "colonial constitutions" of the Mexican Indians – would assist in modernizing and rationalizing the republic.[67]

---

[65] Chávez Chávez, "Retrato del Indio Bárbaro. Proceso de Justificación de la Barbarie de los Indios del Septentrión Mexicano y Formación de la Cultura Norteña," *New México Historical Review* 73, no. 4 (October 1998): 389–424.

[66] José María Luis Mora, *Obras Sueltas*, (México: Editorial Porrúa, c. 1837, 1963), 1, 152–3; Quoted in Lomnitz, *Deep Mexico, Silent Mexico*, 49.

[67] The term *colonial constitution* is borrowed from Lomnitz and is intended to relay the notion that Indian republics after independence were akin to a "nation within a nation," and therefore constituted particular life worlds distinct from those of the Mexican Creoles – whose culture was not exclusively European either. See *Exits from the Labyrinth*, 275.

Another factor that had plagued colonial officials was the disproportionate concentration of the population in a handful of states around Mexico City. Magnus Mörner notes, "[T]he approximately seven million Mexicans who formed the population in 1821 were insufficient for a land that extended from Oregon to Yucatán and from Texas to Guatemala."[68] The presence of the state in the sparsely populated northern regions radiated outward from the center in the form of presidios, military colonies, and citizen–soldiers, while the church extended its influence via the extensive yet waning missions system.[69] Most of the population in Mexico was concentrated in areas where the presence of the state was more visible and most capable of protecting its citizens from the raids that were frequent in areas of low population density, like the north. The millions of Europeans migrating to the Western Hemisphere, it was hoped, would people the north and take up arms on behalf of "civilization."[70] Joining them in this larger national project to settle *terrenos baldíos* would be the Mexicans concentrated in the center of the country. In short, the presence of the state along its peripheries was limited and immigration policy was therefore seen as one of the many remedies to this ongoing concern in post-independence Mexico.

Immigration debates after 1821 thus centered on two questions: whether the Mexican government should focus its energy on inviting Europeans to settle in Mexico or whether it should concentrate on what was then known as "auto-colonización" or "colonization from the interior."[71] The latter entailed the resettling of primarily an indigenous population in locations where the inhabitants were not considered sufficiently loyal to the state. The former entailed the immigration of European settlers to sparsely settled areas in the Mexican republic, offering them lands and then Mexicanizing them. What eventually became settled law was that all subsequent colonies would be mixed with Mexican citizens, and no colony composed of foreigners would be

---

[68] Berninger, "Mexican Attitudes Towards Immigration," 19.

[69] Weber, *The Mexican Frontier*, xv–xxiv.

[70] Enrique Florescano states that the population for the whole northern province (Nueva Vizcaya, Sonora, Nuevo México, Coahuila, and Texas) during the 1780s was around 220,400 in a population that totaled well over 7 million. See "Colonización, ocupación del suelo y "frontera" en el norte de Nueva España, 1521–1750," in *Tierras: Expansión territorial y ocupación del suelo en América (siglos xvi–xix), Ponencias presentadas al IV Congreso Internacional de Historia Económica* (México: El Colegio de México, 1968): 43–76.

[71] González-Polo y Acosta, "Colonización e inmigración extranjera," 4–7.

able to settle twenty leagues from the border in order to prevent another Texas episode. The ideology of colonization in Mexico was based on a number of demographic particulars, and as a result, very different immigration and colonization policies were developed there when compared to Argentina, Brazil, or the United States. Two proposals submitted to the first Mexican Empire provide us with a detailed description of post-independence Mexico and illustrate the ideology behind the colonization policy prior to its transformation into various laws and decrees between 1821 and 1848.

EARLY PROPOSALS FOR COLONIZATION: FROM CONQUEST TO COLONIZATION

The most telling of these proposals was presented on December 29, 1821 to the governing junta following independence from Spanish rule. Entitled *Dictamen Presentado a la Soberana Junta Gubernativa del Imperio Mexicano*, (1821) (hereafter *Naciones Bárbaras*), this extensive document made several observations, recommendations, and other suggestions that would outline colonization policy in the coming years.[72] The policy shift in this document represents a slight departure from the colonial approach with regard to the process of colonizing – and therefore "civilizing" – the indigenous populations of the north. According to this document, "conquest" was out of the question and a different strategy of colonization would have to be employed along the northern corridors populated by Indios Bárbaros.

Beginning with a description of the largest of these indigenous groups in the northern part of the republic, *Naciones Bárbaras* suggests that it is

[72] México, Junta Provisional Gubernativa, Comisión de Relaciones Exteriores. *Dictámenes Números 1 y 2. Naciones Bárbaras de las Indias. Anglo-Americanos. Dictamen Presentado a la Soberana Junta Gubernativa del Imperio Mexicano por la Comisión de Relaciones Exteriores en 29 de Diciembre de 1821, Primero de Independencia.* (México: Biblioteca Aportación Histórica, reprinted 1944); the extended version of this document actually entailed a more detailed foreign policy regarding Russia, Guatemala, England, and the vulnerable coastlines. For the sake of space and in order to focus on the topic at hand, I will focus on the two main focal points of this report. See Juan Francisco de Azcarate, *Dictamen Presentado a la Soberana Junta Gubernativa del Imperio Mexicano por la Comisión de Relaciones Exteriores en 29 de Diciembre de 1821, Primero de Independencia* (México: Publicaciones de la Secretaria de Relaciones Exteriores, 1932). Located at the AHSRE, *Biblioteca José María Lafragua* (hereafter cited as *Naciones Bárbaras de las Indias. Anglo-Americanos*).

"necessary to abandon all projects of conquest" because there were not enough people to settle those lands. The first observation reflects the recognition that – both in the past and at present – there was a sheer lack of bodies to populate and guard the northern frontiers.[73] Employing an early version of cost-benefit analysis, the document noted the costly nature of conquest, suggesting the best prospects for success lay in the establishment of friendly commercial ties with those areas where such ties did not exist, and to maintain ties where they were already established:

> The punctuality in complying with the treaties and good faith in commerce are the magnetism that attracts the Indians, and by this conduct they communicate their fruits and riches, they become civilized, they acquire the better uses and customs; and they are disposed unfeelingly to embrace the religion established in the Provinces and with the inhabitants of the *reducciones* and towns that have a relationship with them. If the Empire would adopt this measure it will achieve greater profits with lower expenses comparable to those realized by the English, the French, and the Anglo-Americans.[74]

The comparison with the French, English, and Anglo-American strategies of conquest is notable and illustrates the power and influence of the Indian nations themselves. Past experience had taught the previous governments that indigenous populations could be employed and coerced by other European powers seeking to advance their expansionist projects in the Americas.[75] The change in policy proposed in this document is that conquest be abandoned in favor of colonization but with the same end results. We can therefore say that the strategy

---

[73] Florescano, "Colonización, ocupación del suelo y "frontera" en el norte de Nueva España, 1521–1750," 43–76.

[74] *Naciones Bárbaras de las Indias. Anglo-Americanos*, 12–13. original: "La puntualidad en cumplir los tratados y la buena fe en los comercios es el magnetismo que atrae a los Indios y por estos conductos comunican sus frutos y riquezas, se civilizan, adquieren los usos y costumbres mejores; y se disponen insensiblemente para abrazar la religión establecida en las Provincias y que siguen los habitantes de las reducciones y pueblos que con ellas tienen parentesco. Si el Imperio adoptarse esta medida, con menos gastos logrará mas utilidades, como las perciben los Ingleses, los Franceses y los Anglo-americanos."

[75] Brian DeLay, *War of a Thousand Deserts: Indian Raids and the US-Mexican War* (New Haven: Yale University Press, 2008).

changed while the intention remained the same, the intention being to forcefully assimilate or acculturate independent Indians into the larger social organism.

These same concerns are voiced in another document by Tadeo Ortiz de Ayala and titled *Resumen de la estadística del imperio mexicano, 1822*, which constitute part of a genealogy to the immigration and colonization policies that emerged in the years following independence. Influenced by the Enlightenment ideas of the day – notably the writings of Adam Smith, Alexander Von Humboldt, and Melchor Gaspar de Jovellanos – Ortiz de Ayala's attitudes toward the indigenous populations mirrored those expressed in *Naciones Barbaras*.[76] Brief and yet erudite, *Resumen de la estadística del imperio mexicano, 1822* covers issues surrounding geography, demography, economics, sources of wealth, and problems with governmentality in the first part and then offers up suggestions for solving these issues in the second part. Here, Ortiz de Ayala provides 115 recommendations on a variety of issues including political thought, foreign policy, public education, labor, agriculture, industry, commerce, transportation, and finally colonization.[77]

With respect to the northern territories with which this chapter is most concerned, Tadeo Ortiz de Ayala remains faithful to the Enlightenment ideals that had so influenced the intelligentsia during the Bourbon reforms as he condemns the cruel treatment of the indigenes by military and ecclesiastical authorities situated along the northern frontiers.[78] His commentary is worth quoting at some length here since he suggests the same recommendations made in *Dictamen*

[76] For other ideological and intellectual influences on Tadeo Ortiz de Ayala, see Tarsicio García's introduction in Tadeo Ortiz de Ayala, *Resumen de la estadística del imperio mexicano, 1822*, vii–xxvii; also Wilbert H. Timmons, "Tadeo Ortiz, Mexican Emissary Extraordinary," *The Hispanic American Historical Review*, Vol. 51, No. 3 (August 1971): 463–77.

[77] Ortiz de Ayala's influence in colonization policy recommendations cannot be overstated. Not only were many of his ideas implemented in subsequent colonization policy, but he also headed a number of colonization projects to Texas and in Coatzacoalcos in the years after the publication of this document. Edith Louise Kelly and Mattie Austin Hatcher, "Tadeo Ortiz de Ayala and the Colonization of Texas, 1822–1833," *Southwestern Historical Quarterly 32*, (February-April 1929).

[78] Weber's recent monograph, *Bárbaros*, provides the best background to those Enlightenment ideals regarding treatment of the indigenes.

Presentado a la Soberana Junta Gubernativa del Imperio Mexicano (1821).
For Ortiz de Ayala:

> The conduct of the cruel soldiers and the ignorant missionaries of
> the northern borders is neither the best means to attract the innu-
> merable nations, whom the missions of the United States solicit
> with other political methods for the commercial advantage and
> growth of that nation. It is very sad to see a continuous and costly
> bloodthirsty war against towns that did no wrong to begin with,
> *and that are called barbarian because they do not wish to be converted*
> *by force*, while the protestant missionaries with their charity and
> sweetness are able to civilize, they convince with their persuasion,
> gaining the friendship of innumerable peoples, to the extent that
> our north provinces could cause incalculable harm in times of war
> with that republic.[79]

The overarching concern of Ortiz de Ayala is that the indigenes be
treated with a benevolent "sweetness" lest they be converted by the
"protestant missionaries" who can later "cause incalculable harm in
times of war with that republic [the United States]." Ortiz de Ayala
advocates abandoning the previous politics of conquest in favor of
a more "benevolent" and "sweet" policy of colonization as the "best
means to incorporate [into the Mexican state] the numerous nations,"
largely in the interest of *realpolitik* and national security. Recognizing
the resistance to Mexican hegemony, or its unsuccessful efforts to pacify these independent indigenous groups, to add just one more detail, is
also a recognition that although the tactics would change, the intention of the state would not. Whether "sweet" or "sour," the Mexican
state would forcibly incorporate or decimate independent Indians.[80]

---

[79] Ortiz de Ayala, *Resumen de la estadística del imperio mexicano, 1822,* 21; Original:
"La conducta de los crueles militares y los misioneros ignorantes de las fronteras
del norte, no es tampoco el mejor medio de atraer a innumerables naciones, que
con otra política las misiones de los Estados Unidos solicitan, con ventajas de su
comercio e incremento de la nación. Es un dolor ver una continua guerra costosa
y sanguinaria contra pueblos que no agraviaron en los principios, y que llaman
bárbaros porque no quieren convertirse a la fuerza, mientras que los misioneros protestantes con su beneficencia y dulzura civilizan, convencen por la per-
suasión, ganando la amistad de innumerables hordas, que a nuestras provincias
del norte pudieran causar incalculables males en tiempo de guerra con aquella
república." My italics.
[80] Chávez Chávez, *Los indios en la formación de la identidad nacional,* 26–7.

As to the question of colonization, Ortiz de Ayala discussed the importance of populating and settling a number of areas throughout the Mexican Empire within the context of his larger imaginings for the nation. These imaginings were directly tied to his main concern regarding populating the vast and rich areas of the country. According to Ortiz de Ayala:

> [T]he integrity of the national territory continues to be weak, [and] risks being lost if there is not a change in the system or an adoption of positive measures to promote its security, by means of a strong local administration that is dependent on and concili- atory towards the federal government, [and] since that frontier point embraces the interests of the entire confederacy, it is the one who should take charge of its care and custody.[81]

His preference for European immigrants is not stated in the section where he makes those recommendations. Instead what is expressed, at least according to article 105, is the author's excitement concerning Chinese and South Indian (the word "Indu" is used) immigrants.[82] These "hard-working inhabitants," according to Ortiz de Ayala, are accustomed to the tropical climate of the Mexican coastal areas.[83] And although "foreign families" are mentioned and favored for colonization, they are mentioned within the same paragraph as "useful nationals," "military veterans," and "federal employees." In short, the question of colonization in the after-math of independence is tied directly to the territorial integrity of the nation and hence the indigenous populations of the republic, but within the context of the global phenomenon of transnational immigration.

[81] Tadeo Ortiz de Ayala, *Resumen de la estadística del imperio mexicano, 1822,* 85. Original: "La integridad del territorio nacional sigue débil, expuesto a perderse si no se cambia de sistema y adoptan positivas medidas de fomento y seguridad, mediante una administración local fuerte y conciliante depen- diente del gobierno federal, puesto que aquel punto fronterizo abrazando los intereses de la federación entera, ella es quien debe encargarse de su custodia y cuidado."

[82] As noted earlier, 12 million South Asians (Indians) and Chinese migrated to various points in the globe between 1820–1930, thus suggesting that Mexican intellectuals were attuned to global migrations.

[83] It is interesting to note that Alberdi specifically points out that the migrations of Chinese and South Indians would not be good for the nation. For example, "Pero poblar no es civilizar, sino embrutecer, cuando se puebla con chinos y con indios de Asia y con negros de África," in *Bases y puntos de partida para la orga- nización política de la República de Argentina,* 18.

IMMIGRATION POLICIES AFTER INDEPENDENCE, 1821–1846

As with much Mexican legislation that followed independence from Spain, several significant issues remained unresolved with the conclusion of hostilities, including a number of pending cases with respect to colonization of the northern frontiers. The Spanish government had been aware for decades of the potential threats posed by the Americans, French, and Russians, so efforts to grant lands for colonization were well under way by the time of independence.[84] Although ambivalence surrounding foreign colonization was voiced as early as 1813, the increasing number of Euro Americans in Texas compelled the Mexican government to legally address the reality at hand.[85]

The best known and most crucial for understanding the evolution of colonization policy was a grant awarded to Moses Austin to settle 300 families in Texas in January of 1821. Spanish officials in Monterrey had authorized Austin to colonize what is now Texas when a number of events led to the reconfiguration of the original agreement between Austin and the fledgling Spanish government. The first was that the Mexican monarchy instituted by Iturbide fell not long afterward, thus rendering all previous contracts null and void. Second was the fact that the elder Austin died before he could act on the grant, which was taken up by his son Stephen F. Austin. The younger Austin began to lead families into Texas in mid-1822 with the knowledge of the governor of Texas at San Antonio de Bexar.

Because the Mexican government was still forming coalitions in the wake of independence, Austin opted to travel to Mexico City to confirm the specifics of his colonization plan. According to historian Andrés Reséndez, "Austin…spent all of 1822 and part of 1823 in Mexico City validating a Texas land grant that the Spanish colonial government had conferred on his father."[86] By the time Austin returned to Texas, the newly independent republic had passed an updated colonization law

---

[84] Spain opened up its lands to foreign settlement in 1820. For an example of early fears of U.S. expansion, see Cortés, *Views from the Apache Frontier*, passim.

[85] Article 10 of *Sentiments of the Nation, or Points outlined by Morelos for the Constitution*, states "Foreigners shall not be admitted, unless they are artisans capable of teaching [their crafts], and are free of all suspicion." English translation located in *The Mexico Reader: History, Culture, Politics*, Edited by Gilbert Joseph and Timothy J. Henderson, (Durham: Duke University Press, 2002), 189–91.

[86] Reséndez, *Changing National Identities*, 65.

that restructured the older law under which the elder Austin had been awarded his grant.[87] The first colonization law, however, is worth going over for the purposes of comparison with the national colonization law published a year later.

The colonization contract that approved the land grant to Moses Austin in 1821 emanated from the northern territories and was subsequently replicated in the Imperial Colonization Law of 1823. Certain features of Austin's contract became standard and were codified in federal law, illustrating the effect of peripheral and regional particularities on federal legislation. We can see in this one example of legislative borrowing the dialectical relationship between the northern territories and Mexico City. This was a legislative pattern that persisted throughout the century as the central government sought to extend its hegemony throughout the peripheries. After independence, all contracts between the Spanish government and other northern state officials were eventually nullified with the publication of the more comprehensive Imperial Colonization Law of 1823.[88] This colonization law was approved during the brief reign of Emperor Agustín I and replaced by a national colonization law a year and a half later. The Austin colony came under this law, as well as most land grants that were awarded henceforth.

Contrary to the claims of historians concerning the whitening of Mexico (similar to what occurred in Brazil or Argentina), at least according to the Imperial Colonization Law of 1823, the articles of the law do not reveal anything that would indicate this particular objective, particularly considering that the law privileges war veterans, Mexicans, and Europeans who had married Mexican women. Moreover, article 18 states that "[n]atives of the country shall have a preference

[87] "The Mexican Colonization Laws," Document No. 23 in Ernest Wallace, David M. Vigness, and George B. Ward, *Documents of Texas History, 2nd Edition*, (Austin, TX: State House Press, 1994), 46.

[88] Austin received his first contract from the Spanish government, but before the Imperial Colonization Law was implemented he secured another grant from the government of Coahuila y Texas. Because of the many colonization laws being passed, there was a need for a more comprehensive and practical standard. Indeed, "with no published compendium of the Mexican laws, administrative and judicial authority rested with Austin, and the result was a mix of Mexican decrees with pragmatic Anglo-American implementation." See Margaret Swett Henson, *Handbook of Texas Online*, "Anglo American Colonization," http://www.tsha.utexas.edu/handbook/online/articles/AA/uma1.html.

in the distribution of land; and particularly the military of the 'Army
of the Three Guarantees,' in conformity with the decree of the 27th
of March, 1821; and also those who served in the first epoch of the
insurrection." And in support of my earlier point regarding the ongoing
Mexicanization of the nation, article 27 injects a third element intended
to incorporate foreigners into the nation when it states, "Those with
the foregoing qualifications who marry Mexicans will acquire particular
credit for obtaining letters of citizenship."[89] This example of legislated
Mexicanization, or assimilation, contradicts some of the interpretations
that I discussed in the historiographical section.[90]

In effect, one could argue that this particular colonization policy
not only sought to provide settlers with lands that would serve collectively as a buffer zone between Mexico and the expansionist United
States, but it also sought to Mexicanize these colonists by requiring
them to convert to Catholicism and later be naturalized as Mexicans.
As for the indigenous populations, it states that "[n]atives of the country shall have a preference in the distribution of land," as suggested
in the *Dictamen Presentado a la Soberana Junta Gubernativa del Imperio
Mexicano por la Comisión de Relaciones Exteriores en 29 de Diciembre
de 1821*. In terms of what this document tells us about how the nation
imagines itself, we can draw the same conclusions from it as from the
Imperial Colonization Law of 1823. And despite the fact that these policies clearly illustrate a preference for Mexicans willing to colonize the
northern frontier, another piece of legislation from the frontier is worth
examining here in order to observe how the incorporation of the indigenous populations was ultimately inserted into the legislative workings
of colonization policy.

The Colonization Law of the State of Coahuila and Texas, 1825 is
the final piece of colonization policy that we will examine in this section
before analyzing the exclusionary law of April 6, 1830, which prohibited further migration of Euro American settlers from the United States
to Mexico. This law illustrates the dialectical relationship between
state and federal colonization policy, particularly the inclusion of local
and regional specifics that demonstrate how the indigenous populations

---

[89] *Codigo de colonización*, 171–6; English translation is available online at
"Colonization Law Decree of 1823," http://www.tamu.edu/ccbn/dewitt/cololaws.
htm#decree.

[90] For example, Bucheneau argued that Mexico had no assimilation process for
immigrants. See "Small Numbers, Great Impact," 23–49.

were incorporated into the nation via colonization policy.[91] One of the main distinctions posited by this particular colonization law is made clear by its open reference to the incorporation of "wandering tribes" of the region. According to article 19:

> The Indians of all nations, bordering on the state, as well as wandering tribes that may be within its limits, shall be received in the markets, without paying any duties whatever for commerce in the products of the country; and if attracted by the moderation and confidence, with which they shall be treated, any of them, after having first declared themselves in favor of our Religion and Institutions, wish to establish themselves in any settlements that are forming, they shall be admitted, and the same quantity of land given them, as to the settlers spoken of in the 14th and 15th articles, always preferring native Indians to "strangers."[92]

Note the double move where the law requires a declaration that favors the religion and institutions of Mexico while at the same time affirming that the colonization and settlement of the indigenes is always more preferable to that of "strangers." The two articles mentioned – the fourteenth and fifteenth – are familiar because they were written into law in previous colonization policies that we have examined.[93] It

---

[91] The translation "natives" has changed over time, but the Spanish version is less ambiguous on its meaning when it clearly states "Se atenderá con preferencia para la distribución de las tierras á los naturales del país.... " The term *naturales* literally translates into "naturals" and was a term first employed by the Spaniards to describe the natives of the land.

[92] A copy of the English translation is available at "Colonization Law of the State of Coahuila and Texas 1825," http://www.tamu.edu/ccbn/dewitt/cololaws.htm#coahuila; a similar law to the Coahuilan legislation is the Colonization Law of Tamaulipas in 1826. See "*Decreto de 15 de Diciembre de 1826 de la Legislatura de Tamaulipas, para la colonización de extranjeros en aquel Estado,*" especially article 25. In *Código de colonización*, 212–18.

[93] Art. 14. To each family comprehended in a contract, whose sole occupation is cultivation of land, one labor shall be given; should he also be a stock raiser, grazing land shall be added to complete a *sitio*, and should his only occupation be raising of stock, he shall only receive a superficies of grazing land, equal to twenty-four million square bars. Art. 15. Unmarried men shall receive the same quantity when they enter the matrimonial state, and for foreigners who marry native Mexicans, shall receive one fourth more; those that are entirely single, or who do not form a part of some family whether foreigners or natives, shall content themselves with the fourth part of the above mentioned quantity, which is all that can be given them until they marry.

seems, therefore, that Indios Bárbaros and foreigners in this regard are "strangers" while "the Indians of all nations (read civilized) are preferred to strangers." More explicit but less talked about is the open reference to the notion of "always preferring native Indians to strangers," and the "Indians of all nations, bordering on the state, as well as wandering tribes." In this case it is evident that the inclusion of the indigenes is intended to work itself out in the form of a policy whereby the local inhabitants are eventually assimilated into the system.

The laws mentioned earlier, despite their overt preference for native Mexicans and indigenous groups, did not have their intended effect, and soon the northern frontiers were populated with thousands of Euro American and American settlers. Just five years after the passage of the 1830 law, the "Anglo-Texas and slave population had grown to about 24,700 inhabitants, outnumbering Mexican Texans ten to one."[94] Encouraged by the enactment of these liberal land policies, Euro American settlers, mostly from the trans-Appalachia states of Tennessee, Missouri, Arkansas, Alabama, Mississippi, and Louisiana, entered Texas to take advantage of inexpensive land and numerous concessions afforded to potential settlers.[95]

The events that transpired thereafter, which ultimately led to the loss of Texas and the defeat of General President Santa Anna in 1836, is a topic of great interest and debate and certainly well beyond the scope of this chapter. Suffice it to say that the growing migration of these Euro American settlers provided the structural conditions (demographically) for what later became known as the Texas Revolution of 1836. Aware of the problem posed by these settlers, the Mexican government passed a law five years earlier prohibiting further migration to Mexico, but to no avail.[96]

TOWARD EXCLUSION: COLONIZATION POLICY DURING THE MID-NINETEENTH CENTURY

This alarming increase in population, along with an 1828 report on frontier conditions submitted by General Manuel Mier y Terán caused

---

[94] Reséndez, *Changing National Identities*, 22.

[95] Mark E. Nackman, "Anglo American Migrants to the West: Men of Broken Fortunes? The Case of Texas, 1821–1846," *The Western Historical Quarterly*, vol 5;4, (October 1974): 441–55.

[96] "Decreto permitiendo la introducción de algunos géneros de algodón; destinos de los derechos que produzcan y providencias sobre colonización y comercio, Abril 6 de 1830," *Código de colonización*, 241–4.

the federal government in Mexico City to implement what has become known as the Law of April 6, 1830.[97] This law, composed of eighteen articles and quite explicit in its intentions, is a project calculated to exclude foreigners from its territory, even as regional authorities argued in favor of continued migration to these areas.[98] Articles 7 and 9 are central to the process of exclusion as they testify not only to a fear of a potential takeover by these settlers, but also to a national hysteria concerning foreigners; another expression of the latter phenomenon was the expulsion orders against Spaniards between 1821 and 1836, coupled with a fear that foreigners were conspiring against Mexican independence.[99]

In order to prevent Euro American demographic dominance, the law called for the introduction of more Mexican settlers to the area. Article 7 states that "Mexican families that voluntarily want to colonize will be helped with the trip; maintained for a year, given lands and other tools for work."[100] This article of inclusion has as its counterpart one of exclusion in Article 9 in the following, "The entrance of foreigners under any pretext without being provided with a passport issued by the agents of the Republic, at the point of origin, is prohibited along the northern border."[101] The entrance of slavers was also explicitly prohibited in this law, even though the practice had been

[97] See Curtis Bishop, *Handbook of Texas Online*, "The Law of April 6, 1830," http://www.tsha.utexas.edu/handbook/online/articles/LL/ngl1.html. Also Mier y Terán's report see *Texas by Terán: The Diary Kept by General Manuel Mier y Terán on his 1828 Inspection of Texas*, edited by Jack Jackson and translated by John Wheat (Austin: University of Texas Press, 2000).

[98] "Decreto permitiendo la introducción de algunos géneros de algodón; destinos de los derechos que produzcan y providencias sobre colonización y comercio, Abril 6 de 1830," *Código de colonización*, 241–4.

[99] See, for example, Berninger's chapter "Rhetoric and Reality," which registers a number of abuses against foreigners. "Mexican Attitudes Toward Immigration," 81–111; also for copies of the expulsion orders see Harold Sims, *Descolonización en México: El conflicto entre mexicanos y españoles (1821–1831)*, (México: Fondo de la Cultura Económica, 1982), 243–56. See also "Se recomienda al Gobernador del Distrito que mande vigilar y guardar las consideraciones debidas a las personas, casas y demás propiedades de los agentes diplomáticas y consulares y súbditos extranjeros, 1833," in *Archivo Histórico de Relaciones Exteriores*, 1-1-47 [Hereafter cited as AHSRE].

[100] "Decreto permitiendo la introducción de algunos géneros de algodón; destinos de los derechos que produzcan y providencias sobre colonización y comercio, Abril 6 de 1830," *Código de colonización*, 241–4.

[101] Ibid., Original: "Se prohíbe en la frontera del Norte la entrada a los extranjeros bajo cualquiera pretexto, sin estar provistos de un pasaporte expedido por los agentes de la República, en el punto de su procedencia."

outlawed nine years earlier. The exclusion of slaves was not intended to keep out African Americans due to any racialized ideology that targeted people of African descent, but was rather a political move intended to discourage the migration of more settlers from the southern United States, many of whom were bringing slaves with them.[102] In the end this law could not prevent the entrance of settlers who had crossed over into Mexican territory in order to colonize the northernmost regions of the republic.

What was worse, the law had the unintended consequence of inciting the colonists to rebellion, which grew into an independence movement leading to the eventual secession of Texas from the Mexican republic and its annexation a decade later by the United States. This action, as many historians in this field have already concluded, ultimately led to a break in diplomatic relations between the two countries and culminated in the Mexican American War of 1846–1848.

But while some Europeans were being invited into the larger Mexican family, others were being asked to leave by force. Anti-Spanish sentiment had come to the surface during the wars for independence when upwards of one-eighth of the white population were violently murdered, culminating in the tragic events of the "Alhóndiga de Granaditas" in 1810.[103] The antagonism directed by Mexicans toward *gachupines* soon shifted to other European groups considered a threat to the nation. When the Mexican government passed a law in the early 1820s reserving the right to expel any foreigner who hindered the struggle for independence, foreign governments requested assurances that their citizens had legal rights as long as they did not meddle in Mexican affairs.[104] And it was precisely this fear of European interference that eventually led to the expulsion of Spaniards on three separate occasions between 1821 and 1836, coupled no doubt, with Spain's reluctance to recognize the independence of its former colony. Although federal expulsions did not begin until 1827, tensions had been building amidst the struggle for independence.[105]

---

[102] Nackman, "Anglo-American Migrants to the West," 441–55.

[103] For an overview of this violence see Marco Antonio Landavazo, "De la razón moral a la razón de estado: violencia y poder en la insurgencia Mexicana," *Historia Mexicana LIV; 3*, (2004): 833–65.

[104] "Se les dice a los comisionados de Inglaterra que los extranjeros que el Presidente puede expulsar, son los que atenten contra la Independencia o sistema de gobierno de México, 1824," AHSRE, 4-24-7070.

[105] Harold Dana Sims, *The Expulsion of Mexico's Spaniards, 1821–1836*, (Pittsburgh: University of Pittsburgh Press, 1990).

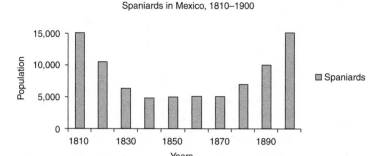

Figure 1.1. Spaniards in Mexico, 1810–1900. Table courtesy of the Author.

Between 1821 and 1836, five national laws and a number of state-level expulsions were implemented in order to rid the newly formed Mexican nation of its Spanish populace.[106] According to Harold Dana Sims, "perhaps a maximum of figure of 10,000 might be reasonable for the *peninsular* community at Independence when the national population had reached about 6,500,000.[107] When the first expulsion took place in late December 1827, 1,823 passports were issued and departure lists recorded 1,771 exiles. The following year 885 *peninsulares* left on their own followed by fifty-three servants.[108] And although strong anti-Spanish sentiment was made visible during the wars for Mexican independence, Dana Sims reminds the reader that "a substantial source of *Criollo* pro expulsionist sentiment was mercantile rivalry between Mexicans and Spaniards during a period of severe economic decline."[109]

SPANIARDS IN MEXICO, 1810–1900

Between the three mass expulsions, the National Colonization Law of 1824, and the break in diplomatic relations between the United States and Mexico in 1846, no other colonization laws or decrees of any substance were passed.[110] The case of Texas loomed large in subsequent

[106] A recent study examines the larger expulsion of Spaniards taking place throughout the Americas, so the trend went well beyond the Mexican experience. See Jesús Ruiz de Gordejuela Urquijo, *La expulsión de los españoles de México y su destino incierto, 1821–1836* (Sevilla: Diputación de Sevilla, 2006).

[107] Sims, *The Expulsion of Mexico's Spaniards*, 10.

[108] Ibid., 35.

[109] Ibid., 18.

[110] Several state laws and decrees are registered; however, they never supersede national legislation. See Sims, *The Expulsion of Mexico's Spaniards*, 37.

colonization policy. This is apparent in a circular published a decade later intended as a reminder to those who would take charge of the *Dirección de Colonización* in late 1846. According to that circular:

> [T]he only one [colonization policy] that has been established and that has prospered, is the one that rebelled in Texas, because the thought of its establishment was not for an economic or commercial venture, but for the usurpation of our territory, taking advantage of the youthful innocence with which the Republic extended its arms to all of the foreign nations without fear during the first days of its independent existence.[111]

The legislation approving the creation of a Department of Colonization in 1846 signaled the importance of having one agency manage and encourage immigration. This law was enacted during the Mexican American War in 1846 – a war that would not end for another fourteen months. It was a case of too little, too late for the inhabitants of the territories that would ultimately be lost to the United States. Until then, little would change in terms of immigration policy. Afterward, Mexican expatriates and Indians were not only specifically mentioned within the national project, but also served as symbols of exclusion in other instances when the territorial integrity of the nation was threatened.

If we take into account the number of immigration and colonization laws that were passed between the war with the United States and the beginning of 1876, at least according to the *Código de colonización y terrenos baldíos de la republica mexicana*, the same pattern regarding the inclusion of the indigenes that I have outlined appears to continue.[112] Postwar immigration and colonization laws seemed to echo the sentiments of José María Lacunza, postwar secretary of the interior, when he noted the following about immigration and colonization policies for the latter half of the nineteenth century,

[111] "Circular de 4 de Diciembre de 1846, recomendando la exacta observancia de las medidas que contiene el decreto expedido para el establecimiento de la Dirección de Colonización," *Código de Colonización*, 360.

[112] De la Maza, *Código de colonización*, 936–45; how these inclusionary measures play out in practice, especially among the various indigenous groups in Mexico, is beyond the scope of this book. Robert Holden comments on two different periodizations for the question of land transfer: 1846 and 1882. See *Mexico and the Survey of Public Lands: The Management of Modernization, 1876–1911*, (DeKalb: Northern Illinois University Press, 1994), 7.

[Regarding the allotment of lands used to invite new settlers,] to liberally grant them would resemble sarcasm, if at the same time indigenous peoples, estranged from their own land, were not deserving of the prudent consideration of the Government. This long standing population should also be attended to, so that it might multiply and prosper; and its prosperity cannot be expected without an easy and abundant means of nourishing itself that, for rural inhabitants, is not possible without productive lands to work.[113]

Even as late as 1898 the great Mexican diplomat Matías Romero maintained that Indians should be converted into "active citizens, consumers, and producers." And when speaking about European immigration he seemingly echoed these mid-nineteenth-century sentiments when he argued, "[B]efore we think of spending money to encourage European immigration to Mexico, we ought to promote the education of our Indians, which I consider the principal public need of the country."[114] In other words, the lack of European migration to Mexico would later necessitate the continued policy of forced, coerced, or implied assimilation or acculturation of the indigenous Mexican population.

Policies favoring Europeans over Mexicans would not be part of the Porfirian project of colonization either, as I will attempt to illustrate in later chapters. The Porfirian period between 1876 and 1911 would partly reflect nationalist ideology in terms of immigration and colonization principles intended to reimplement repatriation of the frontier. Laws encouraging European immigration are almost always accompanied by references to "Mexicanization," or to incentives for incorporating indigenous and Mexican families founded by those few European

---

[113] *Proyectos de Colonización presentados por la junta directiva del ramo, al Ministerio de Relaciones de la Republica Mexicana en 5 de Julio de1848*, (México: Imprenta de Vicente García Torres, 1848), 17–18; Original: "brindándoselas por concesiones liberales, se asemejaría al sarcasmo, si al mismo tiempo la gente indígena no mereciese, extraña en su propio suelo, las miradas de la consideración del Gobierno. La población antigua también debe ser atendida, para que se multiplique y prospere; y su prosperidad no puede esperarse sin medios fáciles y abundantes de alminentarse [sic], que para los habitantes del campo no son posibles sin tierra productiva que labrar."

[114] Matías Romero, *Mexico and the United States: A Study of Subjects affecting their Political, Commercial, and Social Relations, Made with a View to Their Promotion*, 2 vols. (New York: The Knickerbocker Press, 1898), 76.

colonies.[115] New laws, especially the 1883 Land and Colonization Law, would extend invitations for Mexicans in the United States to "return to the homeland" with the most preferential treatment ever written into Mexican immigration and colonization policies during the nineteenth century. Article XVI of the 1883 law demonstrates this new agenda of Mexico's evolving colonization and immigration policies when it stipulates that "Mexicans residing in a foreign country who are desirous of establishing themselves in the uninhabited frontiers of the Republic will have the right to a free land grant, up to an extension of 200 hectares (double that of foreign immigrants) and enjoyed for fifteen years, the exemptions granted by the law."[116] In short, repatriates were allotted twice the amount of land awarded to potential European colonists and any other foreign immigrants.

CONCLUSION

This chapter examined post-independence immigration laws and the role of Indios Bárbaros and Independent Indians, in particular how their demographic and strategic positions influenced the direction and ultimate implementation of Mexican colonization policy throughout the nineteenth century. The conclusions reached in this chapter contradict a view in the historiography that suggests these policies were implemented to whiten the populations like those in Argentina or Brazil, and as such, were failures of Mexican immigration and colonization policy. Mexico's immigration policies emerged in large part as a way to incorporate the majority of the indigenous populace into the larger Mexican family, but also as a way to Mexicanize communities outside of state control.

---

[115] See Robert Holden, "Priorities of the State in the Survey of the Public Land in Mexico, 1876–1911, *Hispanic American Historical Review* 70;4, (1990), 590–592. Holden notes that "Foreign capital played a considerable – if not commanding – role in the modernizing program of the Porfirian period. Thus it was surprising to discover that only 6 of the 59 original concessions was there evidence in the archival record of investments by foreigners; only one concession was awarded outright to a foreigner, Luis Huller." He also states that unlike mininig or railroads, "the survey of public land...was largely a domestic industry."

[116] Secretaría de Fomento, *Memoria Presentada al Congreso de la Unión por el Secretario de Estado y del Despacho de Fomento, Colonización, Industria y Comercio de la República Mexicana. General Carlos Pacheco Corresponde á los años Trascurridos de Enero de 1883 á Junio de 1885*, 5 vols (México: Oficina Tipográfica de la Secretaría de Fomento, 1887), I;185–190; see also De la Maza, *Código de colonización*, 936–45.

Mexico liberalized its immigration policies throughout the nineteenth century, but ultimately a number of factors prevented large-scale immigration of Europeans to that country during this period of mass global movements. I suggest that three Spanish expulsions, unfertile and unsurveyed lands, restrictive immigration policies, religious intolerance toward non-Catholics, and especially low wages all served to discourage immigration from abroad. In the midst of these efforts to attract European immigrants to settle the northern frontiers, Mexico saw a process set in motion by which the loss of its northern territories resulted due to those regions being underpopulated and contested by Independent Indians. Those who eventually did inhabit those regions were Anglo Americans and other Euro American settlers arriving to Texas beginning in the early nineteenth century. Mexicans who remained within the ceded territories were later asked to settle the northernmost regions of Mexico in order to act as a buffer between the latter and the former. This experience would impact colonization and immigration policy thereafter. Nevertheless, European immigrants did come to Mexico during the nineteenth century, although in smaller numbers than was the case in countries such as Argentina, the United States, or Brazil. Most would not settle in government-sponsored colonies but instead chose to live in various urban centers of the republic.

Thus, while Mexico sought to incorporate certain communities within the larger Mexican family, its neighbor to the north undertook a series of Indian removals in the early 1830s that indirectly influenced the forced expulsion of various Mexican communities in Texas and California. In areas where the impact of this global immigration would occur, there appears to be a corresponding expulsion of minority communities, particularly those considered "inferior" or "disloyal." After the Mexican American War, the forced removal of Mexicans would continue during times of economic and political unrest, and the emerging state of Mexico would continue to struggle with the process and practice of repatriation, especially once these repatriates "return[ed] to the homeland."

The President General will not see with indifference a movement that besides naturally awakening his feelings of brotherhood, could be of great utility for our country; thus, there can certainly be no better colonists for our borders, than those instructed with hard experience, as well as with the falsehood of encouraging prom-ises that the Americans are used to making to those that because of their proximity, are found in the most intimate contact with them.

Letter from General Bonilla, Ministry of War and Marine, to the Ministry of Foreign Relations in 1855

CHAPTER TWO

POSTWAR EXPULSIONS AND EARLY
REPATRIATION POLICY

This chapter takes us from the global perspective of the previous chapter to a more hemispheric or binational perspective that examines a series of expulsions that occurred in the lead up to the Mexican American War and then continued throughout the latter half of the nineteenth century. As such, I will not be discussing the coming or process of the war per se, only one manifestation of this event, which shaped the formation of Mexican immigration and colonization policy, particularly for populations outside of state control. Specifically, this chapter also examines a brief history of early nineteenth century expulsions at a moment when immigration policy came face to face with military concerns. Repatriates, especially those expelled from Texas and California, were not only recommended as ideal colonists for the fractured republic, but seen as the most obvious choice for this particular line of defense. "There can certainly be no better colonists for our borders," at least according to General Bonilla of Mexico's Ministry of War and Marine, than those "instructed with hard experience, as well as with the falsehood of encouraging promises that the Americans are used to making...."[1] Mexicans in the United States, the thinking went, would be more anti-American precisely because of their "intimate contact" with Euro Americans.

An important element in this long history is a pattern of what some have termed *ethnic cleansing*.[2] In the 1830s, 1840s, and 1850s, Mexicans

---

[1] "Oficio de la Secretaría de Relaciones a la de Gobernación para que se facilite la inmigración de mexicanos residentes en California, EUA, con destino al departamento de Sonora, por no gozar de sus derechos, Año de 1855," AHMM, XI/481.3/5105.

[2] Gary Clayton Anderson, *The Conquest Of Texas: Ethnic Cleansing In The Promised Land, 1820–1875* (Norman: University of Oklahoma Press, 2005).

residing in the northern territories were the target of a pattern of mass expulsions to Mexico from the borderland regions of California and Texas, areas where Euro American settlers had become a majority. The early expulsions from 1836 through the late 1850s began in the violent aftermath of the Texas Revolution of 1836 and in the wake of the demographic shift in what was once Mexican territory. Similar expulsions took place in the 1840s when the Mexican government tried unsuccessfully to reconquer Texas and again in the 1850s when ethnic Mexicans were often accused of collaborating with freedmen and African American slaves. The government responded by formulating a colonization policy that would simultaneously address the need to repatriate these citizens while fortifying the frontier against further U.S. and Indian encroachment. Much of this discussion would occur in the realm of military colonization favoring Mexicans from the ceded territories.

Although expulsions of Mexicans had taken place since the 1830s, the pretexts for these actions varied. At different times and in different regions, "threats to the nation," "failure to assimilate," "disloyalty," and a host of related notions have been evoked as justifications for removal. To understand the real motives, however, one must look beyond these themes and toward the structural conditions prevailing at the time – labor competition, prior Native American removals, racism, collusion with African American slaves, wage aversion, demographic pressures, the coveting of land, and a perceived terror of Mexican "bandits." A brief look at select archival sources from the nineteenth century highlights some of these structural factors.

Early Mexican Expulsions

The first wave of Mexican expulsions occurred against the backdrop of an increasing migration of Euro Americans to what had once been Mexican territory.[3] Where Mexican settlers were once the majority populace, Euro Americans quickly out numbered these early settlers within a decade. Memories of past massacres by the Mexican Army in Goliad and at the Alamo were still fresh in the minds of Texians, and these recollections provided the psychological setting for these first acts of expulsion in late 1836. Anthropologist and theorist of globalization Arjun Appadurai asserts that "the expelled are often the carriers

---

[3]   Andrés Tijerina, *Tejanos and Texas under the Mexican Flag, 1821–1836* (College Station: Texas A&M University Press, 1994), 137–44.

of the unwanted memories of the acts of violence . . . as new states were formed."[4] The trigger was the so-called Texas Revolution of 1836.

On July 17, 1836, the Mexican consulate reported to the secretary of foreign relations in Philadelphia that over 100 Mexican citizens had arrived in New Orleans after being forced from their homes in Texas. According to the Mexican consulate, Francisco Prianzo Martínez, a U.S. general had issued a warning to all citizens of the León Colony of Texas, Goliad, and Guadalupe Victoria to leave lest they be "put to the knife" by Texas colonists and volunteers, who by then outnumbered the local population.[5] The León Colony was founded by Martín De León, a Mexican empresario who was given a land grant to populate the area in the hopes of thwarting the increasing migration of Euro American settlers.[6] But with the newly arrived Euro Americans outnumbering the local inhabitants almost ten to one by the mid-1830s, these former colonists had a demographic advantage that enabled them to expel those they considered "undesirable." Even though the founders of this particular town, the De León family, fought on the side of Texas and against Santa Ana, their presence and large landholdings generated fear in the burgeoning new state.[7]

The De Leóns were not the only colonists threatened. These early expulsions did not only target individuals; in some cases they were intended to clear the territory of what had become by then a "minority population," namely the early Tejano settlers. General Rusk, the military commander who ordered the expulsion of all Mexicans from this region, issued the following warning to the citizens of the two towns:

> The Citizens of Guadalupe Victoria and Goliad are required, for their own personal safety and security, to march immediately towards the East. They can go as they like, that is, by land or by sea; although the latter is preferable because the trip by land would expose you to inconveniences and labors, and because currently

4   Arjun Appadurai, *Fear of Small Numbers: An Essay on the Geography of Anger* (Durham: Duke University Press, 2006), 42.
5   "Carta de Francisco Prianzo Martínez de Nueva Orleans a Secretaría de Relaciones Esteriores en Filadelfia," July 17, 1836, AHSRE, L-E-1078 (13), 118–19.
6   Ana Carolina Castillo Crimm, *De León: A Tejano Family History*, (Austin: University of Texas Press, 2003), 152–84.
7   Anthony Quiroz, *Claiming Citizenship: Mexican Americans in Victoria, Texas* (College Station: Texas A&M University Press, 2005), 6–7.

there are sufficient boats in the Bay that have been obtained for
this purpose. All will be given Passports and letters of protection,
by means of which you will receive the best treatment. There is
no longer a neutral country; Texas will be free, or it will be transformed into a desert.[8]

Although Rusk confirmed that letters of protection, the best treatment,
and passports would be granted to those individuals, he made clear that
it was not possible to remain neutral in this war for Texas freedom:
"Texas will be free or it will become a desert." He suggested that Texas
would only be free once Mexicans (even those who had demonstrated
their loyalty to Texas) were expelled from their lands, therefore remov-
ing a primary obstacle to further Euro American colonization of the
area. According to the Mexican consulate, Rusk issued another warning six days later: "The families that reside in the Ranchos and in the
immediacies of La Punta, will be transferred aboard in brief time, since
the circumstances require it as such; being the desire, not to detain
the march of the ships, but instead to be most precise." Precision was
necessary because Texas military volunteers were showing "symptoms
of wanting to pass under the knife all Mexicans."[9] A claim filed in the
state of Texas a decade later by Fernando De León asserts that General
Rusk "ordered the removal of the whole De León clan, including the
Carbajal and Benavides families, from Victoria and the Aldretes and
Mancholas from Goliad."[10] These initial acts of expulsion – and those
that followed – were a key component in the formation of the Texas
Republic and a necessary ingredient for thinking *unhistorically*.

[8] "Carta de Francisco Prianzo Martínez de Nueva Orleáns a Secretaria de
Relaciones Esteriores en Filadelfia," 17 de Julio de 1836, in AHSRE, L-E-1078
(13), 118–119; Original: "Los Ciudadanos de Guadalupe Victoria y Goliad son
requeridos, por pedirlo así su seguridad personal, de marchar inmediatamente
para el Este. Podrán ir como gusten, esto es, por tierra ó por mar; aunque se
considera que esta última vía es preferible en razón á que el viaje por tierra los
expondría a inconvenientes y trabajos, y de que en la actualidad hay embarca-
ciones suficientes en la Bahía, que han sido detenidas á este efecto. Se les darán á
todos Pasaportes y cartas de protección, por cuyo medio recibirán el mejor trato.
Ya no hay país neutral; Texas será libre, ó se convertirá en un desierto."
[9] "Carta de Francisco Prianzo Martínez de Nueva Orleans a Secretaría de
Relaciones Esteriores en Filadelfia," 17 Julio 1836, AHSRE, L-E-1078 (13),
118-19.
[10] Castillo Crimm, "Finding Their Way," in *Tejano Journey, 1770–1850*, edited by
Gerald E. Poyo (Austin: University of Texas Press, 1996), 111–23.

The expelled arrived at the port in Louisiana in a miserable state, according to Mexican officials, and their government was unable to provide protection or assistance for their repatriation to Mexican territory. The Mexican representatives in Philadelphia lamented that:

> The position, therefore, of those unfortunates is most pitiful. If at the very least they had been allowed to disembark at some point along the coast of Mexico, they would have at least found aid and consolation; but due to a refinement of cruelty, which public opinion will very soon gauge, they have been sent to a strange land, whose tongue they do not understand, whose customs they do not know, and where because of this, not even their own labor will be able to procure over time the means to prolong their miserable existence.[11]

Compounding the troubles of the repatriates was their inability to speak the language of the region and their unfamiliarity with local customs. Such would again be the case following the end of hostilities a decade later during the Mexican American War (1846–48), particularly in those areas where Mexicans and Tejanos became the minority.

Much of this early violence in the mid-1830s can be traced to the aftermath of the Texas Revolution of 1836. The Euro American population, having suffered severe casualties in that conflict, sought retaliation against Mexican communities and they turned first to the settlements along the Guadalupe and San Antonio Rivers. According to sociologist and historian David Montejano, "in 1837 the Mexican

[11] "Carta de M. E. de Gorostiza y Señor Don Joaquín M. de Castillo y Lanzas," 5 Agosto de 1836, in AHSRE, L-E-1078 (13), 122–4; Original: "La posición pues de aquellos desgraciados es de las mas lastimosas. Si al menos se les hubiera desembarcado en algún punto de la costa de México, hubieren encontrado allí siquiera auxilios y consuelos; pero por un refinamiento de crueldad, que la opinión pública calificará bien pronto, se les ha enviado á una tierra extraña, cuya lengua no entienden, cuyas costumbres desconocen, y en donde por lo mismo ni aun su trabajo personal les podrá procurar en mucho tiempo los medios de prolongar su miserable existencia. En circunstancias tan apuradas, y sin perjuicio de otras medidas que buscaré para socorrer á nuestros infelices é inocentes compatriotas, he dispuesto que se sirva Vuestra Señoría prevenir inmediatamente á los cónsules y Vice-cónsules de la Republica en estos Estados Unidos que haciendo saber este suceso á cuantos mexicanos de ambos sexos residan ó se hallen transeúntes en la demarcación de sus Consulados respectivos estimulen su humanidad y patriotismo para que cada cual contribuya con aquella cantidad que sus facultades les permitan a favor de tan meritorio objeto."

communities of Victoria, San Patricio, La Bahía (Goliad), and Refugio were the first to feel the vengeance for the massacres at Goliad and the Alamo."[12] The town of La Bahía, for example, was razed along with the church and fort built by the Mexican government. One of the biographers of the founding De León family noted that although they were loyal to the Texan cause, "This family like other loyal Mexican families were driven from their homes, their treasures, their cattle and horses and their lands, by an army of reckless, war-crazy people, who overran the town of Victoria." To continue, "these new people distrusted and hated the Mexicans, simply because they were Mexican, regardless of the fact that they were both on the same side of the fighting during the war."[13] The violence of war, as such, became a basis for justifying these early expulsions in Texas.

By 1839 over 100 Mexican families "were forced to abandon their homes and lands in the old settlement of Nacogdoches in what is now East Texas."[14] The individuals who avoided expulsion eventually took refuge further south at the Carlos Ranch. This group lived in constant fear of raids and threats of violence from the burgeoning Euro American population, who recalled the death trap at the Alamo and the massacre at Goliad only three years earlier.[15] During that summer, "these bandits gave warning of their intention to visit Carlos' Ranch (where residents from Victoria and Goliad had taken refuge in 1836) in order to burn it down and kill all the Mexicans belonging to it."[16] These threats were not acted upon until the Mexican government made an effort to reconquer Texas and occupied San Antonio in 1842. At this time, according to historian Arnoldo De León, "Anglos angered over the invasion from Mexico destroyed the ranch and compelled the families to leave the Republic."[17]

These expulsions, not surprisingly, were in many cases responses to real and perceived Mexican violence or carried out for the purposes

---

[12] David Montejano, *Anglos and Mexicans in the Making of Texas, 1836–1986* (Austin: University of Texas Press, 1987), 26–7.

[13] A. B. J. Hammett, *The Empresario: Don Martín de León*, (Waco: Texian Press, 1973), in Ibid.

[14] Ibid.

[15] Jay A. Stout, *Slaughter at Goliad: The Mexican Massacre of 400 Texas Volunteers* (Annapolis: Naval Institute Press, 2008), 174–87.

[16] De León, *They Called them Greasers: Anglo Attitudes towards Mexicans in Texas, 1821–1900* (Austin: University of Texas Press, 1983), 78.

[17] Ibid.

of material gain either political or economic in nature. And here we should recall the context of the period. The Goliad Massacre of 1836 was investigated by contemporaries of the period, and two scholars of that particular bloodbath concluded, "A man-by-man study of Fannin's command indicates that 342 were executed at Goliad on March 27. Only twenty-eight escaped the firing squads, and twenty more were spared as physicians, orderlies, interpreters, or mechanics."[18] At the Battle of the Alamo, between 150 and 250 "Texians" and a number of Tejanos also lost their lives in battle with the Mexican Army headed by Santa Ana, including those who gave themselves up in surrender. Hence, the mass execution of Euro Americans at Goliad, the Alamo, and the rise of the Cordova Rebellion all contributed to the atmosphere of fear and violence in which these initial expulsions of Mexicans took place.[19]

The 1842 effort by the Mexican government to reconquer the lost Texas Republic initiated yet another round of intense expulsions.[20] In the wake of this latter attempt, the Euro American populations of Texas considered banishing all Mexicans from the newly formed republic. According to a newspaper editorial quoted by De León, "There is no faith to be put in them; and until the war is ended, they should be compelled, every one of them, to retire either east or west from the frontier; or if they chose to remain, be subjected to the rigorous treatment due to enemies."[21] No longer considered allies in the cause of Texas independence, these Texas Mexicans were now seen as "enemies" even though it was liberal-minded Tejanos who had initiated this rebellion against the Mexican state.[22]

Now outnumbered and without the protection of either the United States or Mexican governments, numerous families fled south toward Mexico and to areas where familial networks were better grounded. Hundreds of Tejano families, according to historian Andrés Tijerina,

---

[18] Harbert Davenport and Craig H. Roell, "Goliad Massacre," in *Handbook of Texas Online. Texas State Historical Association*, http://www.tshaonline.org/handbook/online/articles/GG/qeg2.html.

[19] Paul D. Lack, "The Córdova Revolt," Chapter in *Tejano Journey, 1770–1850*, Gerald E. Poyo (Austin: University of Texas Press, 1996), 89–109.

[20] Raúl Ramos, *Beyond the Alamo: Forging Mexican Ethnicity in San Antonio, 1821–1861* (Chapel Hill: University of North Carolina Press, 2008), 167–91.

[21] Arnoldo De León, *The Tejano Community, 1836–1900* (Albuquerque: University of New Mexico Press, 1982), 14–15.

[22] Reséndez, *Changing National Identities*, 146–70.

"scattered onto the ranches and eventually to Coahuila," while most Nacogdoches families left for Louisiana.[23]

These difficult conditions were not enough, however, to deter Mexican families from returning to their ranches, and by the end of the war, hundreds had returned and appealed for reinstatement of their land titles and properties. Tijerina points out, for instance, that an 1850 census taken in Texas reveals that "although only about fifteen hundred of the original Tejanos remained in the old Béxar-Goliad region, more than six hundred Mexican-born heads of household had entered the region since the revolution." By the 1850s, the De León and Benavides clans would come to join the fifty Tejano families already residing in "New La Bahia."[24]

Other expulsions followed in those areas of Texas where Euro Americans became the majority and where Mexicans were seen as threats to social, political, and economic hegemony. Austin, Colorado, Matagorda, San Antonio, Seguin, and Uvalde were all sites of expulsion. In the case of Austin, Mexicans were driven out not once but twice. Montejano reminds us that "Mexicans were driven from Austin in 1853 and again in 1855, from Seguin in 1854, from the counties of Matagorda and Colorado in 1856, and from Uvalde in 1857."[25]

Many of these latter expulsions grew out of a fear of alliances between Mexicans and African Americans perhaps influenced by the passage of the 1850 Fugitive Slave Law.[26] In a newspaper of the era, for instance, this fear of a Mexican–Black connection was imagined in both economic and sexual terms:

> Matagorda – The people of Matagorda County have held a meeting and ordered every Mexican to leave the county. To strangers this may seem wrong, but we hold it to be perfectly right and highly necessary; but a word of explanation should be given. In the first place, then, there are none but the lower class or "Peon" Mexicans in the county; secondly, they have no domicile, but hang around plantations, taking the likeliest Negro girls for wives; and, thirdly, they often steal horses, and these girls, too, and endeavor to run them to Mexico. We should rather have

[23] Tijerina, *Tejanos Under the Mexican Flag*, 138.
[24] Ibid., 141.
[25] Montejano, *Anglos and Mexicans*, 28.
[26] Daniel Kanstroom, *Deportation Nation: Outsiders in American History* (Cambridge: Harvard University Press, 2007), 77–83.

anticipated an appeal to Lynch Law, than the mild course which has been adopted.[27]

Here the expulsion of all Mexicans is not seen as problematic; in fact, it is presented as a palatable alternative to lynching. The fact that "Negro girls" and "horses" are both seen as property should not surprise those familiar with the economics of a slave society. However, the accusation that Mexicans endeavored to run slaves and freedmen into Mexico is not without some basis in fact.[28] In an analysis of the 1850 Fugitive Slave Law, for example, legal scholar and historian Daniel Kanstroom suggests that the law "operated as a deportation system" that "caused many to flee the country for Canada and others for Mexico."[29] This collusion (real and imagined) served to further the pretext that Mexicans were disloyal and ought to be expelled.

Paul Schuster Taylor, a noted economist and student of the Mexican American experience in Texas, cited purported Mexican–Black collusion as one of the main sources of conflict between Anglos and Tejanos during the mid-nineteenth century. In the 1850s a plot by African Americans was discovered in Colorado County, and Mexicans were immediately cited as the primary instigators of this rebellion to kill the "white masters." The committee of "whites" announced to their community that "without exception every Mexican in the county was implicated.... They were arrested and ordered to leave the country within five days and never to return. We are satisfied that the lower class of the Mexican population are incendiaries in any country where slaves are held, and should be dealt with accordingly."[30] Delegates from several counties west of the Colorado River met in October 1854 in order to enact stern measures directed against Mexican–Black association in Texas. The convention "resolved that counties should organize vigilance committees to persecute persons tampering with slaves and that all citizens and slaveholders were to work diligently to prohibit Mexicans from contacting blacks."[31] In similar fashion, the town of

[27] For the full text see Olmsted (1857, 502); quoted in Montejano, *Anglos and Mexicans*, 28.
[28] A number of Tejano elites also owned slaves, so this perceived collusion, to the extent that it existed, was certainly not universal. See also Ronnie C. Tyler, "Fugitive Slaves in Mexico," *Journal of Negro History* 57;1 (January 1972): 1–12.
[29] Kanstroom, *Deportation Nation*, 83.
[30] Paul S. Taylor, *An American-Mexican Frontier: Nueces County, Texas* (Chapel Hill: University of North Carolina Press, 1934), 37.
[31] De León, *They Called Them Greasers*, 51.

Seguin "drafted resolutions prohibiting Mexican peons from entering the country and forbidding Mexicans to associate with blacks."[32]

Other locations in Texas also seemed caught up in the spirit of the moment even without a demographic advantage. For instance, to the south in Laredo some Americans "began a movement to clean out the Mexicans," even though the latter constituted the vast majority of the local population and had long held considerable political power. The local "white" population "would rant at public meetings and declare that this was an American country and the Mexicans ought to be run out."[33] Even in the town of San Antonio a writer for the *San Antonio Ledger* suggested in 1855 that "Mexican strangers coming into the city register at the mayor's office and give an account of themselves and their business." Those who could not be vouched for by a "respectable resident of San Antonio" and who were "unable to produce a satisfactory certificate would be required to leave the city premises immediately."[34] Finally, residents of Austin, after accusing Mexicans of horse theft, used this as the rationale to expel twenty Mexican families from their homes in the spring of 1853.

In the case of California, the expulsion of Mexicans from that state began not in the 1830s but almost two decades later, once gold was discovered and settlers began pouring into the area. Indeed, the Gold Rush ultimately overwhelmed the local population, who only a few years earlier had achieved social and political hegemony vis-à-vis the local indigenous populations. Mexicans in California were expelled not only for their "disloyalty" and violent behavior, but because they represented a labor pool that would compete with incoming European immigrants and settlers. This competition was addressed by the 1851 "Foreign Miner's Tax" supported by a mostly male population seeking to put at a disadvantage the experienced Mexican (especially Sonoran), Chilean, and Peruvian miners who migrated to the mines with a particular modality of cultural capital that was informed by centuries of mining under Spanish colonial rule. Jean Pfaelzer's recent study of over 200 Chinese expulsions from California notes that "Latin Americans" also became victims in this climate of "vigilante violence and repressive law," especially after the passage of the Foreign Miner's Tax.[35] Also, the mostly male migration that

[32] De León, *The Tejano Community*, 15
[33] Montejano, *Anglos and Mexicans*, 31.
[34] De León, *They Called Them Greasers*, 51.
[35] Jean Pfaelzer, *Driven Out: The Forgotten War against Chinese Americans* (New York: Random House, 2007), 20–4.

came from as far away as China, Hawaii, Australia, and South America was so intense and economically competitive that "the Sonorans' business activities provoked the bitter ire of local Anglo entrepreneurs," argues sociologist Tomás Almaguer, "who sought the mass expulsion of these business rivals." Almaguer goes further in his observation when he notes that "the bitter strife that followed...led to thousands of Latin Americans fleeing the region and seeking their fortunes elsewhere." In time, "some relocated in bustling urban centers such as San Francisco and Stockton, a few fled south to Southern California, while others simply returned en masse to Mexico or other parts of South America."[36]

Given the relative success of Chilean, Sonoran, and Peruvian miners, threats directed at those groups were not uncommon. The comandancia general of Sinaloa, for instance, pointed out that multiple ships were arriving from Alta California with passengers who were refused entrance into the gold placers of California. The general pointed out that in places like San Francisco, robberies and murders were frequent and a hatred of Mexicans, Spaniards, and Chileans was so intense that locals impeded passengers from living among them. In the words of this military official, "with the greatest of violence, they impede them to reside there, they steal from them, they insult them, and they cause them to embark by force in order to make them leave that territory."[37] When this correspondence reached the Mexican Legation in Philadelphia, Minister Luis de La Rosa wrote to the U.S. secretary of state, contending that this violence in fact constituted an expulsion in violation of the 1849 Treaty of Guadalupe and one that required immediate attention.[38]

For their part, Mexican officials had already begun to adopt colonization policies that favored return migration as a way to settle and develop the northern frontiers of the fractured republic. Numerous pieces of legislation in the Mexican Congress called for repatriates to colonize the northern frontier and assist with state efforts to civilize the numerous Indios Bárbaros who continued to reside along the newly

---

[36] Tomás Almaguer, *Racial Fault-Lines: The Historical Origins of White Supremacy in California*, (Berkeley: University of California Press, 1994), 70.

[37] "Oficio de la Comandancia General de Sinaloa a la Secretaría de Marina y Guerra, 27 Agosto 1849," AHMM, XI/481.3/2972.

[38] "Carta de Legación de México en Filadelfia a Secretario de Estado de los Estados Unidos," October 19, 1849, AHSRE, LE-1095, in Ángela Moyano Pahissa, *Protección Consular a Mexicanos en los Estados Unidos, 1849–1900* (México: Archivo Histórico Diplomático Mexicano, Secretaria de Relaciones Exteriores, 1989), 31–2. [Hereafter cited as *Protección Consular a Mexicanos*].

created boundary. In this context, the expulsion of Mexicans and other Spanish-speaking migrants from the United States were imagined as potential colonists for the fractured Mexican republic. One piece of correspondence from the central government expressed hope that the governors of Sonora and Sinaloa would do "whatever possible to bring this population" into the republic by extending "credit for unculti-vated lands." Moreover, if these states were unable to "cede them for free," uncultivated lands would "nevertheless be provided" later "in the form that the general Congress opportunely authorizes."[39] Here we can see the direct correlation between these expulsions and the practical aspects of repatriating and resettling those expelled. The governor of Sonora responded in kind to the Ministry of Foreign Relations, stating, "This government will freely give of so laudable a resolution inasmuch as the particular legislation of Sinaloa will permit it to do so."[40] These expulsions intensified because of the continued migration of Sonorans to the mines of California almost immediately after gold was discovered. Migration to California, hence, came accompanied by a simultaneous process of expulsion. Thus, as Sonora was losing its population to the Gold Rush, more calls from border governors encouraged repatriation and resettlement along a vulnerable Indian frontier now left unpro-tected and therefore uncivilized.

By 1855, the depopulation of Sonora was in its sixth year and so severe that Mexican military officials began to recommend repatriation not only as a way to thwart northern migration, but also as a means of creating a buffer zone against North American secessionist designs in that area. Writing from the Ministry of War and Marine, General Bonilla suggested to the Ministry of Foreign Relations in 1855 that repatriates from Alta California would be the best colonists because of their negative experiences with American settlers and forty-niners. Bonilla pointed out to the secretary that:

"The President General will not see with indifference a move-ment that besides naturally awakening his feelings of brotherhood, could be of great utility for our country; thus, there can certainly be no better colonists for our borders, than those instructed with hard experience, as with the falsehood of encouraging promises

39 "Se pone en conocimiento de Estados Unidos que los españoles, mexicanos y chilenos son ultrajados en la Alta California, viéndose obligados a emigrar," 3 Octubre 1849, in AHSRE, 6–17–41.
40 "Carta de Gobierno de Sinaloa a Ministro de Relaciones Exteriores," September 22, 1849, AHSRE, LE-1095, f. 186–7.

that the Americans are used to making to those...found in the most intimate contact with them.[41]

Bonilla believed that the government could take advantage of the fact that Mexicans in this region had endured harsh treatment at the hands of Americans, who had enticed them with the false promise of the American dream. Sociologists Alejandro Portes and Rubén G. Rumbaut have described a species of this "hard experience" in their contemporary studies of immigration to the United States as "reactive ethnicity." For them, this reaction is a "Made in America" product of "confrontation with an adverse native mainstream and the rise of defensive identities and solidarities to counter it."[42] Postwar Mexican officials of the mid-nineteenth century seemed aware of this nineteenth-century version of "reactive ethnicity" and naturally sought to capitalize on it. Disillusioned by their negative experiences in the United States, these military officials believed, returning migrants would be the best colonizers for the Mexican frontier. Their experiences in the United States, the thinking went, made them anti-American and therefore loyal to Mexico. In addition, their capacity to thrive in a desert environment made *fronterizos* the ideal Indian fighters. Even someone like Stephen F. Austin recognized *rancheros* as masters of guerrilla warfare. According to Stephen L. Hardin, "Years of bitter conflict with horse-born Comanche and other hostile tribesmen had engendered within Mexican borderlanders cunning, stealth, agility, endurance, mobility, skill with weapons, and the ability to exploit their habitat to military advantage."[43] In contrast to previous historiographies, it seems more likely that the use of repatriates was partly a policy of military resettlement overlaid with the moral patina of nationalism and belonging.

[41] "Oficio de la Secretaria de Relaciones a la de Gobernación para que se facilite la inmigración de mexicanos residentes en California, EUA, con destino al departamento de Sonora, por no gozar de sus derechos, Año de 1855," AHMM XI/481.3/5105, Original: "el General Presidente no vera con indiferencia un movimiento que además de despertar naturalmente sus sentimientos de hermandad, podrá ser de grande utilidad a nuestro país; pues, ciertamente no puede haber mejores colonos para nuestras fronteras, que aleccionados por la dura experiencia, ya como un la falsedad de las halagüeñas promesas que los americanos suelen hacer a los que por la vecindad se hallan en mas intimo contacto con ellos...."

[42] Alejandro Portes and Rubén G. Rumbaut, *Legacies: The Story of the Immigrant Second Generation* (Berkeley: University of California Press and The Russell Sage Foundation, 2001), 284.

[43] Stephen L. Hardin, "Efficient in the Cause," Chapter in *Tejano Journey, 1770–1850*, edited by Gerald M. Poyo (Austin: University of Texas Press, 1996) 52.

In sum, the period from 1836 through the late 1850s marks a period of mass expulsions that emerged in the violent aftermath of the so-called Texas Revolution of 1836. These forced removals continued in the 1840s when Mexico tried unsuccessfully to reconquer Texas, and again in the 1850s when Mexicans were accused of colluding with slaves. The next period of Mexican expulsions encompasses the latter half of the nineteenth century and extends into the twentieth century; these expulsions were justified on dubious grounds similar to those of the early nineteenth century.[44] What was different in this era, however, was that the question of expulsion forced the Mexican government to deal with this once-lost population by formulating a colonization policy that would simultaneously address the need to repatriate these citizens while fortifying the frontier against further U.S. and Indian encroachment. That dialogue about accommodating, or at least addressing the expelled, overlapped with the ongoing debate surrounding military colonization of the northern frontiers.

MILITARY COLONIZATION AS AN HISTORICAL RESPONSE TO EXPANSIONISM AND EXPULSION

One of the most common recommendations and policy suggestions during the mid-nineteenth century came from border governments requesting military colonization of the frontier region. These were only the latest requests for military support, and this particular form of colonization has a longer genealogy in Mexican historiography. Historian Friedrich Katz points out that during the mid eighteenth century "...the Spanish crown had established military colonies along the northern frontier to fend off roaming bands of Apaches and other nomads."[45] But even earlier, and following the defeat of the Mexica-Aztecs in 1521, Tlaxcalan allies would eventually help conquer and colonize various indigenous settlements and towns throughout the territory now known as Mexico.[46] After the Mexican American War several pieces of legislation calling for the establishment of more military

---

[44] See José Angel Hernández, "Contemporary Deportation Raids and Historical Memory: Mexican Expulsions in the Nineteenth Century," *Aztlán: A Journal of Chicano Studies* 52:2, (Fall 2010): 129–33.

[45] Katz, *The Secret War*, 8

[46] Patricia Martinez, "'Noble' Tlaxcalans: Race and Ethnicity in Northeastern New Spain, 1770–1810," (Ph.D. Dissertation, The University of Texas at Austin, 2004).

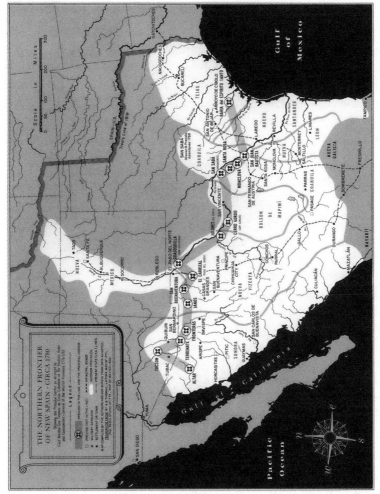

Figure 2.1. The northern frontier of New Spain, ca. 1780. Photo courtesy of the Arizona Historical Foundation.

colonies emerged as many among the elite sought to provide solutions to the continued problems of settling the northern territories. In the case of Mexico, military colonies had been established since the colonial period and were given new life under the Bourbon Reforms of the late eighteenth century when the restructuring and centralization of this institution provided for additional military colonization in the 1770s and 1780s.[47]

That colonial schema, and the limited success – at least from a Spanish point of view – of those military colonies situated along the northernmost corridor of the fledgling empire would continue to be employed with various modifications after the Mexican American War. One could well be inclined to suggest that the formation of these colonies in the eighteenth century unwittingly established the very international boundary that is today shared between the two countries, as the illustration shows.

The Northern Frontier of New Spain, 1780

This particular border has also been described by norteños as a "natural border" because of the very extensive Rio Bravo and the "natural desert" of the Southwest. In fact, one author argues that "with few modifications this chain of forts was to remain unaltered until the 1830's...." and that "no major realignment was made by the following Spanish or Mexican military officials."[48] This argument can be stretched further to add that various independent Indian groups of the northern frontier ultimately determined where the frontier was to be established, and it is apparent from this map that Mexico's contemporary boundary with the United States was established during the end of the colonial period with military forts nestled along the "natural border." The shifting nature of the boundary was negotiated not only by migration and settlement to those areas, but also due in large measure to the many

---

[47] A classic work is Max Moorehead, *The Presidio: Bastion of the Spanish Borderlands*, With a foreward by David J. Weber, (Norman: University of Oklahoma Press, 1975).

[48] The map shows the "presidial cordon as arranged by Field Marshal Don Teodoro de Croix, Caballero of the Teutonic Order and Commandant General of the Internal Provinces, 1776–1783," in Sidney B. Brinckerhoff and Odie B. Faulk, *Lancers for the King: A Study of the Frontier Military System of Northern New Spain, With a Translation of the Royal Regulations of 1772*, foreword by Kieran McCarty, OFM, (Phoenix: Arizona Historical Foundation, 1965), 80.

indigenous empires that controlled this region.[49] It was the presence, occupation, and resistance of Indios Bárbaros to outsiders and invaders that determined for most of the colonial period who paid tribute, took bribes, and ultimately who was in control.[50]

Military colonization was led astray during the independence wars and was replaced by the kind of citizen and immigrant colonization discussed in the previous chapter. After independence, colonization was accomplished to not only curtail the power and threat of local militias, but to convert the Indians and Europeans into productive citizens that would serve to thwart the invasions of "barbarous Indians" and therefore populate those regions threatened by their northern neighbors.[51]

But by the end of 1848, as the war came to an end, Mexican officials finally came to the realization that civilian colonization required the simultaneous establishment of military colonies. The thinking went that military colonization led to very little civilian growth and therefore civilian colonies would subsequently pepper the frontier regions betwixt and between strategically placed military colonies. According to one student of Mexican military colonies in the postwar period, these projects now had several objectives in mind. Lucy Rebecca Watkins, a student of famed borderlands historian Herbert Eugene Bolton, argued that:

> Three distinct border problems faced Mexico immediately following the Treaty of Guadalupe Hidalgo, namely Indian ravages, smuggling, and in the United States, dissatisfaction over the boundary. These problems were of importance to Mexico in the sequence given, and were interrelated because of their common tendency to advance the southwestern frontier of both Indian and Anglo-American.[52]

Thus, Indian raiding, smuggling, and dissatisfaction over the boundary should also include population movements, quelling of Indian raids,

---

[49] Brian DeLay, "Independent Indians and the Mexican American War," *The American Historical Review*, February 2007 http://www.historycooperative.org/journals/ahr/112.1/delay.html (March 10, 2007).

[50] For examples of bribes and paying tribute to independent Indian groups, see Weber, *Bárbaros*, 178–220.

[51] José Angel Hernández, "From Conquest to Colonization: *Indios* and Colonization Policies after Mexican Independence," *Mexican Studies/Estudios Mexicanos* 26: 2, (Summer 2010): 285–315.

[52] Lucy Rebecca Watkins, *Mexican Colonization on the United States Border, 1848–1858*, (M.L. Thesis, University of California-Berkeley, 1912), 1.

and continued – yet failed – filibustering expeditions. This assessment
of postwar military colonization is repeated to some degree in Joseph
Stout's study of filibusterism in Mexico during this period. He argues
that "along the border the Mexican defense against raids of murder-
ous Apaches and lawless *Norteamericanos* remained sorely inadequate"
for protecting the country. Stout goes on to suggest that because the
border was too long, individual border governors made alliances with
natives and sought the protection of the central government to no
avail.[53] Inadequate funding and resources were wanting, according to
his assessment, and the Mexican state accomplished little in providing
for any military colonization. What did emerge was a series of laws and
decrees calling for the militarization of the border with repatriates left
in the ceded territories after the war.

On July 20, 1848, the president of Mexico, José Joaquin de Herrera,
signed into law a decree to establish military colonies along the new
northern boundary of the country, less than six months after the treaty
had been signed. Authored by Mariano Arista, then secretary of war and
marine, the decree "was motivated by a strong desire to populate this
region before the aggressive Americans came back for another slice of
Mexico – a possibility that became a reality just five years later with the
Gadsden Purchase."[54] Herrera called for the establishment of military
colonies in the wake of the "most recent treaty with the United States,
[which] demands special and urgent attention to both preserve our territorial integrity and to defend the frontier states from the frequent and
cruel incursions of the barbarian [Indians]." Bearing in mind the "Texas
experiment," by now Mexican officials stopped short of excluding all
foreigners from this new policy of frontier colonization. Thus, whereas
North Americans and Anglos were imagined with the "steam engine of
progress" at the end of the independence era, now they were considered
persona non grata and therefore reflected in legislation prohibiting their
settlement on Mexican soil. According to article XXIV, "Foreigners will
not be admitted, either as military colonists or as civilians, unless it
be done personally and at the responsibility of the inspector [of the

---

[53]   Joseph Stout, *The Liberators: Filibustering Expeditions into Mexico, 1848–1862
       and the Last Thrust of Manifest Destiny* (Los Angeles: Westernlore Press, 1973),
       27–35.
[54]   José Joaquín de Herrera, *Colonias militares, proyectos para su establecimiento en
       las fronteras del oriente y occidente de la república* (México, 1848); quoted in
       Faulk, "Projected Mexican Military Colonies," 39–45.

military colony], in order that there be no questionable motives behind their joining."[55]

In the following months and years, several proposals for colonization, especially for military colonies in the state of Chihuahua, materialized in the aftermath of the war and in the preceding decades. For example, in an annual military report submitted and read to the Chamber of Deputies in 1852 – only four years following the signing of the decree to establish military colonies – the *memoria* noted that continued problems of Indian raiding impeded the construction and settlement of the northern frontiers. Even so, military colonies were being slowly established and then settled in some cases by repatriates from the United States. The same Department of War and Marine noted only a year earlier that "the colony of El Paso of the North was founded on the fifteenth of December 1849, of a distance of one league from the civil colony of Guadalupe, formed by those emigrants of New Mexico; it occupies ten *sitios de ganado mayor* in vacant lands.... [T]he children of the soldiers cultivated small plots of land where fruits and vegetables were harvested."[56] Although Herrera's call for the need to establish military colonies occurred in the midst of the war, by the early 1850s some progress with settlement was made and articulated in a number of reports to the Chamber of Deputies.

The new boundary served as a safety net for renegades and bandits raiding both sides of the U.S.–Mexico border. Mariano Paredes believed unrest along the Sonoran border served to benefit the already land-abundant Americans because the instability of the northern frontier caused its inhabitants to seek out other alternatives, such as filibustering and illicit trading. In his plan for colonization of the Sonoran frontier, this "obscure deputy from the border state of Sonora" warned of the possible secessionist possibilities engendered because of constant Indian raiding, an unstable environment, and constant violence.

> In a state of abandonment, misery, insecurity [and] lack of protection of rights and liberty [,] She is exasperated, and the possibility is not remote that the delirium of her sufferings may make her surrender herself into the hands of her neighbor who offers her refuge and protection... if the nation leaves the clamor of the frontiers unnoticed, our neighbors will hear them and they will know how to derive

55 Ibid.
56 *Memoria, Secretaria del Estado y del Despacho de Guerra y Marina*, 1851, 24.

advantage from them...These neighbors show us the enjoyment of positive rights, which we do not know in our own country."[57]

Unlike General Bonilla's observations a few years later that articulated the positive aspects of emigrants' negative experiences in the United States, Paredes seems to be suggesting that if the Mexican government failed to do something about populating these regions, American ideology and a stable economy could well curry favor with the local populace of the border region and entice them over to the U.S. side. Note once more his observation that "if the nation leaves the clamor of the frontiers unnoticed, our neighbors will hear them and they will know how to derive advantage from them...."[58]

It is therefore no surprise to read that while Paredes called for heavier fortification of the frontier, military reports emanating from this area were publishing accounts about creating a "buffer zone" with those "immigrant Indians" being pushed toward Mexican territory by U.S. settlers. According to the president of the republic:

> The government should call attention to the Congress about a serious malady that threatens us: the savages that exist and that are disseminated in the territories that today form the United States of the North, pursued by force of that government; they try, without a doubt, to pass the limits of the border and then are introduced into ours; and although the United States has a contract with Mexico regarding the solemn commitment to impede the above-mentioned interaction, it will not be possible to achieve this because of the extension of land they have to oversee, and because our line of defense is guarded very little; thus, the same persecution of them by the United States throws them in our direction.[59]

---

[57]   Mariano Paredes, *Proyectos de leyes sobre colonización y comercio en el estado de Sonora, presentados a la Cámara de Diputados por el representante de aquel estado, en la sesión de extraordinaria de día 16 de Agosto de 1850*, (México, DF: Ignacio Cumplido, 1850), 4–5; quoted in Herring, "A Plan for the Colonization of Sonora's Northern Frontier: The Paredes Proyectos of 1850," *Journal of Arizona History*, vol. 10, Number 2, (1969): 108.

[58]   Ibid.

[59]   *Memoria, Secretaria del Estado y del Despacho de Guerra y Marina*, 1851, 17–19. Original: "El gobierno debe llamar la atención del congreso hacia un grave mal que nos amenaza: los salvajes que existen diseminados en los territorios que forman hoy parte de los Estados Unidos del Norte, perseguidos por fuerzas de aquel gobierno, trataran sin duda de pasar sus límites e introducirse en los nuestros; y

Paredes understood that the settlement of the northern frontier remained essential for Mexico if it wished to create a "buffer zone" between itself and its aggressive northern neighbor.

Without a doubt Native Americans were migrating westward and toward Mexican territory, thus providing an opportunity to settle the northern frontiers. For generations, the country had not been able to settle and therefore colonize this particular region, but with the arrival of particular "immigrant Indians," the state now had an opportunity to create a buffer zone between itself and its northern neighbor. Here, the Seminoles were seen as ideal colonists because, unlike other Indios Bárbaros who made their living from stealing and raiding frontier communities, they were quite effective at trade and accumulating capital. These neighboring tribes, as the report concluded, "have a particular insistence in possessing a fixed home and their distinguishing characteristic is the gratefulness to the nation that welcomes them."[60] In short, these latter groups were civilized in the eyes of nineteenth-century Mexican officials because they had "fixed home[s]." While many Indian groups were incorporated into the larger Mexican family, others actively fought against this imposition by remaining autonomous. So, on the one hand "immigrant Indians" that were "admitted as neighbors in the colonies established in the state of Coahuila," have "responded to the hospitality which they received from the republic, lending themselves and contributing to the military operations with fidelity and profit, as they did when they aided an expedition from Coahuila against the barbarians and in the defense of Cerralvo."[61] By contrast the Tarahumaras, who lived in Chihuahua, "still follow their customs and are found separated from the populations [of] other races either by instinct or because of habit," even though the state had considered them, at least since independence, "as Mexican citizens."[62] Throughout the rest of the nineteenth century, the government would receive a series of requests for repatriation by various indigenous groups in the United States and in Mexico proper. Like many politicians of

aunque los Estados Unidos tienen contraído con México el solemne compromiso de impedir la referida interacción, tal vez no les será posible lograrlo por la extensión de terreno que para ello tienen que vigilar, y porque encontrándose poco guarnecida nuestra línea, la misma persecución de los Estados Unidos los arroja entre nosotros."

60   Ibid.
61   *Memoria, Secretaria del Estado y del Despacho de Guerra y Marina*, 1852, 39.
62   Ibid.

the period, government officials continue to make distinctions between those Indians considered "civilized" and "bárbaros."[63]

Much as was true in propositions advanced before, such as those military reports mentioned earlier, Paredes and others gave preference to Mexicans and Mexican repatriates. According to Patricia Herring, "though colonists were to be Mexican and European, it was hoped that the new settlements would attract primarily Mexicans from the interior or those expatriated by the Treaty of Guadalupe Hidalgo."[64] Paredes, though, also tinged his own proposition with underlying warnings of expatriation and the possibility of migrating to a country where "refuge" and "protection" are guaranteed. These very direct warnings engendered charges of secessionism the following year. Paredes, however, did not allow these changes to deter him from his goal of settling the frontier. In his extensive letter and proposal to the Chamber of Deputies in the fall of 1850, he noted that in order to offset the continued raiding of indigenous groups, capitalists and European immigrants should be allowed to colonize Sonora while at the same time making the port of Guaymas a free zone in order to bring investors and stability to the region. As well, the author echoes the idea espoused earlier regarding the possibility of enticing *fronterizos* to the American side when he notes that "far from them listening to their neighbor," namely the United States of the North, these migrants would then return to a more peaceful and orderly frontier.

Capital investment and the establishment of a free trade zone at the port appeared to be his key concerns, but Paredes was also very familiar with the direct correlation between Indian raiding and the emigration of Sonorans to Upper California. The Apache's "desolating war" had cost the state millions and one need only read the official state paper "in order to see the many victims daily sacrificed to these cannibals."[65] For Paredes:

> The gangrene is spreading, for there are those who will stir the fire; and, in time, with violence, and without losing an opportunity,

[63] The example of Native Americans migrating south toward Mexico would require a separate study. For an early example of Native American requests for colonization see "La legación Mexicana comunica que se le ha presentado al Sr. Juan Rofs, Jefe de la Tribu de Indios Llamados Cherokees, manifestando sus deseos de saber si el gobierno admitiría gustoso en su territorio a dicha tribu, molestada y perseguida por el Ejecutivo de los EUA, 1835" in AHSRE, Exp. 2–13–2965.

[64] Herring, "The Paredes Proyectos of 1850," 109.

[65] Faulk, "A Colonization Plan for Northern Sonora," 300.

the means for Sonora's salvation will not exist. It will be too late to do anything. All may yet to be saved by an opportune law of colonization that will arrest the cancer, giving hope of good things to come to all those Sonorans who are lovers of their nation, if the nation has without itself the flexibility necessary for the salvation of its liberty. Such a law will reanimate the Sonorans, stop their emigration to Upper California, and, in place of complaining against the central government, they will seek its preservation and by it they shall be blessed; far from listening to their neighbor, they will proudly show that the nation has awakened from its lethargy and that foreigners shall also come to our territory to make it great and put up a barrier to ambition – all of this if the law that is urgently needed is frank enough to correspond to that purpose.[66]

This paragraph illustrates the centrality regarding the problem of settling the northern frontiers and the role of the indigenes in that process. Indian raiding affected every element of frontier life along the northern corridor: peace, stability, investment, trade, emigration, and the ultimate security of the region.

Paredes's appeal for settlement along the frontier, apparently, was joined by a chorus of other voices. On August 31, 1850, José María Lacunza, secretary of the interior, came forth with his own decree calling for the colonization of Sonora and the establishment of military colonies. This decree, moreover, directly addressed the appeals of Californios who had been arguing for a cogent and well-ordered colonization program that would facilitate the repatriation of those who sought to return to Mexico. Almost foregrounding the future sentiments of the residents of Alta California in the coming years, Lacunza also addressed some of the same concerns shared by El Clamor Público by inserting his own description of the dire situation of the borderlands in the mid-1850s. Similar to arguments found in Paredes's pleas for assistance, Lacunza described the situation of the borderlands as follows:

Considering the necessity that the government finds itself in attending to the frontiers, of which some run the dangerous risk each day of falling into the hands of adventurers, attending moreover, as is its duty, to the just representation of the

[66] Ibid.

frontier States and to the public clamor of public opinion that
does not cease to manifest the urgent need to colonize, especially
in upper Sonora...that it is now absolutely necessary to procure
in an efficacious mode the colonization of the mentioned state,
finding itself in distinct and special circumstances, due to the new
territorial limits of the Federation.[67]

Lacunza's appeal for action emerged in the wake of several other recommendations for colonizing the frontier and renewed action on the
part of the Mexican government. Such articulations, as well, sought to
respond to the escalating levels of violence reported by the Spanish-
language press in the ceded territories. These concerns would continue
with a cluster of several other proposals for colonizing the frontier;
however, these appeals and laws for colonization would see their full-
est expression during the Porfiriato, which by then converted military
projects into more civilian-like agricultural models intended to civilize
the frontier with modern citizens.

Another example of these early efforts by government officials can
be seen in Juan Nepomucena Almonte's recommendations the following year in 1852. He declared that the states of "Chihuahua, Durango,
Nuevo León, Tamaulipas, Zacatecas, Sonora, and even Sinaloa could
not be more deplorable...for daily its inhabitants are assassinated, its
haciendas plundered, and its fields burned by various tribes of barbarians
who ceaselessly invade that area."[68] Unlike his predecessors, though,
Almonte's colonization plans emphasized the growing need to counter
the increased level of Indian incursions against Mexicans in the frontier
states. These incursions, as we have already pointed out, were caused
in large measure because of the westward migrations that came along
with the "rush for gold." As Anthropologist Ana María Alonso notes,

[67] José María Lacunza, "Circular de Agosto 31, 1850. Se nombra una comisión
que levante planos de los terrenos de Sonora en que pueda establecerse la
colonización," sección in Manuel Dublán y José María Lozano, *Legislación
Mexicana o Colección Completa de las Disposiciones Legislativas Expedidas desde
la Independencia de la Republica, Ordenada por los Licenciados Manuel Dublán y
José María Lozano, Edición Oficial,* (México: Imprenta de Comercio, a Carga de
Dublán y Lozano, hijos, 1876), 734–5.

[68] Juan N. Almonte, *Proyectos de Leyes Sobre Colonización,* (México: Ignacio
Cumplido, 26 Enero 1852); translated in Odie B. Faulk, "Projected Mexican
Colonies in the Borderlands, 1852," *The Journal of Arizona History 10,* (Summer
1969): 115–28.

"although indigenes such as the Apache had engaged in warfare and raiding prior to the conquest, it was the disruption of native society and the displacement of native groups caught between the expansion of the Anglo-American and Hispanic frontiers that turned them into specialists in violence."[69] This in turn precipitated a depopulation of the frontier states, providing the very conditions for easy, and almost unprotected, raiding from all directions. "This colonization," Almonte argued, "is more advisable since in vain do we plan railroads, telegraphs, etc. if we do not begin to found towns in the deserts, which until now, have served only as cover for the wild beasts, assassins, and thieves."[70] As historian Brian DeLay has noted in his recent study on these particular questions, the decades prior to the war exacerbated the level of violence toward communities along the border, and raiding parties traveled deep into Mexican territory in the lead up to war.[71]

The number of deaths and raids at the hands of so-called barbarous Indians is worth noting here in order to get a more balanced view of these concerns put forth in colonization policies and decrees. The state of Zacatecas mentioned earlier is worthy of note because it lies further south of the borderlands, yet the raiding into that state significantly affected that state's population and economy. This latter state suffered 400 dead and wounded in the decade following the Mexican American War. La Villa de Guerrero, between 1836 and 1865, was invaded sixty times while Tamaulipecos counted up more than 35 million pesos in property damages and other losses. The border town of Mier, unlike its counterparts in Reynosa and Camargo, suffered through twenty raids in the fifteen years following the Mexican war and had also been one site of repatriate settlement.[72] The exasperation of this situation is echoed best by the governor of Sonora during the Gold Rush period in the following paragraph: "Of what use can it serve the government when it offers rich

69 Ana Maria Alonso, *Thread of Blood: Colonialism, Revolution, and Gender on Mexico's Northern Frontier* (Tucson: University of Arizona Press, 1995), 24–5.
70 Juan N. Almonte, *Proyectos de Leyes Sobre Colonización*, (México: Ignacio Cumplido, 26 Enero 1852); translated in Odie B. Faulk, "Projected Mexican Colonies in the Borderlands, 1852," *The Journal of Arizona History 10*, (Summer 1969): 115–28.
71 Brian DeLay, *War of a Thousand Deserts: Indian Raids and the US-Mexican War* (New Haven: Yale University Press, 2008), 114–38.
72 Luis G. Zorrilla, *Historia de las relaciones entre Mexico y los Estados Unidos de América, 1800–1958* (México: Editorial Porrúa, 1977), 278–9.

lands in uninhabited lands if one cannot reap the fruits or enjoy them without security? And how can that person be devoted to cultivation or to discovering [mines], if the government doesn't guarantee them an armed force that will free them from these savage occurrences?"[73] These raids, no doubt, weakened governmental and private efforts for decades and underscore the importance of Almonte's proposal.

Like other colonization proposals, Almonte's outline for possible frontier settlers and immigrants included Mexicans and Mexican Americans. Offers of larger tracts and extended tax and military exemptions were offered in hopes of reaching Almonte's goal of populating the country with 25 million souls. Note, for example, one of the articles that states "Mexican families who move from Texas and New Mexico to the northern frontiers of the republic will be a given a quarter more land than the amount designated in the preceding article (one square mile), if they live on it for two consecutive years; in addition, the national government will pay for the cost of their transportation."[74] This example, and the other decrees that outline this particular preferential treatment are not only policies of *realpolitik*, but they also share the common feature of being discussed and proposed during a period when depopulation caused by an increased migration of Mexicans to California and northern Sonora, intense Indian raiding along the frontier, and a continued trepidation over more territorial losses was taking place. Throughout the middle of the nineteenth century, the genealogy of repatriation policy unfolds in the very areas most affected by outward migration and depopulation, which is to say the borderlands.

Conclusion

This chapter has examined an overlooked aspect of Mexican and Mexican American history by analyzing plans for military colonization

[73] Carta de Gobernador de Sonora a Ministerio de Relaciones Exteriores, 3 Octubre 1849, AHSRE, 6–17–41; in *Protección Consular a Mexicanos*, 28–30. Original: "¿De qué servirá que el gobierno ofrezca ricas tierras en despoblado si no se puede disfrutar ni gozar sin seguridad? ¿Y que persona puede dedicarse a trabajar cultivo o descubrir, si el gobierno no les garantiza una fuerza que los libre de los acometimientos salvajes?"

[74] Juan N. Almonte, *Proyectos de Leyes Sobre Colonización*, (México: Ignacio Cumplido, 26 Enero 1852); translated in Odie B. Faulk, "Projected Mexican Colonies in the Borderlands, 1852," *The Journal of Arizona History 10*, (Summer 1969): 115–28.

that sought to take advantage of the expulsion of Mexican citizens from what later became the ceded territories. Or, to follow General Bonilla and the governor of Sonora's observations regarding migrants expelled from the gold placers of Upper California and their potential as colonists, it was believed that the expelled would be ideal settlers for military colonies along the border. After the war, this population would begin to figure into colonization policy intended to further strengthen and develop the northern frontiers. The aftermath of the war affected not only the demography and constitution of those considered citizens versus those that were not, but it also recreated local communities while simultaneously losing territory. Thus, while Mexico lost the ceded territories and a substantial population with them, the United States gained this geographical space and took on a new territorial minority group.

The repatriation and colonization of the population of Mexican origin was codified into law while Mexican government agencies created a discourse and practice that distinguished loyal individuals who were suitable colonists from Indios bárbaros and so-called bad Mexicans. The population that remained within the United States following the war was imagined as ideal for populating the frontiers. In the next chapter, we will examine how colonization policy later came to encompass military, civilian, and political obligations for postwar repatriates in the territories of New Mexico, Texas, and California.

PART II

MÉXICO PERDIDO AND THE MAKING OF POSTWAR REPATRIATION PROGRAMS ALONG THE BORDERLANDS

The direct expression of emigrants from New Mexico, familiarizes Your Excellency with the protection that the government of that period saw itself obliged to extend to the Mexicans, that by virtue of the treaty of Guadalupe, they could be considered foreigners in their own land, wrestling with the religion, language and customs of the new proprietors. Moreover, the points chosen to establish the two colonies of Guadalupe and San Ignacio, are in my humble conception, quite deliberate, together with the conditions imposed on said colonists: given this Department's lack of resources needed to engage in active and tenacious war with the savage, a new wall has been placed between the towns of El Paso and Del Norte that will impede from that point the entry and exit of barbarians that harass this Department and that of Durango.

Carta de Genaro Artalejo a Señor
Ministro de Fomento, Colonización,
Industria y Comercio, 15 Mayo 1855

CHAPTER THREE

Postwar Repatriation and Settling the Frontiers of New Mexico

Introduction: A Dominant Nationalist Discourse

Continuing on to the national level, we now turn to the colonies that eventually made it to Mexico after the war, examining the many problems repatriates encountered in their quest for funds, permission to repatriate and settle, and to figure out who was in charge.

The end of the war brought the creation of a commission dedicated to the repatriation and resettlement of Mexican-origin populations in the United States. To this end, the northern frontier was divided into three regions, and a commission was assigned to each. Because the New Mexico Territory was the most heavily populated, the commission for this region was considered the most important of the three. Postwar instabilities, strapped financial resources, shifting geo-political boundaries, resistance by U.S. authorities, and internal accusations of financial mismanagement and corruption all contributed to the dissolution of these initial repatriation commissions. Yet colonies nevertheless emerged along the northern frontiers between Chihuahua and the New Mexico Territory, due mainly to the will and survival skills of the repatriates themselves.

The history of Mexican American repatriation during the nineteenth century touches equally on the historiographies of the United States, Mexico, the borderlands, and Mexican American Studies, yet this historically significant, but little known episode has been discussed to a limited extent in the academic literature. Nonetheless, repatriation efforts have not received nearly the scholarly attention they merit as transcripts for an alternative reading of national, cultural, and racial formation along the U.S.-Mexico border during this period.

The literature on Mexican American repatriation, as such, straddles a narrative emplotment that extends to both sides of the border. Some historians contributing to the literature on this history have developed several periodizations for it.[1] Though the periodizations and approaches of these scholars vary, they share a general framework that bases the dynamics of repatriation on nationalistic and patriotic impulses. Whether discussing the first repatriation projects in 1848 or the Mexican American colonies founded under the regime of Porfirio Díaz (1876–1911), the conclusions drawn by most of these scholars rely disproportionately on assumptions of nationalist obligations. The articulations of Mexican historian Lawrence Douglas Taylor are illustrative of this particular interpretation, when he concludes in his analysis of Mexican repatriation programs over the past 170 years that:

> The Mexican government has never forgotten the Mexican population that has lived on the other side of this dividing line and it has always stood disposed to resettle them in the event they remain dissatisfied or without the possibility of continuing to reside abroad... it has attempted, and continues attempting to take advantage in the best possible manner of the workforce upon which it relies and, within its limited means, to try to allot to those that have emigrated abroad a viable alternative in the event that they decide to return home, to the country of their ancestors and of their cultural heritage.[2]

[1]   Martín de la Vara, "The Return to Mexico: The Relocation of New Mexican Families to Chihuahua and the Confirmation of a Frontier Region, 1848–1854," in *The Contested Homeland : A Chicano History of New Mexico*, edited by Erlinda Gonzáles-Berry and David Maciel (Albuquerque: University of New Mexico Press, 2000); Manuel Ceballos Ramírez, "Consecuencias de la guerra entre México y Estado Unidos: la traslación de mexicanos y la fundación de Nuevo Laredo," capitulo en *Nuestra Frontera Norte*, compiladora Patricia Galeana (México: Archivo General de la Nación, 1997): 39–59; Lawrence Douglas Taylor Hansen, "La repatriación de Mexicanos de 1848 a 1980 y su papel en la colonización de la región fronteriza septentrional de México," *Relaciones 18*, no. 69 (1997): 198–212; Enrique Cortés, "Mexican Colonies During the Porfiriato," *Aztlán: International Journal of Chicano Studies Research* 10 (Fall 1979): 1–14; Francisco E. Balderrama, *In Defense of La Raza: The Los Angeles Consulate and the Mexican Community, 1929–1936* (Tucson: University of Arizona Press, 1982); Aguila, Jaime R. "Protecting 'México de Afuera': Mexican Emigration Policy, 1876–1928" (Ph.D. Dissertation, Department of History, Arizona State University, 2000), 182–235.

[2]   Taylor, "La repatriación de Mexicanos," 212; Original: "En breve, la repatriación de mexicanos de Estados Unidos ha sido un proceso continuo desde la

Such approaches artificially superimpose a nationalist consensus on a relatively unexamined field that overlooks *how the colonies fared once in Mexico proper.* An analysis of these repatriate colonies allows us to complexify previous historiographies from the singular gaze of hyper-nationalism.[3]

A number of studies on repatriate colonies founded during the twentieth and twenty-first centuries concur with the observations made by noted historian Fernando Alanis that: "In general, the attitude that they [the government] demonstrated was that of not wanting to do anything in the matter; they had reserves to promote repatriation and they ignored requests for return that their nationals sent from the United States; they only made moderate expenditures and the most indispensible in order to help with the return of urgent cases."[4] This brief overview by Alanis applies equally to the postwar period and, I would suggest, to the rest of the nineteenth century.

What follows examines the formation of the repatriate commission charged with encouraging the repatriation of its citizens, its initial efforts at recruiting repatriates, the work of establishing colonies along the frontiers of New Mexico, and the competing interests that pitted the *realpolitik* of state necessities against the pragmatic interests of

delimitación de la frontera entre los dos países en 1848. El gobierno Mexicano jamás se ha olvidado de la población mexicana que vive al otro lado de esta línea divisoria y siempre se ha mantenido dispuesto a reubicarlos en el evento de que se quedaren descontentos o sin posibilidades de continuar en el extranjero. Además, aun cuando ha contado con pocos recursos económicos para satisfacer las necesidades de los ciudadanos que viven dentro de los límites de su propio territorio, en general ha ofrecido cierto apoyo a los que desean repatriarse, en la forma de empleo o pasajes gratuitos para trasladarse a México. Esta actitud confirma la noción de que el gobierno mexicano nunca ha querido o considerado conveniente 'exportar' a sus ciudadanos a otros países. Más bien, ha intentado y sigue intentando aprovechar de la mejor manera posible la mano de obra con que cuenta y, dentro de sus posibilidades limitadas, tratar de proporcionar a los que se hallan emigrado al extranjero una alternativa viable en caso de que decidan regresar a casa o al país de sus antepasados y de su herencia cultural."

3 Prasenjit Duara, *Rescuing History from the Nation: Questioning Narratives of Modern China* (Chicago: The University of Chicago Press, 1995).

4 See Fernando Saúl Alanis Enciso, "No cuenten conmigo: La política de repatriación del gobierno mexicano y sus nacionales en Estados Unidos, 1910–1928," *Mexican Studies/Estudios Mexicanos* 19;2, (Summer 2003): 401–61; Original: "En general, la actitud que mostraron fue la de no querer hacer nada en esa materia; tuvieron reservas para promover el regreso e ignoraron las solicitudes de retorno que sus nacionales enviaban desde Estados Unidos; únicamente hicieron gastos moderados y los más indispensables para auxiliar el retorno en casos urgentes."

repatriates themselves. My analysis of heretofore unexamined archival documents that detail the repatriation experience in the New Mexico Territory argues that continued mismanagement of these first colonies ensured that repatriates and their *vecinos* south across the new border would share a similar experience with land displacement and problematic surveys. In contrast to past interpretations, the Mexican state emerges not as benevolent protector of prodigal sons and daughters, but as an institution distantly attending to repatriation as if it were a colonial afterthought. Our examination of the process of repatriation to Mexico begins with a review of the establishment of the commission charged with this arduous task.

THE FEDERAL REPATRIATION COMMISSION AND ITS MISSION

The decree instituting the repatriate commission contains important stipulations that speak to a more nuanced and accurate view of the period. Particularly telling are those calling for preferential treatment of repatriates and the distribution of authority for the project.

Not long after the end of hostilities, the administration of José Joaquin de Herrera issued a decree on August 19, 1848 addressing "those Mexican families that are found in the United States and want to emigrate to their *patria*."[5] Issued shortly after the important July 5 "*Proyectos de Colonización*" of 1848, the decree was considered an extension of the Treaty of Guadalupe Hidalgo, signed on February 2 of that year.

Consisting of two dozen articles, this comprehensive repatriation decree addressed a wide range of topics. These included the composition of the commission, the states that would accommodate repatriates, the particulars of the repatriates' travel back to Mexico, responsibilities and payments to repatriates, the salaries and duties of the commissioners, and agreements with state and federal officials concerning land.

All potential emigrants were free to make their own travel arrangements according to article 9 of the Herrera decree, but they would still be obligated to notify the "commissioner at the time of enlistment, in order to have him present when making out the budget." Twenty-five

---

5 "Decreto de 19 de Agosto de 1848; para que familias mexicanas que se encuentren en los Estados Unidos puedan emigrar a su patria," en De la Maza, *Código de Colonización*, 407–12.

pesos would be allotted to each repatriate over the age of fourteen and twelve pesos to those aged thirteen and under. At least on paper, local commissioners and state governments did their best to place potential repatriates who did not wish to take up agricultural work in colonies where their skills could be employed.[6]

Article 3 specified that "three commissioners were to arrange the migrations. Mexicans in Alta California were to receive land in Baja California or Sonora; those in New Mexico, land in Chihuahua; and Texas Mexicans, land in Tamaulipas, Coahuila or Nuevo León."[7] It seems more than mere coincidence that the military colonization projects discussed in the previous chapter also divided the northern frontier into these three militarized zones. I would suggest that the repatriation operation should be located within a continuum of the postwar military realignment of the northern frontier as a whole. Repatriation policies, in short order, were co-opted as military policies that included the pacification of the frontier, only this time with returning colonists.

The decree notably granted preferential treatment to repatriates, one of the many hallmarks of repatriation policies as the nineteenth century wore on. Much like the preferential treatment accorded the *indígenas* following independence and to those migrating north from the center of Mexico, the policies outlined in the decree favored Mexicans residing in the "lost territory" over foreign colonists and immigrants. Article one of the decree states:

> All of the Mexicans found in the territory during the celebration of peace that, because of the Treaty of Guadalupe Hidalgo, remained in the power of the United States of [the] North, and want to come and establish themselves in that of the Republic, will be transferred to this one [Mexico] on account of the treasury and in the form established in the following articles.[8]

---

6 Ibid.

7 Thomas Ewing Cotner, *The Military and Political Career of Jose Joaquin de Herrera, 1792–1854* (Austin: University of Texas Press, 1949), 268–69; quoted in Weber, *Foreigners in Their Native Land: Historical Roots of the Mexican Americans*, with a foreword by Ramón Eduardo Ruíz (Albuquerque, NM: University of New Mexico Press, 1973), 141–44.

8 "Decreto de 19 de Agosto de 1848; para que familias mexicanas que se encuentren en los Estados Unidos puedan emigrar a su patria," en *Código de Colonización*, 407–12.

These benefits reflected a perception of repatriates as ideal colonists. Their attractiveness to Mexican authorities came in part from the impression that they could fulfill the dual purposes of displacing foreign colonists and maintaining the northern colonies as military outposts. Article 6 declares: "The Mexicans that emigrate in virtue of this decree will have the right of preference so that all of the concessions that the law establishes or had established in favor of foreign colonists will be made to them." Assistance would be extended to them in a "special manner," and they would receive preferential treatment in the military colonies established by law on July 20.[9] Although foreigners would still be allowed to settle in these colonies, an individual review by the inspectors of the colonies was required in each of their cases.[10]

An abdication of federal authority to the states in the decree presented a major difficulty for repatriates as questions about available land and financial responsibilities were articulated. Whereas the central government wanted the final authority over immigration policy, the responsibility of providing for these migrants would ultimately fall to the states. Article 7 states that "Governors of the states of Chihuahua, Coahuila, Nuevo León, Tamaulipas, and Sonora and the primary political authority of Baja California, shall regulate by law, in the part that corresponds to each of them, the organization of the civil colonies that are to be founded by emigrants." Land for the colonies should come from "arrangements with large landowners, or through whatever other means, that the emigrants find."[11] Article 22 ceded even more authority to the state governors when it noted that the governors had final say in disputed matters. The federal government assigned very significant responsibility to state officials by stipulating that officials would negotiate with local hacendados to secure land for the repatriates. The concentration of land ownership certainly was part of the story behind the weak concentration of settlement in the north, further complicating the possibility of a well ordered repatriation program.[12] In the end, most large-scale landowners did very

---

[9] Ibid.
[10] See Articulo 24 of "Decreto de 19 de Julio de 1848, y Reglamento expedido el día 20 del mismo mes, para el establecimiento de colonias militares en la nueva línea divisoria con los Estados Unidos de América," in *Código de Colonización*, 400–7.
[11] Ibid.
[12] de Vos, "Una legislación de graves consecuencias," 76–113.

little to make land available for repatriates, or any other settlers for that matter.[13]

APPOINTMENT OF THE COMMISSIONERS IN NEW MEXICO

The decree in question was implemented through the appointment of three repatriation commissions. Despite the fact that the decree made a concerted effort to treat the repatriation of the military zones as a whole, the commissions were established at different times, under different circumstances, with different levels of investment, and they ultimately met with differing levels of settlement. This is to state clearly that although we have a law to point to in this instance, the adoption of said law took place at different times and under a varying set of circumstances in each of the three regions that it specified. For example, in the western territory of Baja California, the governor of that state appears to have taken the lead in the designation of a repatriate commissioner with the tardy appointment of Jesús Islas in 1855.[14] In the eastern provinces, Don Rafael De La Garza, a former treasurer for the state of Nuevo León, was offered the title of Commissioner to Repatriate Mexican families to Tamaulipas. In 1850 he declined to accept this position.[15]

---

[13] Holden points out that such practices, at least in terms of claiming public lands (*baldios*) would decrease under the presidency of Benito Juárez as the *Ley sobre Ocupación y Enajenación de Terrenos Baldíos* (1863), but that the rush for public lands commenced during the Porfiriato. See *Mexico and the Survey of Public Lands*, 3–24.

[14] In my own research of these repatriate commissions, I found very little evidence to suggest that a commissioner was ever appointed for Baja California. Not until 1855 is Jesús Islas appointed to the post, and then only seven years later. Instead we find an active governor involved in the repatriation efforts, but only to a limited degree. I would argue that the formation of repatriate societies in California after 1849 is a phenomenon that questions the limits of state efforts to repatriate after the war. See "Disposición de 13 de Febrero de 1856: Promoviendo la emigración de la raza hispano-americana existente en la Alta California, para aprovecharla en la colonización del Estado de Sonora," en *Código de Colonización*, 607–12. This letter and four-point suggestion was also published in the 1856 publication of "Ministerio de Fomento," 10 Mayo 1856.

[15] "Nombramiento para comisionado en Matamoros, hecho en Don Rafael de la Garza, Tesorero que es del Estado de Nuevo León, 1850," in AHSRE, 2–13–1974.

New Mexico, the state with the largest Mexican population, was naturally targeted for repatriation and proved the most fruitful area for recruiting repatriates. Father Ortiz, a leading politician and known patriot, served as the first commissioner in charge of repatriating Mexican families from New Mexico. His tenure seemed without incident, at least until he began to encourage the mass repatriation of Nuevo Mexicanos immediately following the war.

Ortiz's troubles began almost as soon as he set out to the north to begin his commission. As if his task was not arduous enough, he contended immediately with inclement weather. He left for New Mexico in September, but strong snowstorms in northern Mexico forced him to stop over in El Paso del Norte in late November. As local historian Mary Daniels Taylor recounts, by the time Ortiz could make preparations to leave for Santa Fe "to begin to discharge his duty of Commissioner for Repatriation," winter had "come to northern New Mexico, and being a native of that area and knowing firsthand the difficulties of travel in the freezing cold of ice and snow," Ortiz "decided to wait until Spring to go north, making the difficult arrangements for settlements while remaining in his curacy at El Paso del Norte."[16] While waiting for the weather to improve, Ortiz saw no reason why he could not get his recruitment efforts underway right there along the new boundary.

It was precisely along the border where most of the repatriation activity would eventually take place, and Ortiz found no lack of interest on the part of residents. Would-be repatriates in the area eagerly approached the commissioner to have their names placed on the list to migrate to Chihuahua. When Ortiz arrived in the county of Lerdo, New Mexico – where the general opinion of U.S. officials was that only a small portion of the local population wished to return to Mexico – he noted that "the inhabitants enthusiastically presented themselves to me, asking that they be enlisted with their families in order to pass to Mexican territory."[17] Father Ortiz was by his own account received positively wherever he went while serving as commissioner until 1853.

---

[16] Mary Daniels Taylor, *A Place as Wild as the West Ever Was: Mesilla, New Mexico, 1848–1872* (Las Cruces, New Mexico: New Mexico State University Museum Press, 2004), 20.

[17] "Carta de Ramón Ortiz a Ministro de Relaciones Exteriores y Interiores, 22 Junio 1849," in AHSRE, L-E-1975 (XXV), "Asunto: Ramón Ortiz – Nombramiento del citado para que pase a Nuevo México, comisionado para la traslación de familias a territorio de la República, 1848."; see also an English translation of the letter in *Three New México Chronicles: The Exposición of Don Pedro Bautista*

Collecting one's possessions and resettling in another area, whether across a border or across town, is never taken lightly. As psychoanalyists León and Rebeca Grinberg maintain in their study of Spanish immigrants, "In some situations the desire to leave may come from an attempt to escape persecution. In these cases, rather than *heading toward* the unknown because of the good or betterment one believes it has to offer, departure is a matter of *escaping from* the known place and its bad or persecutory experiences."[18] To what factors can we attribute the enthusiastic reception Ortiz received? To answer this question, we must look to the socioeconomic conditions of the repatriates themselves. Ortiz's correspondence provides important information relevant to this question of why people chose to migrate, in this case to a country that historically could not provide safety and order to the frontier.

In one of his first letters to the minister of foreign relations reporting on the conditions in El Paso Del Norte, Ortiz signaled both the enterprise's problems and its promise, that is, the possibility of repatriating thousands of Nuevo Mexicanos. Worthy of note are his references to the kinds of individuals interested in this proposition. According to Ortiz:

> To fulfil the commission that the Supreme Government has seen fit to honor me with, I find myself, after having surpassed the various obstacles that I have had to overcome, at the door of New Mexico, and even before entering I have the satisfaction of announcing to His Excellency that I have received about twenty distinct requests from middle class families to transfer to the territory of the Republic, and that according to the news arriving consistently from the nationals of that country, and according to foreigners that have recently arrived from the same, there should be at least from two to four thousand families disposed to emigrate, yet even though this news favors the generous desires of the Supreme Government of the Nation, it is accompanied by

Pino, 1812; the Ojeada of Lic. Antonio Barreiro, 1832; and the additions of Don José Agustín de Escudero, 1849, (Albuquerque: The Quivira Society, 1942), 144–5; AHSRE, 2–13–2971, "Gobierno del Estado de Chihuahua. Escrito a mano: No. 68: El Gobernador de Chihuahua participa que se ha nombrado agente del Señor comisionado Ortiz al Licenciado Don Manuel Armendáriz para que informe al Supremo Gobierno sobre la inmigración a este Estado de las familias Nuevo Mexicanas, 1849."

[18] León Gringberg, M.D. and Rebeca Grinberg, M.D., *Psychoanalytic Perspectives on Migration and Exile* (New Haven: Yale University Press, 1989), 58–9.

insurmountable obstacles for the emigration to occur this coming Spring.[19]

In this initial report Ortiz clearly indicates that the vast majority of potential repatriates would not be taken from the middle class, but rather from families with more limited means: "twenty requests were made by middle-class families while another potential two to four thousand families were prepared to move south with the Repatriate Commission." Depending on whether we accept the 2,000 or 4,000 figures, the middle class here constitutes a mere percentage of the interested parties. The visits from the repatriate commission clearly generated interest among the least fortunate, or those without lands in the New Mexico Territory.

Nationalist historiographies studying repatriation have suggested that repatriation benefited the region of settlement and provided a means of class ascendancy for repatriates. But the historical record paints a different picture for the first colonies founded by Ortiz. Most of the repatriates who eventually arrived were from the most impoverished classes and saw little improvement in their conditions and freedoms after repatriation. For example, the overwhelming majority of citizens in the colony of Guadalupe "earned less than one peso per day, which restricted them to voting only in the municipal elections." The class system and all of its divisions, as New Mexico archivist and historian Samuel Sisneros has illustrated, "continued in the new colonies, as did class conflicts."[20]

It also appears that for many repatriates, the decision to follow the new political boundaries of Mexico southward was a choice by negation, in other words, a choice favoring the lesser of two evils. Early

[19] "Carta de Ramón Ortiz a Señor Ministro de Relaciones," 8 Diciembre 1848, in AHSRE, L-E- 1975 (XXV), f. 135–7; Original: "Para cumplir con la comisión con que el Supremo Gobierno se sirvió honrarme me hallo ya apenas de los diversos obstáculos que he tenido que vencer a las puertas de Nuevo México y aun antes de entrar tengo la satisfacción de anunciar a V. E. que he recibido ya como veinte solicitudes distintas de familias de la clase media para pasar al territorio de la República y que según las noticias uniformes de nacionales de aquel país y extranjeros que recientemente han venido del mismo, debe haber lo menos de dos a cuatro mil familias dispuestas a emigrar, pero aunque esta noticia es tan favorable a los generosos deseos del Gobierno Supremo de la Nación, se presentan con todo obstáculos insuperables para que la emigración pueda ser en la próxima primavera."

[20] Sisneros, *Los Emigrantes Nuevomexicanos*, 58.

repatriates exhibited doubts about whether their rights would be respected as subjects of the United States if they stayed in place. In a letter to the Ministry of Foreign Relations and the governor of the state of Chihuahua, Ortiz explains that those of El Vado County receptive to repatriation "were willing to lose everything rather than to live in a country whose government gave them fewer guarantees than our own and in which they were treated with more disdain than members of the African race." According to Ortiz, New Mexicans feared that, under a U.S. system of governance, they would be treated as second-class citizens.[21] But as most of the literature illustrates for the nineteenth-century Mexican American experience in the Southwest, the vast majority of Nuevo Mexicanos opted to remain in place, to remain under a U.S. system of government.

Ortiz thus posits two reasons for popular interest in repatriation: more secure rights as Mexican citizens and better treatment than "members of the African race." With respect to the latter, the treatment of African Americans was used as the litmus test of inequality, particularly as it was supported by civil and legal guarantees under the U.S. system. As slaves, African Americans did not have any official rights. If New Mexicans remained in U.S. territory, it was feared they would suffer similar treatment or worse. Although New Mexicans (at least the Hispanic peasantry) had not been subject to enslavement to the extent that African Americans had, it is interesting to point out that, as a native of New Mexico, Ortiz must have been familiar with the well-known traditional practice of indigenous slavery. This practice persisted until it was prohibited only six years after the signing of the U.S. Emancipation Proclamation of 1862.[22]

It should also be considered that the ravages of war and harsh weather had left the local population in desperate straits, and this fact further complicates a simple understanding of the motivations of repatriates as solely based in patriotic loyalties. Potential repatriates had basically lost that year's harvest; grain and seed would have to be brought in from outside. The governor of the state of Chihuahua, Angel Trías, noted

[21] "Carta de Ramón Ortiz a Señor Ministro de Relaciones," 8 Diciembre 1848, in AHSRE, L-E- 1975 (XXV), f. 135-7.

[22] The number of Indians held in slavery in 1862 is estimated at 600. See Loomis Morton Ganaway's doctoral dissertation, "New Mexico and the Sectional Controversy, 1846–1861," *The Historical Society of New Mexico XII*, (March 1944): 73.

in a letter dated June 30, 1849 that his state was "greatly interested in the immigration of any number of citizens who may wish to retain their Mexican citizenship." But in order for this migration to take place, the federal government needed to subsidize transportation costs and at least "one third of the seed crop was needed urgently."[23] It appears that the seed never arrived.

By contrast, it seems, the economic situation in New Mexico was not as bleak as it was in Chihuahua to the south. In particular, the U.S. army and the financial resources funneled to the war zones and lands under occupation – in order to fight the "barbarous Apache" – served as major sources of revenue for local inhabitants, traders, and merchants. By turning their guns on the so-called barbarians, New Mexico's wealthy classes were "able to expand their ranching operations," while *los paisanos* were now able to farm more securely without fear of attacks. Charles Montgomery calculates that between 1848 and 1860, "campaigns against Apache and Navajo bands cost the government some $3 million annually and provided both wealthy and poor Hispanos, who supplied soldiers with food, firewood, and ancillary labor, their major source of revenue."[24] Citing an observation made the year before the Gadsden Treaty of 1853, Montgomery reminds us that Colonel Edwin Vose Sumner said that the only source of money was from the federal government. According to him, "All classes depended on it, from the professional man down to the beggar." Thus while New Mexicans continued to be a majority of the populace, rich and poor alike began to feel the influence and impact of the new American political and economic system. But even as these varied classes made economic gains, they slowly began to lose control of the infrastructure that had sustained the elite for so long – and which they had directly influenced and in some situations controlled. In the end, to quote Montgomery, "Their troubles arose from a confluence of forces, all [of which were] rooted in the structure of the new territorial economy."[25]

Although Ortiz's initial assessment of the prospects for repatriation was generally positive, he stressed the need for more money to offset these unforeseen circumstances having to do with the war and

[23] Carta de Ángel Trías a Ministro de Relaciones Interiores y Exteriores, 30 Junio 1849, in *Three New Mexico Chronicles*, 143–4.

[24] Charles Montgomery, *The Spanish Redemption: Heritage, Power, and Loss on New Mexico's Upper Rio Grande*, (Berkeley: University of California Press, 2002), 42–3.

[25] Ibid.

the winter weather. He made a dramatic appeal to the government of Mexico, sympathetically noting that the situation "makes one feel the hunger of those pueblos and this calamity will be a destructive beating to them after four months."[26] Regardless of whether Ortiz saw these conditions as a liability or potentially a strategic advantage for recruitment, from the perspective of repatriates, the decision to continue in the colonies was perhaps tied as much to questions of survival as to loyalty to the Mexican state. In the balance was Ortiz's standing as savior or scapegoat.

Seven months went by, and still no seed had been provided by either the federal or state authorities. The commissioners would continue to wait for the seeds for years, but to no avail. Many of the more adversely affected voted with their feet and left the repatriate colonies in hopes of improving their living situations elsewhere, most notably north and toward the United States.

COMPETING STATE INTERESTS IN SETTLING THE BORDER REGION

The depopulation and settlement of the border region, or put differently, the "problem of populating the frontiers," continued to be a major concern for both the United States and Mexico after the end of the war. Repatriation, therefore, became a vehicle that trapped Nuevo Mexicanos within seesawing efforts to populate national peripheries. Among the many challenges Ortiz faced with respect to the resettlement of Nuevo Mexicanos was concerted U.S. opposition to his efforts, a fact that flies in the face of ideas that the United States wished to purge Mexicans from its newly won territory. According to Miller Pucket's biography, Ortiz was well aware of the potential numerical impact of repatriation: "so successful was Father Ortiz, at first, that in one town he visited nine hundred of its one thousand citizens agreed to go, and he estimated that the number of abdications would eventually result in seriously depopulating New Mexico."[27] As will be detailed later in this chapter, after Ortiz arrived in New Mexico prepared to recruit a substantial number of Mexican families, he was stonewalled by U.S. authorities who sent him back to Mexico with only a handful of repatriates.

---

[26] "Carta de Ramón Ortiz a Señor Ministro de Relaciones," 8 Diciembre 1848, in AHSRE, L-E- 1975 (XXV), f. 135–7.
[27] Miller Puckett, "Ramón Ortiz," 286.

After Ortiz's initial visit to El Vado, he moved on to La Cañada County, only to be forced to desist when the military governor of the territory, Donaciano Vigil, prohibited the recruitment of repatriates. According to Ortiz:

> The first day I was there about to enlist more than one hundred heads of families, who had appeared before me in compliance with the decree dated August 19, 1848, I received an official letter from the Governor of the territory. In it, with the excuse that the gathering was disturbing the peace, he prohibited my appearing personally in the settlements of the territory.[28]

In no uncertain terms Vigil made it clear that he would not permit "[Ortiz] personally to visit the different points of this territory for the purpose of setting forth [his] commission to the settlers." With the backing of U.S. military officials, Vigil claimed Ortiz had "acted beyond" his "official capacity by making promises which are too extensive and which arouse a great deal of commotion" among the potential repatriates.[29] These accusations of "disturbing the peace," we may recall, were not completely off the mark. Ortiz was known to harbor anti-American sentiments, which had in part led to his appointment as commissioner in the first place. Vigil thus prohibited Ortiz from appearing personally in any of the towns.

However, shortly thereafter, an agreement with Vigil was negotiated whereby agents would replace Ortiz in repatriation activities.[30] Finding that local authorities did little to hinder the work of the repatriation commission, Ortiz appointed agents to recruit families in New Mexico via propaganda and personal visits. Even without the personal appearance of the priest, hundreds of potential repatriates continued to sign up. Within three hours of having posted signs in Santa Fé, Ortiz writes,

---

[28] Correspondence of Ramón Ortiz, *Three New Mexico Chronicles*, 144–9; see also "Asunto: Ramón Ortiz – Nombramiento del citado para que pase a Nuevo México, comisionado para la traslación de familias a territorio de la República, 1848," AHSRE, L-E-1975 (XXV); "Gobierno del Estado de Chihuahua. Escrito a mano: No. 68: El Gobernador de Chihuahua participa que se ha nombrado agente del Señor comisionado Ortiz al Licenciado Don Manuel Armendáriz para que informe al Supremo Gobierno sobre la inmigración a este Estado de las familias Nuevo Mexicanas, 1849," in AHSRE, 2-13-2971.

[29] "Letter from Donaciano Vigil to Ramón Ortiz, 29 April 1849, Santa Fe, New Mexico, in *Three New Mexico Chronicles*, 149.

[30] De La Vara, "The Return to Mexico," 45–7.

his appointed agent "had more than two hundred persons waiting for him at the place selected for the enrollment, the Governor summoned me and prohibited the use of this method."[31] As a result, this method of recruitment was prohibited altogether and Ortiz was ordered to cease all repatriation efforts.

When Ortiz protested in face-to-face interviews with Vigil, the latter argued that Ortiz was inciting disturbances of the sort he had organized after the signing of the Treaty of Guadalupe Hidalgo. Vigil, according to Ortiz, prohibited the repatriation of Mexicans from the territory "under the pretext that the disturbance was growing even in the capital and that he had received complaints from all the prefects in which they said that from the time of my arrival in the territory all the settlements had openly refused to obey them."[32] Ortiz emerges as a figure caught between his regional loyalty to the territories of the north, his patriotic sentiments toward the Mexican government, and his concern for a repatriate population more interested in pragmatic concerns than ideology.

The Mexican American War, Anti-American Sentiment, and Father Ramon Ortiz

According to one study of the period, Ortiz "appeared to be the person best qualified for the job" of heading the first repatriate commission from New Mexico to Chihuahua after the Mexican American War. Ortiz was quite familiar with the territory of New Mexico, and apparently the regions of Durango and Chihuahua as well. Born in 1814 in Santa Fé, where he lived for his first eighteen years, he then traveled south to study theology in Durango under the guidance of Bishop José Antonio Laureano de Zubiría, also known for his anti-American stance.[33] Anti-Americanism in Mexican politics has a long history in

[31] Correspondence of Ramón Ortiz, *Three New Mexico Chronicles*, 144–9; see also "Asunto: Ramón Ortiz – Nombramiento del citado para que pase a Nuevo México, comisionado para la traslación de familias a territorio de la República, 1848," AHSRE, L-E-1975 (XXV); "Gobierno del Estado de Chihuahua. Escrito a mano: No. 68: El Gobernador de Chihuahua participa que se ha nombrado agente del Señor comisionado Ortiz al Licenciado Don Manuel Armendáriz para que informe al Supremo Gobierno sobre la inmigración a este Estado de las familias Nuevo Mexicanas, 1849," in AHSRE, 2–13–2971.

[32] Ibid.

[33] Sisneros, *Los Emigrantes Nuevomexicanos*, 23–5. Zubiría continues to reemerge in the period following the U.S. occupation and will figure prominently in the local politics of southern New Mexico until the 1870s.

the political life of the country, and one marked especially after the war. Catholic priests, more important, were essential for their leadership roles in many communities.

Part of the qualifications that helped Ortiz gain the position of commissioner in late 1848 certainly included his long record as a "staunch opponent of North American intervention in the months leading up to the war."[34] After reading the correspondence between Father Ortiz and various government officials from Mexico, it requires no great stretch of the imagination to construct an image of Ortiz as a Mexican nationalist. As a representative of New Mexico, Ortiz opposed the terms of the Treaty of Guadalupe Hidalgo.[35] After his participation in a failed rebellion against the treaty in the spring of 1848 at the Battle of Santa Cruz, Ortiz was obliged to concede defeat. But he continued to fight on behalf of Nuevo Mexicanos in a number of different capacities.

Only five months after the Battle of Santa Cruz, Ortiz accepted the position as one of the commissioners in early August 1848, and he was on his way to New Mexico via Mexico City the following month.[36] Describing his acceptance of his appointment as repatriation commissioner, Ortiz conveys his sense of obligation to the nation, to his "native country" of New Mexico, and to the "less fortunate" residents of the area. As he stated in his letter to Mariano Otero, the minister of foreign relations who communicated the appointment:

> I see nothing in the commission [to New Mexico] that Your Excellency [the President] has conferred upon me but a demonstration of the kindness of His Excellency which greatly engenders my gratitude, pertaining as it does [to] matters of such great importance for the entire Republic and in particular for my state, for the less fortunate inhabitants of my native country. I find myself in this case unable to deny my services for the fruition of an undertaking as just as it is beneficial, even as I recognize the challenges with which I must contend, I am greatly humbled to accept such a charge.[37]

---

34 González de la Vara, "The Return to México," 44.
35 Fidelia Miller Puckett, "Ramón Ortiz: Priest and Patriot," *New Mexico Historical Review* XXV;4, (October 1950): 265–95.
36 González de la Vara, "The Return to México," 44.
37 "Carta de Ramón Ortiz a Señor Ministro de Relaciones," 9 Agosto 9 de 1848, in AHSRE, L-E- 1975 (XXV), f. 124–6; Original: "[N]o veo en tal nombramiento que V. E. se ha servido comunicarme, sino un efecto de la bondad de S. E. que grava profundamente mi gratitud, tratándose de intereses de tan alta

Ortiz wasted no time in asking for clarification of particular aspects of the decree that provided for his commission and of general points and promises of the law. Two thousand pesos were set aside for his salary, and a sum of $23,000 was sent ahead of Ortiz to the state of Chihuahua for the purchase of seeds, tools, and other items repatriates would need for resettling the northern frontiers.

The Legal Argument in U.S. Opposition to Repatriation

Vigil's affronts to repatriation efforts echoed a broader set of arguments that appealed directly to interpretations of the Treaty of Guadalupe Hidalgo, and thus reflected the still fresh wounds of battles over national sovereignty and border territory. Some in Washington, D.C. echoing the concerns expressed by local officials interpreted the repatriation of New Mexicans to Chihuahua as counterproductive to the normalization of relations between the United States and Mexico, and a violation of the Treaty of Guadalupe Hidalgo. The past of Father Ramón Ortiz, integral to this history, became a factor in the way repatriation efforts would play out.

Strictly speaking, the repatriation of the population of Mexican origin was not part of the agreement reached in February 1848 when both nations came together to sign the Treaty of Guadalupe Hidalgo. U.S. Secretary of War George W. Cranford pointed out to the Mexican minister of foreign relations that "it is not perceived, examining the material, that Mexico has acquired any right, not even when it can be inferred that it possess it, to entice those inhabitants in the ceded territories to emigrate and conserve their citizenship returning to establish themselves within Mexican territory."[38] The treaty excluded the possibility of repatriation and consequently, so the argument went, the entry

importancia para toda la República y en particular para mi estado, para los desgraciados habitantes de mi país natal, me hallo en el caso de no rehusar mis servicios para el logro de una empresa tan justa como conveniente, por más que el conocimiento de las dificultades con que tengo que luchar me infunda la mayor timidez al aceptar semejante encargo."

[38] "Carta de George W. Cranford a Ministro de Relaciones Exteriores y Interiores, 5 Octubre 1849," in AHSRE, 2–13–2971, "Gobierno del Estado de Chihuahua. Escrito a mano: No. 68: El Gobernador de Chihuahua participa que se ha nombrado agente del Señor comisionado Ortiz al Licenciado Don Manuel Armendáriz para que informe al Supremo Gobierno sobre la inmigración a este Estado de las familias Nuevo Mexicanas, 1849."

of a foreign representative such as Ortiz into New Mexico to encourage repatriation was prohibited. This unauthorized travel to depopulate a region of its inhabitants could then be framed in stark terms as an invasion in violation of the treaty. In a remarkable political move, here the treaty was interpreted to include not only the physical landscape, but also extended to the inhabitants of the ceded territories.

Opposition to Ortiz, or to his leadership of the first repatriation campaigns, did not deter ongoing efforts at repatriation by the national government or state governments across the new international boundary. The repatriation of Mexican nationals to the state of Chihuahua did not end with this first commission. It became a state-level initiative thereafter. The states of Sonora, Baja California, Chihuahua, Coahuila, and Tamaulipas each did their part to encourage and in some cases implement repatriation initiatives.

Ortiz resolved to try other avenues that encouraged return migration, as federal efforts were thwarted and subsequently suspended. Where he was removed from New Mexico for encouraging repatriation, he was now hired by the government of Chihuahua to receive and settle those repatriates that had crossed into Mexican territory.

THE RIVER CROSSED US?:
THE FATEFUL REDIRECTIONS OF EL RIO BRAVO/
THE RIO GRANDE

After Ortiz was prohibited from recruiting repatriates in New Mexico by national and state officials, the priest returned to Chihuahua where in mid-1849 "Governor Frías granted him the power to announce and give possession of the land needed to form new towns."[39] Frías simultaneously appointed Vice-consul Lic. Manuel Armendáriz the liaison between the repatriation commission and the president of Mexico. The governor noted that Armendáriz had been assigned to said position "so that the Supreme Government can receive the itemized reports in a verbal manner as instructed by the events witnessed in New Mexico and the instructions taken to carry out his commission."[40] The change made by the governor

---

[39] De La Vara, "The Return to Mexico," 47.

[40] "Carta de Ángel Frías a Ministro de Relaciones Exteriores e Interiores, 30 Junio 1849," AHSRE, 2–13–2971, "Gobierno del Estado de Chihuahua. Escrito a mano: No. 68: El Gobernador de Chihuahua participa que se ha nombrado agente del Señor comisionado Ortiz al Lic. Don Manuel Armendáriz para que

of Chihuahua not only appeared genuine, but one could argue that the policy of repatriation now had the direct ear of the Mexican presidency.

MAP OF GUADALUPE AND SAN IGNACIO, CHIHUAHUA

While some communities were offered "twice their lands" by the Mexican government in areas where settlement and the protection of sovereignty was deemed especially critical, in other areas there was not as much commitment to the process of repatriation, particularly toward the center and south of the republic. Here the continued activity of Ortiz helps us to understand why Chihuahua would receive most of the repatriates. In the same letter in which Governor Frías appointed Armendáriz as a liaison to Mexico City, the governor commented that his state "has great interest in verifying the immigration of citizens that want to conserve their nationality."[41] For this to happen, at least one-third of the seed would be required for the new repatriate colonies, adding costs to the repatriation effort. Earlier that year, the state assembly had ratified an initiative introduced by Frías creating the first colony on the opposite side of the Rio Grande to be named Colonia Guadalupe de los Nobles.[42]

Perhaps affected by a large snowstorm in the winter of 1849 (and the subsequent snowmelt), the main river relied upon in the aftermath of hostilities to mark the political division between the United States and Mexico, El Río Bravo/Rio Grande, shifted course. It was also possible to redirect the course of the river during this politically volatile period by means of strategically placed dams. Thus, the question of whether the geographic location of a given border colony vis-à-vis the agreed upon border was naturally or artificially shifted becomes critical to disentangling the loyalties of would-be and actual repatriates. Natural disasters, in effect, could also serve as opportunities to shift loyalties. A desire to remain under U.S. sovereignty could be masked as due merely to the serendipities of natural causes or even divine intervention. Failure to muster the resources to build dams that would correct for southerly detours in river flow could be read as an indication of satisfaction by residents

informe al Supremo Gobierno sobre la inmigración a este Estado de las familias Nuevo Mexicanas, 1849."
[41] Ibid.
[42] De La Vara, "The Return to Mexico," 47; Sisneros, *Los Emigrantes Nuevomexicanos*.

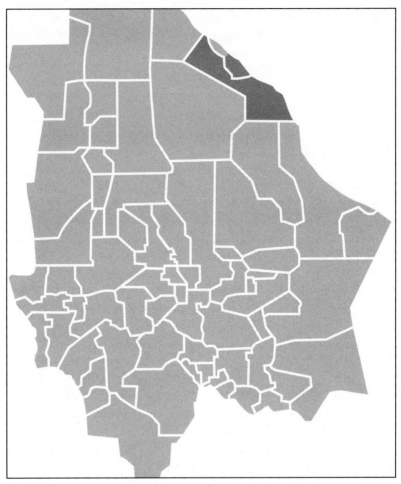

Figure 3.1. Map of Guadalupe and San Ignacio, Chihuahua. Map courtesy of Cambridge University Press.

with a newly carved political status as American citizens. The map below illustrates this river flow, and one can clearly see that La Mesilla sits in a very unusual geographic location, depending on the shift of the river.

1863 Map of La Mesilla and Changing Course of the River

In a letter from the ministry of foreign relations to the boundary commission sent to oversee the surveying of the border, the minister

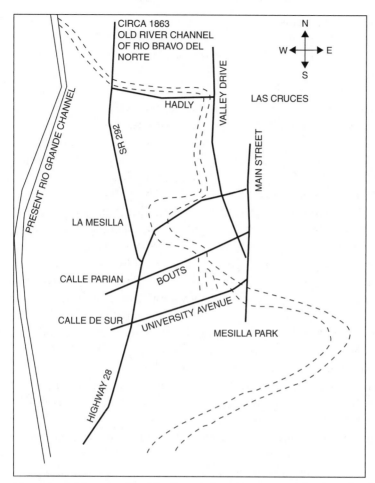

Figure 3.2. 1863 map of La Mesilla and changing course of the river. Courtesy of Judge Lionel Cajen Frietze.

observed that towns threatened by "natural causes" of the river were of great importance to the nation, and efforts to maintain territorial integrity faced natural and man-made obstacles.[43] He noted that "the flooding produced a change in the course of the waters" that resulted in the "disputed territory of the pueblos" becoming U.S. territory. As

[43] "Carta de Ministro de Relaciones Interiores y Exteriores a Don Pedro García Conde, 18 Febrero 1851," in AHSRE, 17–11–102, "Se dan órdenes para que al atrasar la línea divisoria de Norte queden en territorio Mexicano los pueblos San Elizario, Isleta, Socorro, y Sénecu, 1850."

can be seen from this 1863 map, these particular colonies also shared the unique distinction of shifting borders due to an overflowing of the main river that formed a "natural" division between the United States and Mexico.[44]

Given that a natural disaster had been responsible for the shift of the repatriate towns of San Elizario, Ysleta, Socorro, and Senecú (down river south of La Mesilla) to the U.S. side of the border, Mexican authorities were puzzled that local and state authorities did little to manipulate the course of the rivers to prevent the shift. This had the effect of placing them on the "left side of the river" and therefore within the new territorial limits of the United States.[45] As Francisco Urquidi pointed out, "[T]he local authorities in that district did nothing, and in subsequent years the principal course of the river has continued by the arm of the river that leaves those mentioned towns on the left side."[46] Neither human intervention nor natural disasters could be clearly blamed for the change in the course of the river, but Urquidi was positive that those towns situated along the northern frontier were "indisputably the right of the Mexican Republic." Discussing efforts to ensure territories remain within the republic, Urquidi questioned the loyalty of local inhabitants, as some were reportedly allied with the Americans: "It is very well known and above all I too would ask: have some measures been taken, in order for the river to move each time more towards us, or by the cunning of our own compatriots united with the Americans?"[47] It seems that local residents – at least in this case – spoke through their lack of action to damn the river upstream and therefore remained on the U.S. side of the river.

Ortiz took an active role in such matters when he directed repatriates of La Mesilla to dam the river upstream. A letter from the Jefe Politico of the area noted that the neighbors of La Mesilla, under the guidance of "Don Ramón Ortiz," had changed the direction of the river

[44] An example of Rio Bravo shifting in the Mesilla Valley, circa 1863; Graph Located in Frietze, *History of La Mesilla and Her Mesilleros,* 2nd Edition.
[45] "Se dan órdenes para que al atrasar la línea divisoria de Norte queden en territorio Mexicano los pueblos San Elizario, Isleta, Socorro, y Sénecu, 1850," AHSRE, 17–11–102.
[46] Ibid.
[47] Ibid. Original: "Demasiado conocidas son y sobre todo yo también preguntaré, ¿se han tomado algunas medidas, para que el Rio se lance cada vez más sobre nosotros, por las astucias de nuestros mismos conciudadanos unidos á los Americanos?"

by moving dirt from one side of the riverbed to the other. They did their work so well no water remained for people living downstream or for the colony of La Mesilla itself.[48]

If the inaction seen in most of the border towns impacted by the shifts in the course of the river signaled a local preference to remain subject to U.S. sovereignty, what lay behind this preference? In an 1851 letter to the Chihuahuan governor and the minister of foreign relations, General Don Pedro García Conde pointedly observed: "They were not the arguments, nor the subtleties of the intelligence of those that could conserve in our power the referred towns, after the treaty of peace; but the material struggles."[49] In the mind of the top military general of the region, the loyalty of borderlanders had shifted because of material struggles, or *luchas materiales*. Material struggles involved the issue of taxation and the best option in terms of costs and benefits to individual families, and which nation could provide better security. This is why "without the loss of perhaps one day, the towns sought the protection of the American authority, for further injury, by virtue of the treaty, so as to not pay taxes; and this latter [authority] sheltered them...basing it on the principle that the western arm of the isle was much deeper."[50] The loss of these border towns illustrates that a number of individual communities opted to try their luck as U.S. possessions because of material interests like tax concessions, privileges, business ties, and general safety.

In like fashion, the eventual founders of the colony of Guadalupe were driven by "material struggles" with which the Chihuahuan state offered assistance. As a way to induce settlers from the borderlands to migrate south and populate the Mexican side of the newly established boundary, the Chihuahuan legislature issued a decree in the spring of 1850. The text began, "To Chihuahuan residents of Doña Ana, Isleta, Socorro, and San Elizario, the government will provide lands, double in size to those given to other Mexican immigrants of New Mexico or

[48] "Contestaciones habidas por haber cortado algunos norteamericanos las aguas del Río Bravo que utilizan algunas poblaciones mexicanas, 1851–1852." AHSRE, 17–11–8.

[49] "Señor General Don Pedro García Conde a Gobernador de Chihuahua y Ministro de Relaciones Exteriores y Interiores," 11 Febrero 1851," en AHSRE, 17–11–102, "Se dan órdenes para que al trazar la línea divisoria del Norte queden en el territorio mexicano los pueblos de San Elizario, Isleta, Socorro y Senecú, 1850–1851."

[50] Ibid.

California." These lands, the decree outlined, would be "from unculti-
vated sections on the right bank of the Rio Bravo." In accordance with
the state decree of January 17, 1849, repatriates who chose to return
would also be granted "the same privileges and conditions that are
established by decree, and without prejudice of financial assistance to
those who have said right granted by the laws of the Republic."[51] The
arrival of repatriates on the Mexican side of the international boundary,
though, entailed a different story that belies the nationalist discourse of
these decrees.

A Pueblo United?: Issues with Funding and Favoritism

As already described, the desire to repatriate was much stronger than
initially expected. It is not surprising, then, that the original amount
of money allotted for repatriation was but a fraction of what Ortiz pre-
dicted would be needed for resettlement.[52] The problems associated
with finances, favoritism, and the cronyism of regional politics contributed to the early problems with repatriation.

In April 1849 a small group of settlers occupied the area which
would become the Colonia Guadalupe de los Nobles, and successive
waves of repatriates would foster resentment and competition for land
in the years to come. In his study of contemporary rural violence in
Mexico, sociologist Andrés Villarreal concludes that "because the
loss of land, or loss of good quality land, has a direct impact on the
livelihood of the peasant and may indeed be life-threatening, conflict
over land may be expected to turn more violent."[53] Resentment and
competition between the first settlers and later colonists is a univer-
sally known source of social conflict, and the distinctions can become
harsher when these particularities are being resolved along a violent
and volatile frontier. These first settlers had "emigrated from the towns
of Senecú, Ysleta, and San Elizario" – locations and settlements that

---

[51] De La Vara, "The Return to Mexico," 49; Taylor, *A Place as Wild as the West*, 25;
and *Código de Colonización*, 535–51.

[52] Ortiz was estimating that the total costs of repatriation would entail some
1,653,342 pesos for all the potential migrants.

[53] See "The Social Ecology of Rural Violence: Land Scarcity, the Organization of
Agricultural Production, and the Presence of the State," *American Journal of
Sociology 110*, number 2, (September 2004): 313–48.

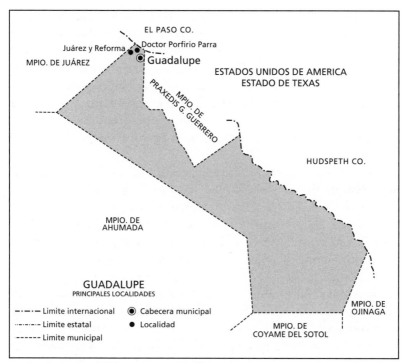

Figure 3.3. Map of modern day municipalities of Praxedis G. Guerrero and Guadalupe, Chihuahua. Map courtesy of Cambridge University Press.

had been part of Chihuahua prior to the U.S. occupation. Although the commissioner articulated an objection to preferential treatment, the material promises of the decrees undermine such a caveat. Favoritism and extortion, whether real or imagined, emerged as a constant theme in almost every repatriate colony I located. Gregorio Gándara, the commissioner of emigration from the border town of San Elizario, stipulated that the emigrants from just across the river should be treated the same as those coming from further away in New Mexico.[54]

By April 1850, it is estimated that 600 families from New Mexico had migrated to the colonies of Guadalupe and San Ignacio. Governor Frías noted in the middle of March that migrants were arriving at the border towns of San Elizario and Isleta every day, and that more were to

[54] Sisneros, *Los Emigrantes Nuevomexicanos*, 46–54.

be expected. Frías estimated that "[t]wo thousand five hundred people to date exist in the colony of Guadalupe of those that have emigrated from New Mexico and of the towns of San Elizario, Socorro and Isleta belonging to this Villa; and new emigrants are arriving most of the days."[55] Two years later the population of Guadalupe appears at 1,015 individuals, while that of San Ignacio was at 232. Of this total, upwards of 550 colonists had come from the New Mexico Territory to these two colonies, according to the 1852 census and per the analysis provided by Sisneros.[56]

The reassignment of Ortiz from a national to a state-level commission may indicate that the federal government to some extent abandoned repatriation efforts after U.S. authorities challenged the repatriation commission. But the cost of this enterprise must certainly have been daunting to federal officials with perennially empty coffers. During his trip in the spring of 1849, Ortiz indicated to the ministry of foreign relations that he would need a great deal more than the first payment of twenty-five thousand pesos.[57] According to his calculations in early June of that year, Ortiz estimated that in addition to the 900 families that had already signed up to help found the colonies in Chihuahua, another sixteen thousand families totaling upwards of fifty-three thousand souls could migrate south if monies were set aside for this endeavor. An additional 1,653,342 pesos would be necessary if all of the potential repatriates opted to leave, or about 1,628,342 pesos more than the original twenty-five thousand initially extended. Around ninety-two thousand fanegas of corn and almost twenty-five thousand fanegas of beans, roughly an eight-month supply of food, would be needed until the colonies could become self-sufficient.[58] By the end of 1850 accounting

55 "Carta de Ángel Frías a Ministro de Relaciones Exteriores, 27 March 1850," AHSRE, 2–13–2977, "El Gobernador de Chihuahua transcribe una comunicación del Comisionado en que pide fondos para la empresa de traslación de familias, 1850."
56 Sisneros, *Los Emigrantes Nuevomexicanos*, 158.
57 Del La Vara, "The Return to Mexico," 50.
58 Correspondence of Ramón Ortiz, in *Three New Mexico Chronicles*, 148–9; AHSRE, L-E-1975 (XXV), "Asunto: Ramón Ortiz – Nombramiento del citado para que pase a Nuevo México, comisionado para la traslación de familias a territorio de la República, 1848"; AHSRE, 2–13–2971, "Gobierno del Estado de Chihuahua. Escrito a mano: No. 68: El Gobernador de Chihuahua participa que se ha nombrado agente del Señor comisionado Ortiz al Licenciado Don Manuel Armendáriz para que informe al Supremo Gobierno sobre la inmigración a este Estado de las familias Nuevo Mexicanas, 1849."

by the government of Chihuahua showed Ortiz as being at a deficit of almost 3,000 pesos. He had spent 39,110 pesos since the start of his mission, and various governmental officials and agencies had forwarded around 36,167 pesos.[59]

The government acknowledged that funding for repatriation was an ongoing problem, and that it may have had an effect on where individuals chose to live after the war. The forty-three-page Memoria report submitted to the Chamber of Deputies in 1851 addressed this matter somewhat vaguely:

> *Transfer of Mexican families*: The government has given some quantities more for this object and has the satisfaction of announcing that there have already been formed in the territory of the Republic, new populations composed in their larger part by Mexicans that have emigrated from the lands given by the last treaty to the United States of the North. I should mention here that Don Gregorio Mier y Terán graciously ceded some lands for this object. The government believes that if it had been able to dispose of larger sums, the number of those that would have transferred to Mexico would have been greater.[60]

The use of "some additional amounts" really means a total of a few thousand pesos, surely not more than one percent of the $15 million the U.S. government provided for the lands ceded to them after the war. To make matters worse, the "the civil colonies' first years were arduous ones for its inhabitants."[61] Given that government support was limited at best, it seems clear that repatriation was much more a matter of individual decision that requires a more complex analysis of repatriation than one that relies solely on nationalist sentiment.[62]

[59] "El Gobernador de Chihuahua transcribe una comunicación del Comisionado en que pide fondos para la empresa de traslación de familias, 1850." AHSRE, 2–13–2977.

[60] México, *Memoria del Ministro de Relaciones Interiores y Esteriores Leída en las Cámaras en 1851*, (México: Imprenta de Vicente García Torres, 1851), 29.

[61] De La Vara, "The Return to Mexico," 52.

[62] Taylor is the historian that claims: "The Mexican government has never forgotten the Mexican population that has lived on the other side of that dividing line and it has always been disposed to resettle them in the event they were left unhappy or without possibilities to continue residing abroad." See Lawrence Douglas Taylor Hansen, "La repatriación de Mexicanos de 1848 a 1980 y su papel en la colonización de la región fronteriza septentrional de México," *Relaciones* 18, no. 69 (1997): 198–212.

The preferential treatment of migrants from right across the river would serve to fuel internal tensions between earlier and newly arrived migrants. The early settlers were the keenest to secure better lands, the most abundant watering holes, and other advantages. The division between earlier and later settlers, as was the case in La Mesilla – and later La Ascensión, Chihuahua – created a situation analogous to what historian Emilio Kourí described in his "pueblo divided" thesis concerning Papantla in the state of Veracruz.[63] In other words, and in contrast to nationalist historiographical readings that paint the repatriate experience as a "pueblo united," social divisions within these colonies were transferred to the new locales and further complicated by successive waves of settlement. New arrivals are always treated with resentment by earlier colonists.

Repatriates Within the Colonial Periphery

Although repatriates were theoretically not limited as to where in Mexico they could settle, a number of the decree's articles directed repatriates to the frontier states of Tamaulipas, Sonora, Chihuahua, Coahuila, and Baja California. In the context of military strategy, it is not hard to understand why repatriates were directed toward the northern frontier states, especially when various indigenous groups were pushed to the region during and after the war. Mexican state efforts at repatriation emerged in large part out of the long tradition of trying to settle the region with "civilized Indians" and Mexicans from the interior. At this time, according to anthropologist Ana María Alonso, "[A]lthough indigenes such as the Apache had engaged in warfare and raiding prior to the conquest, it was the disruption of native society and the displacement of native groups caught between the expansion of the Anglo-American and Hispanic frontiers that turned them into specialists in violence."[64] The diaspora from the ceded territories would provide border governors with an additional pool of loyal settlers effectively placed on the front lines of indigenous resistance. Repatriation, therefore, was envisioned as part and parcel of the militarization of the frontier and the repatriates' role was to further the development, settlement, and pacification of the region. It was a common belief of the time

---

[63] Emilio Kourí, *A Pueblo Divided: Business, Property, and Community in Papantla, Mexico* (Stanford: Stanford University Press, 2004).

[64] Alonso, *Thread of Blood*, 24–5.

that repatriates were somehow more civilized because of their tenure abroad, and so their resettlement along these frontiers accomplished a number of long-term objectives. The repatriate-cum-colonists' obligation to defend the frontier for Mexico was based in large part on an historical social contract that the Mexican government had employed for generations. Historian Friedrich Katz reminds us that during the colonial period in Mexico extraordinary benefits were granted to Spaniards, Mexicans, "as well as to local Indians who were willing to settle in these Military Colonies" situated in the north.[65]

Underscoring the military approach to repatriation, one of the final articles (Article 23) of the 1848 decree offered additional incentives like land and tax concessions to repatriate for all government employees and military officials who found themselves in the ceded territories.[66] Thus, the official state paper of Chihuahua, El Faro, noted in November 1849 that "In regard to the transfer of families who wish to emigrate from New Mexico and establish themselves in Chihuahua...this commission believes it to be very important, since this method will augment the population useful for the war [against the Indians]. They will populate, in a permanent way, a portion of the area along the banks of the rivers and by springs and watering places."[67] Anthropologist Daniel Nugent offers an interesting example of this social conflict in his historical ethnography of Namiquipa, Chihuahua. In that study, he points out that a number of these original settlers also displaced indígenas from their lands. The "Despojo de Tierras (dispossessions of land) of indígenas in the Sierra Tarahumara committed by New Mexicans and other recent settlers to Chihuahua followed soon thereafter in the 1850s."[68] New repatriates, unlike Euro American settlers and "civilized Indians," were less likely to be disloyal, or so the thinking went, since they were Roman Catholic, spoke Spanish, and were experienced Indian fighters.

Throughout the nineteenth century, requests for land regurgitated this trope of pacification and civilization. For example, in his

[65] Katz, The Life and Times of Pancho Villa, 12.

[66] See Articulo 23 of "Decreto de 19 de Julio de 1848, y Reglamento expedido el día 20 del mismo mes, para el establecimiento de colonias militares en la nueva línea divisoria con los Estados Unidos de América," in Código de Colonización, 400–7.

[67] El Faro, Chihuahua, 24 November 1849; quoted in Taylor, A Place as Wild as the West, 20.

[68] Nugent, Spent Cartridges of Revolution, 52

extended correspondence with the central government, Vicente Ochoa requested lands on which to colonize the margins of the Rio Bravo and stipulated that over 200 families from the La Mesilla region wished to settle in the lands of "Canutillo, San Emilio, and San Joaquin" in the state of Chihuaha. To 160 families from the region of La Mesilla were added another twenty-five "poor Mexican families" and twenty-five families composed of Tarahumara Indians.[69] All three of these groups would fight on behalf of the nation, Ochoa noted several times throughout the file. One of the supporters of his request noted, "Besides, the establishment of this colony, because of its convenient situation, will powerfully influence and impede in this way the invasions of the barbarians, as well as contraband."[70] In the end, the project was not funded because the request was considered too expensive.

Divisions between the earlier and subsequent repatriates became a major factor in the colonization process. We see this play out in the repatriate colonies of La Mesilla, La Ascension, and elsewhere again and again in the Porfirian period. Sisneros agrees with this latter point and observes that those "who wished to repatriate from San Elizario and Doña Ana were to receive twice the amount of property, caus[ing] some heated dispute."[71] Problems with land, water, wood, and land surveys became so acute for the colonists that by the middle of the 1850s they were not only abandoning their homes in Guadalupe, but doing exactly the opposite of what Chihuahuan authorities hoped for: They were returning to the United States!

Through the lens shaped by the ambitions of colonization, we can interpret the difficulties faced by the colonies of Guadalupe and San Ignacio as a poor fit between the skills of the residents and the goals of postwar nation building. San Ignacio, for instance, was established as a military outpost to counter Indios Bárbaros. It "was almost entirely populated by *Nuevomexicanos*; 214 out of the 232 residents (40 out of 52 families) were from New Mexico."[72] Of these 232 individuals,

[69] See "Vicente Ochoa – Presupuesto para colonizar los terrenos baldíos de las márgenes del Bravo, con familias Mexicanas. 2 Diciembre 1878," in *Archivo Histórico de Terrenos Nacionales*, 1.29 (06), Exp. 28. [Hereafter cited as AHTN]

[70] "Carta de José González Porras a Secretaria de Fomento," 15 Octubre 1878, in ibid.

[71] Sisneros, *Los Emigrantes Nuevomexicanos*, 47.

[72] Ibid., 49.

approximately 120 were male while 112 were female and together they formed around fifty-two households. Most of these repatriates were from southern New Mexico and not from the northern areas of the territory where Ortiz had done much of his recruiting.[73] The result was that only sixty-three of the 120 men registered in the 1852 census were able soldiers. These men became the San Ignacio Cavalry and Infantry, and two-thirds of them were armed with small handguns, while another thirteen carried swords, pistols, and one carbine. Those without arms (nine men) were to act as the only logistical support for the other sixty-three "Indian killers." The tally of such armament suggests that their primary function was military in nature.

As noted previously, while some in American political circles have held that the postwar U.S. government wanted the newly acquired territory sans Mexicans, the evidence points to a general consensus that repatriation should be prevented. Underlying this consensus was a belief that only Nuevo Mexicanos, the original settlers of the occupied area, were capable of preventing the "incursions of the barbarians."[74] Their numbers were also seen as vital to obtaining statehood, the ultimate goal of the U.S. government as the territory transitioned from military governance to civilian rule. The colonial perspective deepens our understanding of U.S. opposition to Mexican efforts to retrieve former citizens through repatriation. Secretary of War George W. Cranford pointed out that "it would be a disgraceful event that now when Indian depredations along the frontiers of that territory demand their punishment, that order and peace are agitated by the Mexican part of that population."[75] Indian raiding, as Brian DeLay has recently argued, increased as a result of the war.[76] The

---

[73] See appendix 2 in Ibid., 158.

[74] Nona Barrick and Mary Taylor, "The Mesilla Guard, 1851–1861," *Southwestern Studies, Monograph No. 51,* (El Paso: University of Texas at El Paso Press, 1976); For problems arising among Mesilleros and Apache conflict see "Asesinato del Jefe Apache 'Cuentas Azules,' Cometido por mexicanos los que huyeron a la Mesilla; Lista de los prisioneros en el fuerte Webster, Nuevo México, 1853," AHSRE, Exp. 30–16–58.

[75] Carta de George W. Cranford a Ministro de Relaciones Exteriores y Interiores, 5 Octubre 1849, in AHSRE, 2–13–2971, "Gobierno del Estado de Chihuahua. Escrito a mano: No. 68: El Gobernador de Chihuahua participa que se ha nombrado agente del Señor comisionado Ortiz al Licenciado Don Manuel Armendáriz para que informe al Supremo Gobierno sobre la inmigración a este Estado de las familias Nuevo Mexicanas, 1849."

[76] Delay, "Independent Indians and the U.S.-Mexican War," 35–68.

commotion caused by Ortiz only served to agitate a common enemy at the time when the new U.S. territory and its way of life were being destroyed. Here – unlike in Texas and California – the United States opposed these first repatriation efforts, at least in the case of New Mexico.

Much like the settlers of Guadalupe, the repatriates of San Ignacio were required to defend the nation against all enemies. In two land titles awarding José Anaya a lot for housing and a lot for raising crops in exchange for at least four years of land settlement, and with the stipulation that those lands not be ceded to any "dead hands" (church, priest, community corporation, monastery, etc.), we can clearly see the social contract between state and citizen. The contract given to Anaya also mentioned that he could do as he pleased with the land "if and whenever as citizen of the frontier he is quick to defend the Country from the enemies that harass it and to track them in their persecution when the authority deemed it." In exchange, the state would do its best to provide the colonists with "weapons and horse" and also the lands on which a colonist such as Anaya would be required to "reside with his family in the new population for the space of four years."[77] The requirement to pursue enemy combatants targeted the Indios Bárbaros specifically, whose attacks almost always consisted of hit-and-run maneuvers. The defense of the frontier naturally required horses and guns, hence the government's promise to supply these items. This was a normal expectation in the other repatriate colonies as well, and was usually part of colonization contracts throughout the nineteenth century.

The colony of Guadalupe was founded in the aftermath of the Mexican American War and grew to be much larger than San Ignacio. The 1852 census shows Guadalupe with a total population of 1,015, of whom 612 were male while 403 were female. Interesting, there were fifty-seven widows and widowers among the adults; female widows were the overwhelming majority (they numbered forty-one) whereas there were sixteen male widowers. If these widows constituted individual households in the colony of Guadalupe at this time, this would mean

---

[77] "Títulos de José Anaya, 28 Febrero y 8 Mayo de 1854," in AHTN, 1.29 (06), Exp. 239, "Don Juan Vigil, emigrado de Nuevo México como apoderado de los demás emigrados en la colonia de Guadalupe y San Ignacio en el Paso del Norte pide se concedan a dicha colonia varias tierras baldías. [El Agente remite 287 Títulos], 1849–1855."

that of the 215 households documented, over twenty-five percent were headed by widows, 26.5 percent to be precise.[78] I have not been able to determine why in this particular colony the number of widows and widowers was so high, or if there might have been a benefit to claiming property as a widow as opposed to a family unit. The high number of female widows may also serve as a reminder of life expectancy for frontier males, the dangers of everyday life in the postwar borderlands, or the impact of Indian killing and violence during this particular period in time.

Of the 612 males, 189 served in the Guadalupe infantry (108) and cavalry (81). One hundred twenty-four men were armed with small handguns, 104 with pistols, sixty-four with lances, thirty-three with rifles, seven with long rifles, and fourteen with swords. And much like their counterparts in San Ignacio, many of the repatriates of Guadalupe came from southern New Mexico and not from the northern territories or from California. Today Guadalupe de los Nobles has a population of 9,148 persons and still dedicates approximately ninety-three percent of its lands for livestock grazing, according to available state statistics.[79] Like many towns and cities along the border, the modern municipality of Guadalupe is experiencing the current violence of President Calderón's war against the "Narco Terrorists," and has made national news recently.

At the local level, these concerns were addressed through the stipulations in land titles that we saw earlier in the case of José Anaya. An exchange between government officials at the Department of Fomento in 1855 regarding the distribution of land titles revealed the purpose behind the founding of San Ignacio and Guadalupe, the absence of funding notwithstanding, as being the civilizing of the Indios Bárbaros. An examination of this exchange is worth going over in detail so as to remain grounded in the reality of repatriation during the middle of the nineteenth century. For the local representative of the department:

The direct expression of emigrants from New Mexico, familiarizes Your Excellency with the protection that the government of

[78] Sisneros, *Los Emigrantes Nuevomexicanos*, See appendix 2, 158.
[79] Secretaría de Gobernación y Gobierno del Estado de Chihuahua, *Los Municipios de Chihuahua* (México: Secretaría de Gobernación y Gobierno del Estado de Chihuahua, 1988), 139–42.

that period saw itself obliged to extend to the Mexicans, that by virtue of the treaty of Guadalupe, they could be considered foreigners in their own land, wrestling with the religion, language and customs of the new proprietors. Moreover, the points chosen to establish the two colonies of Guadalupe and San Ignacio, are in my humble conception, quite deliberate, together with the conditions imposed on said colonists: given this Department's lack of resources needed to engage in an active and tenacious war with the savage, a new wall has been placed between the towns of El Paso and Del Norte that will impede from that point the entry and exit of barbarians that harass this Department and that of Durango.[80]

These new colonies, outfitted as they were with infantry and cavalry, would be the first lines of defense at the newly established boundary between the United States and Mexico. The obligation of these repatriates is made clear and the benefits of the state are clearly outlined: kill for the state in exchange for land, which explains why I belabor the point of the settlers' weaponry and military positions.

These repatriate colonies were therefore founded not solely for nationalist reasons related to the aftermath of the Mexican American War, but grew out of a fairly straightforward discourse driven by concerns of national security, pacification of the border, development of the region, *realpolitik,* and territorial sovereignty.

---

[80] "Carta de Genaro Artalejo a Señor Ministro de Fomento, Colonización, Industria y Comercio de la República de México, 15 Mayo 1855," in AHTN, 1.29 (06), Exp. 239, "Don Juan Vigil, emigrado de Nuevo México como apoderado de los demás emigrados en la colonia de Guadalupe y San Ignacio en el Paso del Norte pide se concedan a dicha colonia varias tierras baldías. [El Agente remite 287 Títulos], 1849–1855"; Original: "La simple enunciación de emigrados de Nuevo México, da a conocer a Vuestra Excelencia la protección que el gobierno de aquella fecha se vio en la obligación de prestar a los mexicanos, que en virtud del tratado de Guadalupe, se podían considerar como extranjeros en su propio suelo y pugnando con la religión, idioma y costumbres de los nuevos propietarios. Además, los puntos escogidos para plantear las dos colonias de Guadalupe y San Ignacio, son en mi humilde concepto, muy a propósito, juntamente con las condiciones impuestas a dichos colonos: pues careciendo este Departamento de los recursos necesarios para hacer una guerra activa y tenaz al salvaje, se ha puesto entre los pueblos del Paso y del Norte otra nueva muralla, que impedirá por ese punto la entrada y salida a los bárbaros que hostilizan este Departamento y el de Durango."

Persistent Mismanagement Plagues
the Mexican Border Colonies

Mismanagement, abuse of authority, and questionable land surveys were the hallmarks of the repatriate experience in the middle of the nineteenth century. Such practices called into question the Mexican state's ability to deliver on the promises found in its benevolent rhetoric of national belonging, and they contributed to a simultaneous migration northward to the United States. Early migration to the United States not only took advantage of economic incentives, but also reflected the ability of the two nations to protect their citizens, particularly those living along the frontier regions.

By 1853 the residents of San Ignacio had lodged a series of complaints against the justice of the peace (Juan Antonio Trujillo) for not managing the colony in accordance to the law. Trujillo's incompetence earned him a description as a *retonto* among one of the correspondents of San Ignacio.[81] In the mid-1850s similar allegations of mismanagement of the colonies, including the fabrication of land titles and the selling of fictitious properties (since they had not been surveyed) were common in the colony of Guadalupe. The outcry grew so great that Mexican authorities opened an investigation concerning land issues in both colonies on June 27, 1854.[82] De La Vara seems to suggest that a number of the difficulties had to do with resentment over this preferential treatment: "[A] confrontation among the colonists of Guadalupe erupted, perhaps owing to a lack of sufficient natural resources."[83] Upset about the best lands allotted to repatriates from Socorro, Ysleta, and San Elizario – and in grants twice the size of the repatriates' holdings in the ceded territories – emigrants from New Mexico threatened to leave the colony. The abundant harvests in 1851 and 1852 mollified their discontent, however. Questions about land titles and continued

---

[81] The use of the term *retonto* has a particular meaning that can be described as "really dumb" or "double dumb." In *Ciudad Juarez Municipal Archives Microfilm Collection*, MF513, Pt. 2, Reel 37, 10 May to August 9, 1853; quoted in Sisneros, "An Annotated List of Documents on the Towns of Guadalupe and San Ignacio in the Ciudad Juarez Municipal Archives, 1849–1859," located at the UTEP Special Collections.

[82] In *Ciudad Juarez Municipal Archives Microfilm Collection*, MF513, Pt. 2, Reel 38; quoted in Sisneros, "An Annotated List of Documents on the Towns of Guadalupe and San Ignacio in the Ciudad Juarez Municipal Archives, 1849–1859," located at the UTEP Special Collections.

[83] De La Vara, "The Return to Mexico," 52.

mismanagement continued to be raised well after these good harvests, but the origins of the conflict can be traced back to the moment when later repatriates began to arrive.

By the spring of 1856, continued allegations of abuse of authority threatened the peace of Guadalupe to such a degree that many repatriates decided to return to the United States. Justice of the Peace José Maria Carvajal and the municipal president of Guadalupe, Joaquin Molina, were accused of going beyond their jurisdiction in extending land titles to their associates. According to the commissioner of the Guadalupe colony, Guadalupe Miranda, these two officials were:

> bothering the colonists of this [colony] and those of San Ignacio, with excesses and abuses of their authority, seeking to extend beyond the powers demarcated to them by the laws in its boundary and annul agendas, such as those of destroying some acts of this Commission, confirmed already by the Supreme Government, trying to remove or to diminish the property that this Commission has adjudicated to the Colonist, with the purpose of giving it away or to cultivate relationships with favorites; in truth unlawful proceedings and offensive to the delicacy of the Commission, that when it has exercised its faculties in these acts, it has been guided by no other principles than those of justice and equity recommended by the law, attending to the requirements and considerations that these poor unfortunate emigrants rightly deserve and who have had the difficult necessity of being displaced from their Country, to come to beg for a living, only so as to continue the condition of their race, exposing themselves to fight daily with the savage to oust him off land that they still dispute with him, and to resist the hunger, the misery and the inclemency's resulting from this businesses of establishing new colonies.[84]

---

[84] "Carta de Guadalupe Miranda a Señor Agente del Ministerio de Fomento y Colonización, Don Anastasio Nava, Chihuahua, 18 Marzo 1850," in AHTN, 1.29 (06), Exp. 239, "Don Juan Vigil, emigrado de Nuevo México como apoderado de los demás emigrados en la colonia de Guadalupe y San Ignacio en el Paso del Norte pide se concedan a dicha colonia varias tierras baldías. [El Agente remite 287 Títulos], 1849–1855"; Original: "Molestando a los colonos de ésta y la de San Ignacio, con demasías y abusos de su autoridad, pretendiendo extenderse más allá de las facultades que se les demarcan por las leyes en su [linde] y abrogarse agenas [sic], tales como las de destruir algunos actos de esta Comisión, confirmados ya por el Supremo Gobierno, intentando quitar o disminuir la propiedad que por esta Comisión se le ha adjudicado al Colono,

Miranda clearly recognized the great sacrifices made by the repatriates and noted the contradiction on the part of the municipal president and the justice of the peace in this matter. Cases of this type, as the following chapters will illustrate, were not unique to these first repatriate colonies, but would plague later colonies as well. These allegations were contested by Carvajal, and ultimately the request for titles appears to have been granted despite the charges of fraud and abuse of authority.

CONCLUSION

The fact that the Mexican government – operating through various state and federal agencies – made generous offers of land to Mexicans to repatriate across the new international boundary should not blind our analysis to the matters of *realpolitik* and state efforts to populate an area that historically had suffered from a lack of settlement, at least according to U.S. and Mexican perspectives. The Mexican government of the postwar period came to realize what others had recognized before them: that "La Gran Chichimeca" would be difficult to conquer, colonize, and civilize. A more nuanced and accurate understanding of repatriation is needed beyond that of the sympathetic alignment of state, local, and individual interests suggested by hyper-nationalist historiography.

A host of problems with the founding of Guadalupe and San Ignacio appear to have emerged shortly after the federal government placed Ortiz in charge of repatriating Mexicans from the ceded territories. These allegations did not, however, deter Ortiz, charged with the duties of commissioner, from continuing to encourage repatriates to settle in colonies such as Guadalupe, Zaragoza, San Ignacio, Los Amoles, and La Mesilla – all of which he helped to establish.

con el fin de darla o a crecer a otros de sus favoritos; procedimiento a la verdad contrario a las leyes y ofensivo a la delicadeza de la Comisión, que cuando ha ejercido en estos actos sus facultades, no ha sido guiada por otros principios que los de justicia y equidad recomendados por la ley, atendiendo a las exigencias y consideraciones que justamente se merecen estos pobres desgraciados emigrantes que han tenido la dura necesidad de desalojarse de su País, para venir a mendigar en que vivir, por sólo seguir la condición de su raza, exponiéndose a combatir cotidianamente con el salvaje para desalojarlo del terreno que aun hoy todavía disputan con él, y resistir la [sic] hambre, la miseria y las intemperies consiguientes a estas empresas de plantear nuevas colonias."

The potential depopulation of the New Mexican Territory was viewed unfavorably by the new U.S. authorities, especially the military government installed after the war. The United States responded to the departure of Mexicans from the state of New Mexico with the claim that this violated the Treaty of Guadalupe Hidalgo. In Texas and California, however, the expulsion of Mexican families continued despite protests, and the governments of these two territories did nothing after the war to prevent attacks on Mexicans or to retain them as residents. By contrast, New Mexico's largely Mexican population was not driven out against its will; many desired to leave, but due to tensions on a national level, repatriation became the province of state-level initiatives.

In the absence of the Mexican government following through with what its laws had promised, New Mexicans had no incentive for making the short but significant trip south into Mexico. In short, and quoting from the repatriate commissioner himself, why should New Mexicans choose to undergo hardship in Chihuahua if the only benefit was being "subjects of the government of Mexico"?[85] Father Ortiz understood that material benefits, tax concessions, and other forms of remuneration would be required if the government wished to see the northern frontiers settled to any degree. As it happened, the government did not offer much help and most repatriates found that they could only depend on themselves. Although Ortiz did not have a prior history of trouble with the Mexican political establishment, the general ambivalence, incompetence, and disregard manifested by federal authorities must have tested his loyalty.

To end, although important towns like La Mesilla, Los Amoles, San Joaquin, Guadalupe, Socorro, Zaragoza, and Santo Tómas were founded by repatriates from the ceded territory of New Mexico, the process owed much to the material conditions and tenacity of the repatriates themselves and little to the state's capacity to fund repatriation and ensure the protection of its citizens. The vast majority of Nuevo Mexicanos ultimately chose to remain under a U.S. system of governance – one that offered better incomes, more safety, and trade – rather than become "subjects of the government of Mexico."[86]

---

[85] "Carta de Ramón Ortiz a Ministro de Relaciones Exteriores y Interiores, 23 Diciembre 1849, AHSRE, 2–13–2977, "El Gobernador de Chihuahua transcribe una comunicación del Comisionado en que pide fondos para la empresa de traslación de familias, 1850."

[86] Ibid.

Preferential treatment along the northern frontier did not ameliorate life in a harsh environment marked by conflict with *indígenas* for several more decades. The perceived threat represented by Indios Bárbaros on either side of the Rio Bravo/Rio Grande served as a primary reference point, turning the non-indigenous residents and potential repatriates of the border region into little more than useful placeholders on the colonial map of the region.

This government does not doubt the patriotic feelings of His Excellency, who will double his efforts with the suitable object, and that he will have at present that the unfortunate ones that today implore aid to return to their homeland are sons of Mexico, and they have been citizens of the State of Coahuila: that this same State did not only lose the immense and considerable possession of the Department of Texas, but also the part that made up its limits among the Río de las Nueces and Río Bravo: that this immense loss has not been reimbursed by the federation even though it be a considerable part of the land given to the neighboring Republic, and for which was reimbursed to the Nation the sum of fifteen million pesos; that for these circumstances the children of Coahuila are entitled to be aided with preference in the necessary expenses for their adjournment to the territory of the Republic.

Governor of Coahuila to
Minister of Foreign Relations, May 19, 1851

CHAPTER FOUR

REPATRIATIONS ALONG THE

INTERNATIONAL BOUNDARY

THE CASES OF TEXAS AND

CALIFORNIA

INTRODUCTION

Approximately "25 percent of the total Mexican American population of the Southwest in the 1850s" was repatriated in the four decades following the end of hostilities, according to noted historian of the Mexican American experience Professor Richard Griswold del Castillo.[1] Although accurate figures would be almost impossible to determine because of the imprecision of statistical data then and now, studies have surfaced over the past few years that shed light on repatriation and return migrations.[2] According to one author, for instance, the total number of Mexicans that "returned" to Mexico between 1848 and 1880 from the ceded territories amounted to 3,000.[3] Yet one Mexican commissioner sent to recruit Mexican families in New Mexico places the number much higher noting: "I have the satisfaction of being able to inform your Excellency that . . . at least eighty thousand persons are ready to emigrate to the territory [Chihuahua] of the republic."[4] Hence,

[1] Richard Griswold del Castillo, *The Los Angeles Barrio: A Social History, 1850–1890* (Berkeley: University of California Press, 1979), 120.

[2] Some comparison with other cases might be of use for gauging the number of return migrants during the middle to late nineteenth century. For instance, historian Mark Wyman notes for the case of return immigrants in Europe that "During this era of mass immigration, from approximately 1880–1930 when restriction laws and the Great Depression choked it off, from one-quarter to one-third of all European immigrants to the United States permanently returned home." See *Round Trip America: The Immigrants Return to Europe, 1880–1930* (Ithaca and London: Cornell University Press, 1993), 6.

[3] Douglas Taylor, "La Repatriación de Mexicanos," 198–212.

[4] Ramón Ortiz to Angel Trías, 9 June 1849; copy of letter in *Three New Mexico Chronicles: The Exposición of Don Pedro Bautista Pino, 1812; the Ojeada of Lic.*

the number of Mexicanos that migrated south in the decades after the Mexican American War continues to generate debate accompanied by a variety of conflicting numbers, but Griswold's estimate of thirty-one thousand appears to be the most thoughtful of the lot.[5]

Regarding the seventy-five percent of Mexicans who chose to remain in the United States, the discipline of Mexican American studies has focused a disproportionate amount of its scholarship on those north of the Rio Bravo. The modest but growing historiography on the repatriation of Mexicans has also concentrated by and large on repatriation from New Mexico to Chihuahua, thus contributing to

Antonio Barreiro, 1832; and the additions of Don José Agustín de Escudero, 1849, translated with introduction and notes by H. Bailey Carroll and J. Villasana Haggard (Albuquerque: The Quivira Society, 1942), 144–9.

[5] See Griswold del Castillo, *The Los Angeles Barrio,* 120; William Douglas Taylor places the number at 3,000, however, he only cites the [Chihuahuan] study undertaken by Martín González de La Vara (1994), and then only this one case. Douglas states that "Aunque no se sabe con exactidud el número de mexicanos que eventualmente se hayan mudado a México, se calcula que alrededor de tres mil personas aceptaron la oferta y volvieron." See "La Repatriación de Mexicanos de 1848 a 1980 y su papel en la colonización de la región fronteriza septentrional de México," *Relaciones* 18, no. 69. (1997), 198–212. A more comprehensive study of this process will require more research and demographic sampling, which is difficult given the periodization and paucity of documentation. Even with today's technology, the United States and Mexico do not have the capacity to record the number of undocumented Mexicans in the United States, nor is the Mexican government able to estimate the number of return migrants in today's world. Interestingly, González Navarro also provides conflicting numbers, but his study of only analyzing "official colonies" during the Porfiriato does provide for some appropriate samples, which this manuscript attempts to articulate for the mid-nineteenth century. He states "During the long government of Porfirio Díaz there were established, with very unequal success, 16 official colonies and 44 private, 60 in total; eight of the official and 10 of the private (colonies) were formed by Mexicans; three of the first and two of the second with repatriates." In other words, ethnic Mexicans (native and repatriated) composed sixty-nine percent of the official colonies (11/16) during the Porfiriato and they constituted over twenty-seven percent of the private colonization projects, or 12/44. If we combine both the private and government-sponsored colonies, ethnic Mexicans constitute 38.8 percent of the grand total. The author does not take into account as he points out his examples of "foreign" and "American" colonies the number of ethnic Mexicans that not only composed each of these colonies, but that were written into the colonization contracts for almost every single case. See *Los extranjeros en México II,* 133.

our understanding of the complex experience of *fronterizos* during the nineteenth century.[6] Scholars, understandably, have been drawn to the New Mexico Territory region due to its high population density and the fact that the largest institutional representation dedicated to repatriation in the Mexican government focused on New Mexico – an aspect of which I described and outlined in the previous chapter.[7] Yet the repatriation of ethnic Mexicans in the ceded territories took place beyond New Mexico and continued through the close of the nineteenth century, but those particular narratives seem to be overlooked in several bodies of literature that this chapter will attempt to address. This chapter begins to contribute to a historical record for these neglected areas, particularly with respect to return migrations to Mexico from the modern day states of Texas and California.

Repatriations from Texas

According to the research that I conducted in Mexico City, Chihuahua, and the United States, the repatriation of the Mexican population in the region of Texas began in 1831 and saw a substantial increase with the many expulsions that occurred after so-called Texas Independence in 1835. According to sociologist Davíd Montejano, there was "considerable repatriation after the Mexican War," in which "refugees" moved across the Rio Grande and settled "among the old established towns of El Paso del Norte, Guerrero, Mier, Camargo, Reynosa, and Matamoros."[8] The towns of Piedras Negras, Coahuila, and Nuevo Laredo, Tamaulipas were also founded immediately following the war, and several locales in Coahuila would become the sites of repatriation as the century came to a close.

The government, a decade later, as stipulated in the 1830 law prohibiting the migration of Euro American settlers to Texas, did in fact subsidize the repatriation of Mexicans and other people of color

---

6   Martín de la Vara, "The Return to Mexico," 9-21; Ceballos Ramírez, "Consecuencias de la guerra entre México y Estado Unidos," 39–59; Taylor, "La repatriación de Mexicanos," 198–212; Cortés, "Mexican Colonies During the Porfiriato," 1–14; Aguila, "Protecting 'México de Afuera," 182–235.

7   An exception are the micro-studies done on particular Tejano families forced to leave after the defeat of Santa Anna at San Jacinto in 1836. Handbook of Texas Online, s.v. "Mexican Americans and Repatriation," http://www.tsha.utexas.edu/handbook/online/articles/MM/pqmyk.html.

8   Montejano, *Anglos and Mexicans in Texas*, 30.

from Louisiana.⁹ Like previous colonization schemes of the period, this action should be seen as yet another effort to settle the frontier regions of Mexico. The 1830 law specified where the repatriates should settle and allocated 1,500 pesos for this process, which according to article 14, were to be used for the "transfer to the Republic of helpless Mexican families that are found in New Orleans and other parts, transporting them to the locations they elect; provided they are no more distant than the residence before."¹⁰ It is important to note that the funds earmarked for the 1831 repatriations had been set aside for military fortifications in a previous law. Only one year later, orphans and widows of Mexicans residing outside the republic became eligible for repatriation as well.¹¹ As seen in previous immigration and colonization policy, restrictions on immigration for certain groups were codified into law while the inclusion of others was facilitated.

Throughout the rest of the nineteenth century other important towns were founded and grew just across the new border, towns such as Nuevo Monterrey, Tamaulipas (now Nuevo Laredo), Piedras Negras, San Diego, San Juan, Palo Blanco, Agua Dulce, El Sauz, Los Olmos, San Luis, Pansacola, Zapata, San Ignacio, and Los Saenz.¹²

Many of the repatriates settled in towns that were already well established and sat right across the new international boundary. For example, Piedras Negras, Coahuila, sits across the border from modern day Eagle Pass, Texas.¹³ It was a notable repatriate destination. A local historian mentions that thirty-four repatriates arrived on June

9 "Numero 74: Enero 18 de 1831: Resolución facultando al Ejecutivo para invertir la cantidad necesaria en el regreso de las familias mexicanas pobres existentes en Nueva Orleáns," in De La Maza, *Código de Colonización.* 244.
10 Ibid., 244.
11 "Numero 76: Resolución de 14 de Abril de 1832 Sobre pagos por la traslación a la República de las viudas y huérfanos Mexicanas residentes en países extranjeros," in ibid., 245–6.
12 De León, "Life for Mexicans after 1836," passim. The total number of towns founded or repopulated after the war requires an amount of detailed research that is not always easily accessible. Indeed, one way in which to analyze this phenomenon would be for a research team to identify, quantify, and analyze the number of settlements established along the Mexican frontiers in the years following the war.
13 A succinct historical overview is provided by Carlos Flores Revuelta and Álvaro Canales Santos, *Piedras Negras: Reseña Histórica, Protagonistas,* (Saltillo: Club del Libro Coahuilense, Editora el Dos, 2004).

15, 1850 to settle in what was then called Colonia Militar de Guerrero en Piedras Negras.[14] Five years later, this settlement lost its military character and became an ordinary civilian outpost named simply Piedras Negras. Today the population of Piedras Negras numbers over two hundred thousand in the larger metropolitan area and constitutes its own city and municipality. Contrary to what historian González Navarro argued about which colonies were or were not successful, the city of Piedras Negras today generates millions of dollars in revenue as a major port of entry between the United States and Mexico. A similar phenomenon has taken place in the case of Nuevo Laredo, Tamaulipas – today one of the most important trade routes between the United States and Mexico – which we turn to next.

Nuevo Laredo: An Archetypical Patriotic Town, or Repatriate Exception?

Regional and state historian Manuel Ceballos Ramírez notes that "the population that with the greatest drama preserve the memory of repatriation to this very day is New Laredo."[15] Directly across the border (and river) from Laredo, Texas, the border town of Nuevo Laredo still holds celebrations that hearken to its foundational 1848 repatriations. On the surface, it appears repatriation across the new international boundary in this locale took place uneventfully, but this state of affairs should be scrutinized more closely and placed within the broader context of postwar repatriation as a whole.

Nuevo Laredo does distinguish itself in its historical memory and patriotic myths. In 1958 presidential candidate Adolfo López Mateos characterized Nuevo Laredo as a town so entangled with a notion of *Mexicanidad* that those who had chosen to settle in that border town over a century earlier brought with them "the venerated remains of their ancestors."[16] López Mateos was referring to a local myth that maintains that Nuevo Laredo was founded by zealously patriotic individuals who took the initiative to repatriate the remains of their dead. "Tradition assures us," recounts local historian Ceballos Ramírez, "that not content with being transferred themselves to the Mexican side; they also

14 Otto Schober, "Breve historia de Piedras Negras," http://www.piedrasnegras.gob.mx/contenido05/conoce-pn/historia/.
15 Ceballos Ramírez, "Consecuencias de la Guerra," 43–4.
16 Ibid.

unearthed their dead, made the sign of the cross over their remains, and then reburied them in New Laredo in order that they not lay on foreign territory."[17] Yet because no evidence is provided by this historian to support this extraordinary claim, we can neither confirm nor deny this local myth.

Archival evidence does exist that money and land were provided to support repatriation to Nuevo Laredo and also to the town of Mier in neighboring Coahuila. According to some sources, the governor of Tamaulipas wrote to the minister of foreign relations to "receive and distribute the ten thousand three hundred and seventy-nine pesos destined for the Supreme Government for the aid of 502 individuals from Laredo that should form a colony on the land ceded for this purpose by Don Gregorio de Mier y Terán," the area of modern Nuevo Laredo.[18] Some records also exist pertaining to the establishment of the town of Mier in modern day Coahuila. According to the governor of Tamaulipas, in April 1850, fifty families "left in the territories ceded to the United States of America" were granted lands close to the town of "Villa de Mier."[19]

The founding of Nuevo Laredo and Mier are remarkable grassroots efforts considering that they occurred without the benefit of a government representative leading the effort. Yet rather than blindly accept places like Nuevo Laredo as representative of the unflagging loyalty along the border at the time, one must consider the relative ease with which the local population and the government could align in this case of repatriation. To relocate in Nuevo Laredo repatriates needed only to transfer their belongings to the opposite side of the river. One must also consider other, better recorded cases in which repatriation did not appear to proceed nearly as smoothly, a situation we turn to next.

[17] Ibid., 44.

[18] "Carta de Payno a Ministro de Relaciones Interiores y Exteriores, 27 Diciembre 1850," AHSRE, 2–13–2974, "Nombramiento para comisionado en Matamoros, hecho en Don Rafael de la Garza, Tesorero General. Del Estado de Nuevo León, 1850." Don Gregorio de Mier y Terán is probably one of the few individuals who donated a substantial amount of his land for repatriate colonization.

[19] "Carta de Gobernador de Tamaulipas a Ministro de Relaciones Interiores y Exteriores, 15 Abril 1850," AHSRE, 2–13–2976, "El gobernador de Tamaulipas pide se nombre al comisionado que haya de entenderse con la traslación de familias que soliciten venir a México y que vivido en E.U. de A. De acuerdo con el Tratado de Guadalupe, 1850."

"Denied Equal Grace": Antonio Menchaca
and the Problematic Repatriation from
Nacogdoches, Texas to El Remolino, Coahuila

The 1850 repatriation of 618 individuals from Nacogdoches, Texas to El Remolino, Coahuila, approximately 150 kilometers away, presents an interesting test case for gauging the Mexican government's commitment to the cause of repatriation. Aside from being one of the best documented of the cases I located, it also has the distinction of having its correspondence overlap in three different archival depositories. In essence, the experience of this case, and a number of the examples that I pull from the material, are an illustration of the repatriate experience after the war. The repatriation from Nacogdoches was shaped largely from the problematic execution of appointing a repatriation commissioner for the eastern provinces. There was no government champion to spearhead the effort for the case of Texas as there was with Ortiz in New Mexico. In the end, the success of repatriation over this considerable distance relied much more on local intervention than the economic and political support of government authorities. Without being blind to a certain amount of self-interest in colonization, that success seems to have rested largely on the shoulders of a prominent local official, Antonio Menchaca.[20]

Menchaca composed a list that provides the bare facts of the Nacogdoches to El Remolino repatriation.[21] From it we learn that 200 families intended to settle in El Remolino. The total number of persons was 618, and 146 of these were under the age of fourteen, while the

[20] I have done some research on the life of Antonio Menchaca, but there appeared at least three possible candidates, two of which are father and son. The letters written by Menchaca never mention his background, his qualifications, or any titles bestowed upon him in the past. This is interesting to point out because all three Antonio Menchacas (sometimes written as José Antonio Menchaca) that I have researched have interesting, well-documented, and politically active lives. In the absence of more research on this individual, I am reluctant to speculate any further as to his extensive biography.

[21] *Nominal list of Mexican families from Nacogdoches who remained on territory transferred to the United States in the Treaty of Guadalupe Hidalgo, and due to said treaties and the Decree of August 19, 1848, are conceded the right to transport themselves in Mexican territory*, in "Carta de Menchaca al Presidente de México, 4 Diciembre 1850,"in AHSRE, 2–13–2975, "El Gobernador de Coahuila acompañando una solicitud de Don Antonio Menchaca vecino de Nacogdoches para trasladar a la República familias mexicanas. Se nombra comisionado al Gobernador de Nuevo León, 1850."

remaining 472 were over the age of fourteen. Only three female heads of household were listed by Menchaca in his correspondence with officials in Coahuila and Mexico City.

The appointment of a repatriation commission for the eastern provinces (as outlined in article 3 of the decree of August 19, 1848) ended in temporary disarray when the nominee, José Rafael De La Garza, rejected his appointment. Among the several candidates proposed initially was José María Carvajal, who years later would be accused of fraud and going beyond his jurisdiction by attempting to extend land grants to friends and cronies.[22] De La Garza was the ultimate choice for commissioner.[23] It was specified that "the quantity of ten thousand three hundred and seventy-nine pesos " should be allotted to him for the repatriation of individuals to Nuevo León if he were eventually named as repatriate commissioner for the region. Unfortunately for the officials in Mexico City, De La Garza declined his appointment that fall because of his current employment and other personal business matters. In his response to the officials, De La Garza stated: "I can barely and badly attend to [my own affairs] because of my public [obligations]."[24] Feeling overburdened, he resisted taking on any additional public duties and commented that "[M]y employment as Chief Treasurer of this State absorbs all of my attention, [and] my responsibility toward the same State and the circumstances of my private business would interfere with the work of the Repatriate Commission."[25]

Unaware as yet that De La Garza had turned down the position of commissioner, Menchaca went to the port of Matamoros in hopes of speaking with him in person. There he contacted the Mexican consulate in Brownsville about De La Garza, waiting three months for information. Menchaca was finally able to meet with De La Garza in late November, only to be shown a copy of the letter in which the appointee had formally (and respectfully) declined his appointment as repatriation commissioner for the region. Oddly, neither Menchaca nor the

---

[22] See case in *Ciudad Juarez Municipal Archives Microfilm Collection*, MF513, Pt. 2, Reel 38; quoted in Sisneros, "An Annotated List of Documents on the Towns of Guadalupe and San Ignacio in the Ciudad Juarez Municipal Archives, 1849–1859," located at the UTEP Special Collections.

[23] "Nombramiento para comisionado en Matamoros, hecho en Don Rafael de la Garza, Tesorero General. Del Estado de Nuevo León, 1850," AHSRE, 2–13–2974.

[24] Ibid.

[25] Ibid.

consulate in Brownsville was ever informed through official channels of De La Garza's rejection of the appointment. This lack of communication and other problems must surely have frustrated Menchaca and the hundreds of repatriates waiting to resettle across the border. The frustrations of Antonio Menchaca with respect to repatriation along the Texas border typified the kinds of relations that often developed between local officials and the central Mexican government in such efforts. At first it seemed as though government officials in Mexico City and the foreign ministry were warm to the mutual benefits of repatriating experienced frontiersmen as settlers of the northern frontiers. Only later when money became a factor did national interest waver, and patriotism as well. Menchaca invested a total of fourteen months traveling and petitioning the government for a repatriation commission to assist him in a serious case of postwar repatriation in the mid-nineteenth century.

On various occasions Menchaca attempted to use the power of the pen and a varied arsenal of arguments to solicit help from relevant authorities. In correspondence with the president of Mexico, Menchaca minced no words, describing the De La Garza appointment as "illusory" and insisting that Herrera's government comply with the laws already on the books. Presumably this was a reference to the decree of August 19, 1848, which "while being of use for the nation, also alleviates [the] misfortunate [emigrants]."[26] Menchaca also wrote to the governor of Coahuila, Rafael De La Fuente. From this correspondence we learn that Menchaca was aware of the Nuevo Laredo repatriation a few months earlier, and he could use the case to good advantage. He described it as an "identical case that presented itself this year, regarding the emigration and establishment of the colony of Mier y Terán by Mexican families from Laredo."[27] In addition to being fair, a repatriation colony was due in order to "fulfill the aims of unfortunate Mexicans [and] to ease their difficult situation" and to realize the "noble and patriotic objectives" of the repatriation commission. This feat would engender

[26] "Carta de Menchaca al Presidente de México, 4 Diciembre 1850,"in AHSRE, 2–13–2975, "El Gobernador de Coahuila acompañando una solicitud de Don Antonio Menchaca vecino de Nacogdoches para trasladar a la República familias mexicanas. Se nombra comisionado al Gobernador de Nuevo León, 1850." See also "Sobre el establecimiento de 200 familias emigradas de Bejar en el punto del Remolino en Coahuila (1850)," Expediente 1819, VOl. SLVI, pp. 93–127, in *Saltillo Archives, Center for American History, University of Texas at Austin* (hereafter cited as *SACAH*).

[27] Ibid.

"undying gratitude toward the sponsors," argued Menchaca, if only the Mexican government would respond in the positive.[28]

De La Fuente jointly took up the cause with Menchaca and relied similarly on notions of precedent, fairness, humanitarian concern, patriotism, and pragmatic grounds. On behalf of Menchaca, De La Fuente composed a pointed appeal to the minister of foreign relations in May of 1851 that included material culled from Menchaca's correspondence. Menchaca asked, "[I]f Nuevo León [Laredo] was granted ten thousand pesos to transfer the neighbors of Laredo to a new colony inside its jurisdiction, should Coahuila be denied equal grace?" Monies gained from the treaty, it was argued, should rightly be applied toward the welfare of patriotic individuals who only circumstantially found themselves across the border from their homeland. "This government," began De La Fuente, "did not doubt the patriotic sentiments of the national government in rescuing and assisting the return of Mexico's sons back to the homeland." Referring to the value of the lands lost after the Mexican American War, he continued:

> [T]hat this immense loss has not been reimbursed by the federation even though it be a considerable part of the land given to the neighboring Republic, and for which was reimbursed to the Nation the sum of fifteen million pesos; that for these circumstances the sons of Coahuila are entitled to be aided with preference in the necessary expenses for their adjournment to the territory of the Republic.[29]

As seen in much of the documentation of the period relating to repatriation and colonization, practical concerns are also glossed over with the moral patina of national belonging and postwar suffering. But such appeals were usually met with responses of scant treasuries and its accompanying discourse of "administrative disorder." Appealing to the nation's sense of suffering and oppression, Menchaca seemed to implore that Mexico should "transfer to her bosom the unfortunates that reside in Texas today reporting as Mexicans the injustices of the proud Americans that, with weapons in hand, required and obtained from Mexico those fertile lands."[30] At the very least, argued the governor

[28] Ibid.
[29] Ibid.
[30] "Carta de Gobernador de Coahuila a Ministro de Relaciones Exteriores, 19 Mayo 1851," in AHSRE, 2–13–2975, "El Gobernador de Coahuila acompañando una solicitud de Don Antonio Menchaca vecino de Nacogdoches para trasladar a la

of Coahuila, the government should do everything in its power "to rescue the unhappy Mexicans that by virtue of the treaty of Guadalupe remained foreigners in their own land, and of the misfortunes that afflict them."[31] In short order, the monies granted to the nation should be applied to the very victims who had suffered the loss of land, namely the now fractured state of Coahuila y Tejas.

The back and forth between the federal government and those on the ground dragged on for eight years and tested the patience of Menchaca and the governor of the state of Coahuila. For years to come the *Diario Oficial de Coahuila* and various newspapers would continue to publish advertisements promising government support for the repatriation of Mexicans to the state. But repatriates also grew tired of waiting, and many decided to deal with administrative matters at a later date. Some matters were in fact never resolved. In other cases, as with the repatriation of La Ascensión, Chihuahua, land titles were issued more than a decade later, though this did not end controversy over land matters.

Although little government aid came forward to contribute to the formation of this settlement, the repatriate colony of El Remolino, Coahuila would return to Mexico under difficult conditions and circumstances. Part of these conditions were motivated by the government's desire to populate the northern regions with loyal citizens to fight off Indios Bárbaros and to serve as a buffer zone against its northern neighbor, not to mention other entrepreneurial filibusters from both the United States and Mexico. The colony would subsequently be renamed Resurrección and then settled in a location that had earlier been called La Colonia Militar de San Vicente, attesting to the military concerns of postwar colonization policy. Repatriation throughout the nineteenth century was therefore not a policy based on nationalist sentiment or impulse, but one more interested in maintaining territorial hegemony and a military presence along the frontier.[32]

The case of El Remolino illustrates several important issues. First, arguments in favor of supporting repatriation in the eastern provinces could be made based on A) legal/treaty obligations, B) precedent in comparison with other repatriations, and/or C) on humanitarian

República familias mexicanas. Se nombra comisionado al Gobernador de Nuevo León, 1850."

[31] Ibid.

[32] See "Sobre el establecimiento de 200 familias emigradas de Bejar en el punto del Remolino en Coahuila (1850)," Expediente 1819, VOl. SLVI, pp. 93–127 in *SACAH*.

grounds. Second, the inadequate response of the Mexican government in this case supported widespread claims of "administrative disorder" of the Herrera government as well as the divide between regional and federal authorities in mid-nineteenth-century Mexican politics. At the national level, the Menchaca case shows us that state governments had little power or influence in postwar Mexico. If states had difficulty in their appeals for federal aid or assistance, then surely repatriates would suffer a similar fate. Finally, and perhaps most important, a persuasive argument could be made that there was an unresolved contradiction in repatriation policy in the years after the Mexican American War, namely, that the very monies intended for supporting those within the ceded territories were never appropriately distributed to the direct victims of the war. Of the $15 million paid by the United States as recompense for the ceded territories, less than one percent made its way into the hands of the victims. Guillermo Prieto, former finance minister, perhaps said it best: "If you ask what use Mexico made of all the money it got from the United States as a result of its national tragedy, you should answer, without hesitation, that it wasn't in material improvements, defending the borders, or for public safety. It went, almost entirely, to our creditors, foreigners mostly."[33]

Some thirty-eight months after Menchaca composed his nominal list, the number of repatriates and their families was unchanged when Menchaca billed the federal government for 20,632 pesos. He broke down his expenditures in the following manner: 1,752 for the 146 persons under the age of fourteen (allotted twelve pesos each) and 11,800 for the 472 persons over the age of fourteen (allotted twenty-five pesos each). To this Menchaca added 7,080 pesos in unforeseen expenses as he financed and led this particular repatriation project. The Ministry of Foreign Relations responded to Menchaca's request by saying that due to the "scantiness of the treasury" the government was currently not in a position to "make the proposed expenditure."[34] This kind of exchange typified relations between repatriates and advocates following the Mexican American War. Menchaca's case is one of the best

33 Guillermo Prieto, *Informes leídos en la Cámara de Diputados por el Secretario de Hacienda*... (México, 1852), p. 40. Quoted in Richard J. Salvucci, *Politics, Markets, and Mexico's 'London Debt,' 1823–1887*, (Cambridge: Cambridge University Press, 2009), 200–201.

34 See "Sobre el establecimiento de 200 familias emigradas de Bejar en el punto del Remolino en Coahuila (1850)," Expediente 1819, VOl. SLVI, pp. 93–127 in SACAH.

documented and archived that I have found, and illustrative of at least a dozen other cases that concluded with explanations of a depleted treasury. The government response in this and many other cases was near universal: There is no money.

ORGANIZED REPATRIATION FROM BELOW IN CALIFORNIA

In contrast to the cases of Texas and New Mexico, California support for repatriation seemed to sprout from the ground amidst government inaction, or if you prefer, "administrative disorder." In this case repatriation would be buttressed by the institutional interests of a secularized Catholic Church, by the accessible and mobile wealth of California gold, and by an accompanying redistribution of labor involving significant ethnic-based expulsions from California. As in other regions, the indigenous population fighting for survival formed a common enemy for U.S. and Mexican national boundaries that continued to be contested. In California, the prime movers of repatriation were not prominent individuals like Menchaca, but a variety of religious and secular societies that formed during the period to fulfill the aforementioned interests of returning to Mexico during times of economic and social stress.

The central government in Mexico City appears to have administered the repatriation of Alta California as it did in Coahuila and Chihuahua – that is to say not very efficiently or effectively. With respect to repatriation, Griswold del Castillo has noted that Californios in particular "had little financial help from the Mexican government in these ventures."[35] Yet repatriation was successfully conducted to Sonora and to various locales along the northern Mexican frontiers mostly because of the repatriates themselves. So who or what lay behind these resettlements? Part of the answer lies with the way repatriation mediated the interests of the Catholic Church, the depopulation of northern Mexican states, and the violence and opportunity of the Gold Rush in California.

REPATRIATION SOCIETIES AND LOCAL PROTECTION

Mexicans in search of work and riches in gold country entered a frenzied field composed not only of Euro American and Chinese miners, but also Peruvian, Chilean, Spanish, and other "Latins" who drew successfully

[35] Griswold del Castillo, *The Los Angeles Barrio*, 119.

from the mining expertise they had acquired in their home countries. On the ground, reaction to "foreign" competition in the mines took the form of an escalated level of violence in various locales in Gold Rush era California. The courts reacted by passing the Foreigner Miner's Tax of 1851, which levied a $20 per capita fee on all "foreigners" wanting to stake claims in the gold placers of Upper California. This racially targeted legislation applied to non-Euro Americans, that is, those not of the white race, thus fueling the number of potential repatriates for the states of Baja California, Sonora, and Sinaloa.

The Mexican government recognized that such legislation and perhaps border violence as well could serve its interests by curtailing emigration and forcing its citizens to remain in those lands "infested by Indios Bárbaros." With this background in mind, the governor of Sonora, Ignacio Pesquiera, initiated some of the first colonization policies for Mexican Americans in that state. "Incensed by outrages committed [in the goldmines] by the Anglo Americans against...Mexican Americans," Pesquiera "offered lands to the victims, aiding them and at the same time colonizing the lands." In the process, according to historian Enrique Cortés, the governor "set the stage for a pattern that was repeated throughout the rest of the century."[36]

Pesquiera was not alone in his condemnation of Euro American ill treatment of the working classes and the migrant populace. Several other politicians and government officials put forth proposals to hasten the repatriation of Mexican Americans while others supported the establishment of military colonies on the northern frontiers of the decapitated country. But very little assistance was forthcoming from the central government. As in Texas, the most vocal and articulate advocates for repatriation were governors and politicians from the border region itself. But their outrage did not translate into material assistance or an organized repatriation process. The answers were always the same: The treasury is depleted.

In the face of government neglect, Californios and Mexican residents in California responded to the violence and land displacement in a highly organized fashion by forming repatriation societies. Independent and self-funded repatriation societies such as Jesús Islas's La Junta para Promover la Emigración de Todos los Hispanos-Americanos Residentes en California (The Steering Committee to Promote Immigration of All Hispanic-Americans Living in California) and Andrés Pico's La Sociedad

---

[36] Cortés, "Mexican Colonies during the Porfiriato," 1–14.

de Colonización de Nativos de California para el Estado de Sonora (The Colonization Society of Native Californians for the State of Sonora), founded in 1855 and 1858 respectively, sprang up and established a trend in California that we will not see for the other regions: the patriotic naming of colonization and repatriation societies. By the time of the Porfiriato several more organizations of this kind had come into being, such as Compañía de Colonos para la Republica Mexicana (1875), Compañía de Colonos "La Esperanza" (1878), and Sociedad de Colonización Benito Juárez (1880). Many of the colonization schemes, like Pico's La Sociedad de Colonización (1855) were advanced "during the height of racial conflict and violence." Neither Mexico nor the United States could respond, it was articulated at the time, so locals out of necessity took matters into their own hands and moved south to Mexico in what can only be termed a "back to Mexico" movement of sorts.

In 1855 Jesús Islas founded a colonization society in San José that managed to recruit hundreds of people throughout California "by running advertisements in the newspapers." According to Griswold Del Castillo, Islas's success "spurred others to imitation." La Junta para Promover la Emigración de Todos los Hispanos-Americanos Residentes en California offered a similar rationale for returning to Mexico in an 1855 announcement. "Their major purpose," accordingly, "was to escape the inhospitable social and economic climate of Anglo-American dominated California."[37]

To promote repatriation, Islas published an extensive broadside titled *Situacion de los Habitantes Ispano-Americanos en el Estado de la Alta California*, printed in Mazatlan on June 26, 1855, which was carried by at least one newspaper in California, *El Clamor Público*. Written as a kind of manifesto, this document detailed how Mexican American repatriation would benefit potential colonists and the Mexican government. A close reading reveals not only references to humanitarian concern for the mistreatment of patriotic Mexican Americans, but also the contradictory nature of that discourse when gauged against state concerns for its failing economy and threatened northern perimeters.

Islas begins his appeal for repatriation, not by mentioning the violence visited upon the Mexican population, but by sketching the larger structural forces that compelled him and other Californios to seek better economic opportunities elsewhere. In effect, Islas was patently aware of a global economic crisis that had subsequently impacted the lives of a

---

[37] Griswold del Castillo, *Los Angeles Barrio*, 119–24.

population which now sought repatriation in Mexico. As his opening salvo states, "[T]he epoch has arrived in which the extravagance of the [gold] speculations, and the great importance of foreign products, has brought a great monetary crisis, that has caused the ruin of most of the bankers and innumerable mercantile stores, as well as the complete annihilation of agriculture in general."[38] The collapse of the agricultural sector to which he refers had hit the "Ispano-Americanos," made up of "*Californios*, Mexicanos, Chilenos, and Peruanos," particularly hard.

Perhaps it is no coincidence that in this document "Ispano-Americanos" are framed as only suited to performing agricultural labor, thereby ignoring the legislation and racist climate that excluded even the highly skilled from work in the mining sector: He states:

> It should be observed that most of the Hispanic-American population, which includes *Californios*, Mexicans, Chileans, Peruvians, etc. etc. had been dedicated to the work of agriculture, that, due to the complete paralysis of and lack of appreciation for the productivity of the country, they have all been obliged to abandon their fields and labors and they are today found ruined and unable to secure a destiny; and being the only work that the Spanish class can dedicate itself to, given that in no other industry would they be able to compete with the Saxon race, because they lack the necessary know-how, they are seen today therefore in the saddest situation and without hope for the future. Besides it should be added that one of the causes of the discontent and general displeasure is the mistreatment that the Hispanic-American population has received from certain classes of the American populace.[39]

[38] Jesús Islas, *Situación de los habitantes Ispano-Americanos en el Estado de Alta California*, 26 Junio 1855 (Puerto de Mazatlán: Imprenta de Rafael Carreon, 1855).

[39] Jesús Islas, *Situación de los habitantes Ispano-Americanos en el Estado de Alta California*, 26 Junio 1855 (Puerto de Mazatlán: Imprenta de Rafael Carreon, 1855); Original: "Debe observarse que la mayor parte de la población Ispano-Americana, que comprende *Californios*, mexicanos, chilenos, peruanos, etc. etc. Se habían dedicado al giro de agricultura, las que por causa de la completa paralización y ningún aprecio de las producciones del país, se han visto todos obligados a abandonar sus labores y trabajos y se encuentran hoy arruinados y sin poder obtener destino; y siendo el único giro al que la clase española puede dedicarse, pues en ninguna otra industria podrían competir con la raza sajona, por carecer de los conocimientos necesarios, se ven hoy pues en la más triste situación y sin esperanzas en lo futuro. Además debe agregarse que una de las

Reminders of the injustices this population had suffered could play well on the patriotic sentiments of border officials and private land-owners across the border. Yet this bad treatment by the Americans could also align with an ongoing military strategy. Islas states that these potential colonists alone are "able to contain the advances of the barbarous apache." Officials who hoped to contain the "Barbarous Indians" simultaneously sought to make use of Mexicans residing in the United States for this purpose, and would offer them lands, tax concessions, and free passage to government-sponsored colonies as enticements.

The designs harbored by Mexican officials can be discerned by the manner in which Mexican American labor is framed in contra-dictory ways. The "energy" and "strength" of new migrants and their families is always noted in the archival record, but the unique position of Californios as potential repatriates was presented with a particular regional twist. Islas advanced the idea that, among the different candidate populations available to occupy the northern territories, only Mexican American repatriates would thrive given their existing "compatibilities" with Mexico:

> And what better time for Sonora to take advantage of the circum-stances, which under its liberal and protective laws, is the only emigration that is acceptable because of its language, religion and customs? Right now is the time to populate its frontiers with a population that is useful, energetic, and trained by contact with the Saxon race, the only one that is able to contain the advances of the barbarous apache.[40]

Thus, even after decrying the mistreatment of Mexican Americans and framing them suitable only for agriculture, he also posits that it is precisely "contact with the Saxon race" that makes his potential repatriates so desirable for Mexico in general, and Sonora in particu-lar. Notably, the discourse that paints Mexican migrants in the United States as somehow better that those who never left continues to this very day, and here we have a future leader of the repatriate commission articulating this folk belief in the mid-nineteenth century.

causas del descontento y disgusto general, es el mal tratamiento que la población Hispano-Americana ha recibido de ciertas clases del pueblo americano."
[40] Ibid. Reprinted in "Situación de los Hispano-Americanos en California," *El Clamor Público*, 23 Octubre 1855, no. 19.

This double discourse of lauding the United States while at the same time demonizing the "Saxon race" for its negative treatment of Mexicans runs through much of the correspondence that appeals for repatriation in the case of California. The aforementioned case is one example of this particular narrative trope, but it is also an example of how a private initiative was later co-opted by government officials in Mexico City when they appointed this individual to lead the repatriate commission for the western region in the late 1850s.

ISLAS'S COLONY AND THE MIXED MESSAGES OF REPATRIATION

In October 1855, Francisco P. Ramírez, editorial writer for *El Clamor Público*, criticized the Mexican government and wrote an extensive editorial that "encouraged [California] Mexicans and Chileans to join Isla's *Junta Colonizadora de Sonora* and return to Mexico." Disillusioned by the U.S. government's lack of concern about Euro American racism, Ramírez continued to promote "the emigration society even when it was evident that it was not getting the proper support from Mexico."[41] The commotion and enthusiasm for the project attracted the attention of local and federal officials who noted the benefits of this migration to the frontiers of the Mexican republic. According to Islas's report published in the local paper, the project was received with "great enthusiasm by all of the populations of the state," including the governor and the large landowners, "to protect the emigrants that settle along the frontiers of the state." For instance, locals came to the aid of Islas's project in Sonora. The village of Ures donated 200 fanegas of wheat, 100 head of cattle, and land for those cattle as well as for the production of cotton, sugar, and indigo.[42]

Recognizing the enthusiasm for Islas's project earlier that year, the federal government encouraged the state of Sonora to cooperate with this "patriot" and appointed him as the colonization agent for the same state. Always mindful of useful anti-American sentiment, Minister of Fomento Manuel Siliceo maintained that there were "great advantages" to welcoming these Gold Rush repatriates: "they do not mix with the

---

[41] Acuña, *Occupied America: A History of Chicanos*, 4th ed. (New York: Longman, 2000), 148.

[42] "Emigración a Sonora: A los Mexicanos, Hispano Americanos y *Californios*; Manifiesto," *El Clamor Publico*, 16 Febrero 1856.

Anglo-Saxon race," with whom they lacked a common culture, and would fare much better as colonists in Sonora.[43] Thus, unlike the relatively organized repatriate commission of New Mexico or the botched appointment of the eastern provinces, the case of the repatriate commission for the western states was a case where government officials in Mexico City co-opted the most visible leader of a repatriation society and appointed him as repatriate commissioner for the region.

In early 1856 Islas recruited 300 people for his colonization project and headed out for Sonora. News of the Islas colony reached the Californio audience via El Clamor Público. By June 1856, El Clamor Público noted that "more persons than could conveniently be taken" continued to arrive and were awaiting financial support for the journey. For the time being, Los Angeles would serve as their base of operations.[44] As success of the colony became widely known, more and more repatriates set out for the colony, now known as Saric, Sonora. At this time, according to Griswold del Castillo, "it appeared that this colonization venture was succeeding" and Islas reported the following: "We are living peacefully and breathing the pure and agreeable air of this beautiful climate."[45]

But negative reports also surfaced, including one that alleged that the Islas colony had joined in a rebellion against the central government.[46] The prosperity of the Islas colony in Sonora opened a space among the Mexican community in California to debate the merits of this process, and it appears that not all were in favor of resettling in a country that had already abandoned them once. Making a case that had been raised in New Mexico (and later in San Antonio, Texas) locals questioned the logic of returning to a government so fraught with "administrative disorder" and a history of abandoning the frontier regions to "barbarous Indians" and then North Americans. In an extensive and critical letter signed by "California," the author noted the past history of the Mexican state left much to be desired. Colonists returning to Sonora would be subjected to "undisciplined military officials and mercenaries"

[43] "Disposición de 13 de Febrero de 1856: Promoviendo la emigración de la raza hispano-americana existente en la Alta California, para aprovecharla en la colonización del Estado de Sonora," en Código de Colonización, 607–12. This letter and four-point suggestion was also published in the 1856 publication of "Ministerio de Fomento," 10 Mayo 1856.

[44] "La Colonia," El Clamor Publico, 7 Junio 1856.

[45] Griswold del Castillo, Los Angeles Barrio, 121.

[46] "Sonora," El Clamor Publico, 13 Diciembre 1856.

that ruined the local population with levies and forced contributions, according to his view.

The "failed colonizations" of Texas and Coatzacoalcos in the 1820s, the author reminded the readers of *El Clamor Público*, were proof enough of the government's incompetence. These past failures occurred "for the very simple reason that although the government of Mexico has judgment and discernment, the Mexicans do not have it and with their anarchic craziness do not allow the realization of useful business," as the example of past colonization projects had effectively proven.[47] Living under U.S. rule was much better than living under a Mexican regime that only a few years earlier had passed their fate into the "hands of strangers." "When were we the most happy, when we pertained to the Mexican Republic or now?" asked the author. And although wishing the colonists and the enterprise well, the letter writer echoed the sentiment expressed by previous critics who argued that Los Angeles was historically the refuge of Sonorans. The government of Mexico, always in constant revolt and in "administrative disorder," made promises that it could not keep, and any repatriate would probably be swept up in one of the many uprisings.[48] Several exchanges for and against return migration were recorded in *El Clamor Público* between a number of authors, but in the end, the Islas colonization project proceeded and settled repatriates.

Little is known about the details of the Islas colony, and a more thorough regional study is necessary to deepen our understanding of this important case. For instance, the municipal archives of Guaymas, or the state archives in Hermosillo, might reveal a difference in living standards when compared to the Californios who opted to remain in Alta California. For now, I think it is fair to suggest that repatriation societies like the kind organized by Islas were a direct response to government inaction in both the United States and Mexico. The United States could not protect Californios against various abuses related to labor competition, xenophobia, economics, and bigotry, while Mexico could not protect Californios because of empty coffers, "administrative disorder," and continued war against the Indios Bárbaros. Local organized "back to Mexico" movements like Islas's project, therefore, became the proverbial "third way" out of this particular condition in postwar California.

[47] "Comunicado," *El Clamor Publico*, 24 Mayo 1856.
[48] "Mas Sobre la Emigración a Sonora," *El Clamor Publico*, 17 Mayo 1856.

The Catholic Church and Repatriation Problems

Written at the height of the California Gold Rush in the spring of 1849, a letter from the finance minister to the Ministry of Foreign Relations highlights church secularization efforts and repatriation as a new sort of church mission. Fray Miguel Molina y Pacheco of Mexico City's Colegio Apostolico de San Fernando presented a bill from the California missions on behalf of Don Ignacio Cortina Chávez for 601,576 pesos in back pay. He also made an additional request for one hundred thousand pesos for repatriation costs. According to the request:

> 601,576 pesos are owed…to the cited school for the stipends of the Missions of California, conquered since the year of 1811 to the present, as well as for the supplies that the same missions have provided, before and after Independence, for the troops that guarded the borders and prisons of those territories, and ultimately, by the capitals and credits of the diverse impositions that the government recognizes in favor of the aforesaid convent of San Fernando.[49]

According to church authorities in Alta California, the secularization of the missions in 1811 meant the end of governmental support of the church. As the charges to the state are outlined, it is clear that the church in Alta California performed the functions of a state institution and possessed the power to impose order and secure the frontiers; however, the thinking went, now that the war was over and the church was being forced to relocate, it was time to parcel the $15 million given for the Mexican cession.

The cost of repatriating Mexican families and the religious orders was calculated to be much higher than the 25,000 pesos earmarked for Ortiz in New Mexico, which had the largest Mexican population of the regions along the border. The initial request by these officials was roughly one hundred thousand pesos: twenty-five thousand pesos for the repatriation of Mexican families and "religious missionaries that were left in Alta California," and seventy-five thousand pesos

[49] "Carta de Ministro de Hacienda a Ministro de Relaciones Exteriores y Interiores, 28 Marzo 1849, AHSRE, 2–13–2967, "El Ministro de Hacienda comunica el convenio celebrado con el Sindico y guardián del Convento de San Fernando, sobre traslación de familias Mexicanas de la Alta California, de acuerdo con el Tratado de Guadalupe, 1849."

worth of unoccupied lands with "healthy climates," along the coasts of Sinaloa or Jalisco if possible. A repatriation commission appears to have approved the initial twenty-five thousand pesos, yet nothing more exists in the archival record. What follows instead is a constant stream of letters from the consulates and Norteño government officials recommending repatriation and offering suggestions about how to stem the tide of Mexican miners northward into the United States in search of gold. Hence, although we have evidence of postwar migrations to the state of Sonora, the rush for gold simultaneously and disproportionately pulled migrants from the northern border states and toward California.

The finance minister prophetically cited the potential future role of the church in repatriation. He argued that no other method could be "more proper and efficient to achieve the means of transferring to the Republic the Mexican families that are found in those remote and already foreign lands."[50] The wholesale repatriation of these missions, it was suggested in the correspondence, was likely to serve the republic's repatriation goals effectively since the missions were already organized into settlements and had common cultural attributes. To repatriate whole missions, the idea went, translated into resettling fully formed colonies in Mexico proper.

Future research in ecclesiastical archives would be necessary to reveal a more concrete picture of exactly what took place with the repatriation of these particular communities from Alta California following the war. Clearly the church took a different approach in California than in New Mexico or in Texas.

GOLD AND DISTRIBUTED WEALTH IN EL NORTE

After gold was discovered in newly lost California in 1849, a number of government officials pondered how Mexico could benefit from some of the riches being extracted. The damage in the aftermath of war was not only measured in lost potential, but in material terms. Gold, in this context, functioned like a magnet that attracted groups of Mexican miners from their posts occupying the northern frontier. Already burdened by the need to populate the deserts of Sonora, Mexico now saw the Gold Rush pull these very settlers away from the sparsely populated frontiers that cleared the way for easier raiding by independent Indians.

[50] Ibid.

Alluding to the silver lining in the cloud of the depopulation of the frontiers, General Ignacio Pesquiera, the governor of Sonora, noted that, although return migration was evident, the "returning citizens appear to be motivated to return to the next station of the works," and many of them returned with vast amounts of wealth. They in turn "excited many others" to make the trip northward. If this work was not "absolutely impeded" by local authorities, the governor estimated that "next year's emigration from this state will be surpassed in a somewhat greater number by this year's emigrants."[51] Unless they were prevented from working in the mines, this northern migration could spiral out of control and bring dire consequences.

Still, a northern circuit with a lid on it presented a significant potential benefit to the Mexican state. The unusual wealth available to prospecting potential repatriates was well recognized by those of the frontiers and those far removed from the border. Pesquiera observed, "It can be calculated that more than 300 [migrants] have returned and others are arriving daily, to such a manner that it can be expected that that we will not lose all of this part of the emigrated population."[52] And, even in the face of long and dangerous journeys, returning Sonorans "come very satisfied with the wealth of those bonanzas and they report that except for the crime of robbery, all the others enjoy immunity." Many documents relating to Sonoran history point out that Sonorans returned from the gold placers of California with millions of pesos worth of gold.[53]

However, the borders drawn between the United States and Mexico were also superimposed on land still claimed by many indigenous groups willing to die and raid in its defense. This presented a dilemma for any who had designs on the wealth in the region's natural resources. Pesquiera correctly pointed out the three factors that hindered the successful colonization of the frontier – Indian raiding, depopulation caused by emigration, and insecurity. These issues were intertwined and not easily resolved. Unless the government solved the question of

---

[51] "Carta de Gobernador de Sonora a Ministerio de Relaciones Exteriores, 3 Octubre 1849," AHSRE, 6–17–41; in *Protección Consular a Mexicanos en los Estados Unidos*, 29.

[52] Ibid., 28.

[53] Ibid., 29; Original: "Los ciudadanos regresados aparecen estar animados para volverse en la próxima estación de los trabajos, esta animación ha alborotado a otros muchos, de manera que si en California no se les embarga absolutamente el trabajo en otros placeres de oro, para el próximo año se superara una emigración de este estado en un numero algo mayor del emigrado este año."

Indian raiding first, neither repatriation nor long-term stability would have much of a chance along the northern frontier. For the governor, it was clear that "the day that those incursions of the barbarians are finished, at that same moment the state will remain populated." While the Indios Bárbaros were still not under the control of the state and "the border is found in the abandonment that it is currently found, it is impossible to be able to stimulate the population with any kind of offers."[54] And so the process appeared to be a self-perpetuating mechanism which only an end to raiding and attacks could interrupt.

Though framed from the perspective of government interest, the governor provided a remarkable early recognition of the ironic predicament of having to leave Mexican roots in the hope of one day returning better able to sustain them. He noted that those with property "abandon it" and then migrate to the United States, while "the ones that do not have it, seek it to leave it... in the hopes that at some time they will have it."[55]

CONCLUSION

In this chapter we have examined a number of regional cases of repatriation beyond those from New Mexico, specifically a series of repatriations from the territories of Texas and California. They illustrate how, in the absence of genuine central government support, grassroots efforts were left to contend with the influence of forces such as geography, the institutional interests of the Catholic Church, an economic boom due to gold mining in the north, legislation enacting a racialized division of labor, and continued Indian raiding along the frontiers. Nestled in government duplicity and contradiction, repatriate towns in these areas managed to form and fend for themselves.

While proximity made patriotic settlement in Nuevo Laredo relatively straightforward, the Antonio Menchaca case of the 1850s, in which approximately 200 Mexican families (618 persons) from Nacogdoches, Texas repatriated to Coahuila in 1853, testifies to the internal problems of the repatriation commissions. Menchaca by default took the initiative and called for the naming of a repatriation commissioner, basing his appeal on the law passed to protect and resettle Mexicans who

---

54 Ibid., AHSRE, 6–17–41; in *Protección Consular a Mexicanos en los Estados Unidos*, 28.
55 Ibid.

wished to retain their Mexican citizenship after the war.[56] But given the "administrative disorder" of the period, funds would not be forthcoming for years after the repatriates settled on Mexican soil.

The governor of Coahuila noted the ironic aspect of the situation when he pointed out that the "immense loss has not been reimbursed by the federation even though it is a considerable part of the land given to the neighboring Republic." The compensation for this loss was fifteen million pesos, causing the governor to ask the president of the republic, "[Were not] the children of Coahuila...entitled to be aided with preference in the necessary expenses for their adjournment to the territory of the Republic?"[57] This brief question encapsulates the very paradoxical nature of repatriation policy and the concern that the state supposedly felt for this now "lost population." Are the children of that "lost Mexico" not entitled to the protection and organized repatriation from the territories lost in the war? Did not the state of Coahuila y Tejas become the first state to lose Tejas to its northern neighbors, thus warranting a direct legal claim to the monies in question?

In California, by the mid-1850s, the continued lack of government-sponsored repatriation commissions resulted in the integration of the Catholic Church and the founding of independently funded repatriation societies. The emergence of repatriate societies in California illustrates that, in the absence of state-sponsored repatriation programs, local initiatives were organized and in some cases ultimately forced the Mexican government to implement repatriation policies. Still, the government did not follow through on a number of proposals, and many of the efforts and resources expended by later repatriation societies would be for naught.

It is well worth noting that in California, despite the well-documented violence against Californios, migration continued northward toward the gold placers, and a long historical pattern had been established consisting of migratory circuits between Mexico and those areas in the United States that were undergoing rapid economic development involving railroads, agriculture, and mining. This occurred within a hostile climate of expulsion. The expulsion of workers, miners, and

[56] "El Gobernador de Coahuila acompañando una solicitud de Don Antonio Menchaca vecino de Nacogdoches para trasladar a la República familias mexicanas. Se nombra comisionado al Gobernador de Nuevo León, 1850," AHSRE, 2–13–2975.

[57] Ibid.

nonwhites was directly related to the demographic changes taking place at the time, labor competition, and the Gold Rush. New Mexico did not see a significant wave of Euro American migration until the middle of the 1890s; moreover, people of Mexican origin would remain the majority there until the 1930s.[58] This latter aspect partly explains why major expulsions like those in California or Texas did not occur in New Mexico in the postwar period.

What has not been discussed thus far were how these repatriate colonies, affected by the postwar environment, fared under a Mexican system of governance. In order to outline that particular history, we turn now to an in-depth study of repatriates in La Mesilla, New Mexico as they were resettled three times within a generation. Their experience, first under U.S. and then Mexican rule, will provide us with a window into the experience of one repatriate colony after the end of the Mexican American War. Where our approach commenced at the level of global migrations, and where these previous chapters have focused on the national level, the final chapters will be dedicated to a local analysis.

---

[58] John M. Nieto-Phillips, *The Language of Blood: The Making of Spanish-American Identity in New Mexico, 1880s-1930s* (Albuquerque: University of New Mexico Press, 2004), 111–13.

PART III

THE LOCAL MIXING, UNMIXING, AND REMIXING OF A REPATRIATE COLONY IN CHIHUAHUA

Se van...
Se van...
Los Republicanos...
Se van para La Ascensión...
Porque los Demócratas...
Ganaron la elección...
They leave...
They leave...
The Republicans...
They leave to La Ascensión...
Because the Democrats...
Won the election...

Gamboa Band
(Democratic Party)
to the Bull Band
(Republican Party),
ca. 1871

CHAPTER FIVE

THE 1871 RIOT OF LA MESILLA,
NEW MEXICO

INTRODUCTION

This chapter constitutes the first of three final chapters that will narrate the local history of one repatriate colony that made its way back to Chihuahua, Mexico on three separate occasions. I focus on Chihuahua for the following reasons. First and foremost, of all the repatriate colonies founded throughout the nineteenth century, the case of La Mesilla, New Mexico (later to become La Ascensión, Chihuahua in 1872) is the best documented and has provided the most data to date. Second, because of this key consideration, this local, more nuanced perspective allows me to begin completing my threefold approach from the global, to the national, and ending with the local. Finally, this thick description provides us with a series of opportunities to examine and analyze the early process of return migration after the war, particularly how one specific colony fared under a Mexican system of governance.

The town of La Mesilla was founded in Mexican territory in 1850, resettled in the United States as part of the Gadsden Purchase in 1853, and reconfigured in 1871 when part of its population migrated back to Mexican territory. These resettlements have been the subject of several historiographical interrogations by students of nineteenth-century New Mexican history, specifically as this history relates to the electoral violence that engulfed the town in 1871.[1] The narrative in each of these interpretations usually ends in 1872, and they do not follow the

---

[1] George Griggs, *History of Mesilla Valley or the Gadsden Purchase, Known in Mexico as the Treaty of Mesilla* (Mesilla, NM: Bronson Print Company, 1930); Joe Frietze, *A History of La Mesilla and Her Mesilleros, Written and Compiled by a Native Mesillero* (La Mesilla, NM: privately printed, 1995); Anthony Mora,

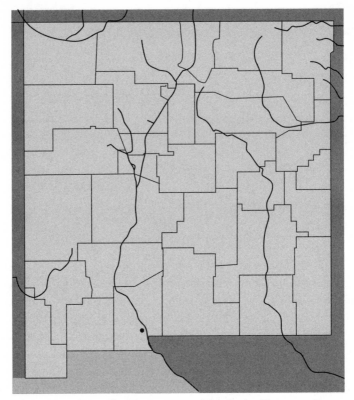

Figure 5.1. La Mesilla. Map courtesy of Cambridge University Press.

contingent of Nuevo Mexicanos that left for Mexico after the election. In short, their narrative ends where the border begins, and hence misses an opportunity to apply a truly transnational approach to this growing body of research. In this chapter I will broach this historiographical gap and discuss how the colony of La Mesilla was founded, including its early history in the postwar period. I dedicate the latter half of the chapter to elaborating on the events that led to this particular episode of political violence only twenty years after the end of the war.[2] But

"Resistance and Accommodation in a Border Parish," *The Western Historical Quarterly* 36 (3); Taylor, *Mesilla, New Mexico*, passim.

[2] For instance, one of the main participants in the electoral violence was Atilano Baca, who would later be indicted as one of the main conspirators of the 1892 Revolt in La Ascensión only two decades later. Baca was the nephew of Padre José Jesús Baca, another one of the main protagonists of the Riot of La Mesilla in 1871.

first, let us turn to the founding of La Mesilla and the violent event that would split the loyalties and fates of residents thereafter.

THE FOUNDING OF LA MESILLA, CHIHUAHUA IN 1850

About forty miles northwest of the El Paso/Ciudad Juarez border area sits the valley of La Mesilla, New Mexico – a crossroads of sorts where the Chihuahuan desert and the Organ Mountains meet. The valley sits in the floodplain of the Rio Grande, which slices its way through the region north to south. On the eastern side of the river lies modern day Las Cruces, New Mexico with a current population of seventy-five thousand. Across the river, on the western side, La Mesilla was founded in the mid-nineteenth century, after the war between the United States and Mexico. A contemporary eyewitness described the founding as follows: "[S]ix or eight miles below Doña Ana, on the opposite side of the river, is the town of Mesilla, containing between six to eight hundred inhabitants, a place which owes its origin to circumstances growing out of the late war with Mexico."[3] The colony was located at the southernmost region of the New Mexico Territory and tenuously clung to by Mexico in the face of postwar encroachment and resistance from Euro American and indigenous groups who also claimed the area as their own. Following the usual nationalist trope, most historians have argued that the founding of La Mesilla after the war was one of several attempts to counter subjection to U.S. rule in this area. According to New Mexico historian Carlos R. Herrera, whose work best epitomizes this particular approach, the colony sprang largely from nationalist loyalty: "citizens from San Elizario, Isleta, Doña Ana, and Socorro, communities that had found themselves on the U.S. side of the border after the war established this colony as an expression of their allegiance to Mexico."[4] Yet, as I will

---

3   John Russell Bartlett, *Personal Narrative of Explorations and Incidents in Texas, New Mexico, California, Sonora, and Chihuahua, Connected with the United States and Mexican Boundary Commission, During the Years 1850, 1851,1852, and 1853*, 2 vols. (New York: D. Appleton & Company, 1854; republished in facsimile by Rio Grande Press: Chicago, 1965), I: 212–14.

4   Moreover, both Mexico and the United States made fantastic offers to lure people to one side of the border or the other. See Carlos R. Herrera, "New Mexico Resistance to U.S. Occupation during the Mexican American War of 1846–1848," chapter one in *The Contested Homeland: A Chicano History of New*

discuss later in this chapter, competing familial relations and a desire to improve material conditions complicate such claims considerably. The case of La Mesilla, and the experiences of those who actually left to colonize Mexican lands, mirror the experience of other cases we've covered thus far.

ACCOUNTING FOR THE GROWTH OF LA MESILLA

At its founding La Mesilla was part of concerted competing efforts to populate, and thereby possess, the area. The changing demographics in Doña Ana County, fairly typical of the New Mexico Territory as a whole, played an important role in shaping the course of repatriation. Before the arrival of immigrants and settlers from the United States, the population of New Mexico hovered at a little over sixty thousand. Of these 90.9 percent were longtime resident Nuevo Mexicanos, five percent were Native Americans, 0.6 percent were Mexicans from Mexico, and 2.6 percent of the population was composed of American and European immigrants concentrated in Santa Fe and Las Vegas.[5] The strategically located area grew quickly after it was founded; it drew immigrants from Europe and Euro Americans from New York, Texas, Missouri, and Pennsylvania, especially after the railroad arrived. At mid-century La Mesilla was a composite of immigrants, servants, army deserters, debtors, *peónes*, repatriates, and emigrants – a demographic mosaic with competing loyalties and interests. They gathered on this relatively fertile tangential strip for various reasons, but together they comprised a fast growing and thriving community. By 1851 La Mesilla had become "the most important immigration zone in Northern Chihuahua."[6] The migration was mostly internal for the next half century given that "foreigners composed a rather small share of New Mexico's population, and never exceeded 7.3% between 1860 and 1910."[7]

Mexican repatriation efforts would contribute during these years to both populating and depopulating the area as political, economic, and

---

Mexico, edited by David R. Maciel and Erlinda González-Berry (Albuquerque: University of New Mexico Press, 2000), 23–42.

[5]   Nieto-Phillips, *The Language of Blood*, 111–13.

[6]   Martín González de la Vara, "El traslado de familias de Nuevo México al norte de Chihuahua y la conformación de una región fronteriza, 1848–1854," *Frontera Norte* 6; *11*, (Enero–Junio 1994): 9–21.

[7]   Nieto-Phillips, *The Language of Blood*, 111–13.

social loyalties ebbed and flowed in this mix of competing interests.[8] Local historian of La Mesilla, Mary Taylor, mentions at least three different waves of immigration to the area between 1849 and 1851: from El Paso del Norte in 1849; from Doña Ana in 1850; and in 1851, a group of colonists arrived and received lands from Mexican commissioner Father Ramón Ortiz, charged with granting lands to repatriates.[9] Ortiz, who had strongly opposed the Treaty of Guadalupe Hidalgo, first attempted to secure the area as Mexican *in situ*. As we saw in Chapter three, he made a heroic but ill-fated effort to recruit Mesilleros to redirect the course of the Rio Grande to keep La Mesilla on the Mexican side.

Ortiz's strategy also included attempts to populate the area with resettled Mexicans from other parts of the republic. During the period when it still seemed uncertain whether La Mesilla would belong to Mexico or the United States, Ortiz began to grant lands to repatriates such as Esmeregildo Guerra, Juan Ortega, Teodoso Dominguez, Miguel Ortega, and Agaton Avalos, saying, "the state guarantees your property and always the free use of it as a citizen of the frontier... always be quick to defend the country against enemies who are hostile and who persecute you. Take care to have arms and a horse with you at all times."[10] Such language mirrors the decrees and appeals that guaranteed repatriates lands and tax concessions in exchange for their settlement in Mexican territory after the war.

So immediately following the war, and in an effort to populate lands with Mexican bodies, Ortiz took active steps to populate La Mesilla with residents loyal to Mexican interests. At times, this meant taking aggressive actions against Euro American residents. For instance, he compelled Americans to "move back across the river to the east bank where they settled in the more peaceable and sympathetic towns of Las Cruces and the now quiet Doña Ana."[11] According to Taylor, "[I]n a fever of patriotic zeal, Father Ramón Ortiz took away lands from Americans in Mesilla," and a customs house was set up along the river to charge duties on all goods "coming across the border." By February 1852, Ortiz made land grants to eighty-three migrants from Mesilla; by the fall of 1853, under the new commissioner, Guadalupe Miranda,

---

[8] The best study of these competing ideals and ideas is Reséndez, *Changing National Identities*.

[9] Taylor, *Mesilla, New Mexico*, 26–7.

[10] Ibid., 32.

[11] Ibid.

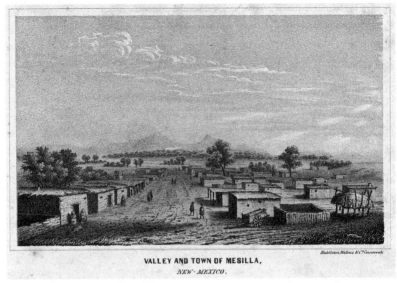

VALLEY AND TOWN OF MESILLA,
NEW-MEXICO.

Figure 5.2. Early View of La Mesilla, 1854. Photo courtesy of New Mexico State University Library Archives and Special Collections.

the La Mesilla colony increased to such an extent that it was divided into two distinct towns, the new town being named Santo Tomás de Yturbide.[12]

As the likelihood that the La Mesilla strip would become U.S. territory grew stronger, Ortiz shifted his energies to resettling individuals to points further south in Chihuahua territory. Recruitment was so successful (3,000 repatriates opting to move, with some 8,000 individuals expressing interest), American officials demanded Ortiz be removed from the territory along with outside "agitators" who sought to disturb the "peaceful conquest" of southern New Mexico.[13]

By 1853 the population of La Mesilla was around 2,000.[14] Immediately after 1853 the population of the general region grew as individuals

[12] González de la Vara, "El traslado de familias de Nuevo México al norte de Chihuahua," 9–21.
[13] See "Gobierno del Estado de Chihuahua. Escrito a mano: No. 68: El Gobernador de Chihuahua participa que se ha nombrado agente del Señor comisionado Ortiz al Licenciado Don Manuel Armendáriz para que informe al Supremo Gobierno sobre la inmigración a este Estado de las familias Nuevo Mexicanas, 1849," AHSRE, 2–13–2971.
[14] See Bailey Carroll and Villasana Haggard, *Three New Mexico Chronicles*; Fidelia Miller Puckett, "Ramón Ortiz: Priest and Patriot," *New Mexico Historical Review*,

continued to arrive in significant numbers until the end of the century. The repatriate colonies of Guadalupe, San Ignacio, and Zaragoza, Chihuahua were also primary destinations.

It is tempting to see these resettlements as pure nationalist resistance to American occupation, but such claims require a transnational examination in the areas the settlers left and the locations where they ended up. Granted, some Mesilleros desired to be free of U.S. hegemony after the Mexican American War and this contributed to a decision to resettle. Ortiz reported a strong nationalist sentiment at La Mesilla and throughout the northern border region. Sensing that occupation by the United States was a real possibility, Mexicans began mounting a defense of the territory in the 1850s. According to Ortiz, even while the treaty was still being negotiated, colonists at La Mesilla "gathered to determine what should be done in case the Governor of New Mexico should attempt to take possession of the colony for the United States."[15] However, when it became known that Mexico legally ceded the territories in the Gadsden Treaty with a proclamation "turning over the purchased country to the jurisdiction of the United States authorities," the effort was abandoned.[16]

Yet Ortiz seemed not only to overlook northern migrations to the west and east of New Mexico, but also to overlook the northern migration of Mexicans to the United States at precisely the same time. As discussed in previous chapters, northern migrations to California and Texas mirrored those to New Mexico, but were due to differing structural factors, like those having to do with the ongoing war. In the colony of La Mesilla itself, some Nuevo Mexicanos "fled at once to the other side of the Río Grande into that part of the United States which Mexico recognized as American territory... when its young men were conscripted into the Mexican Army which might do battle in this very place."[17] Apparently a willingness to fight and die for the Mexican *patria*

vol. 25, no. 4, (1950): 287; González de la Vara, "El traslado de familias de Nuevo México al norte de Chihuahua," 9–21.
[15] Taylor, *Mesilla, New Mexico*, 36.
[16] Ibid., 39.
[17] Migratory flows in both directions, as has been mentioned, occurred simultaneously during this period, and Mesilleros were not immune to these dynamics. Thus, the "problem" of runaway slaves was further exacerbated by the bifurcation of the border as Mexicans rendered aid, in some cases for small sums of money, to those escaping one form of slavery in exchange for another. According to Greber, this "aid to runaway slaves assumed [such] large proportions" that several extradition treaties were proposed and negotiated between Mexico and

was lacking for some border residents; these opted to take their chances with the Norte-Americanos.

LEGAL MANEUVERINGS IN THE STRUGGLE TO SETTLE LA MESILLA

If not entirely feelings of nationalism, then what lay behind the move to populate or depopulate the valley of La Mesilla? Part of the answer stems from the way some residents were not so much *drawn to* La Mesilla and other repatriate colonies as much as they were *forced out* of their traditional homes by colonial and bureaucratic American practices.

The push-pull dynamics governing the changing demographics in southern New Mexico can be discerned from the writings of John Russell Bartlett, a surveyor for the U.S. Boundary Commission constructing the international boundary line. In the aftermath of the Mexican American War, he wrote an intriguing account of his work and travels through the region. The following passage begins to describe the local expression of how Mexican repatriation efforts capitalized on grievances against the United States:

> On the 1 March, 1850, sixty Mexicans, with Don Rafael Ruelas at their head, most of whom had been domiciled at Doña Ana, abandoned their homes on account of their many grievances, and moved to the lands known as the Mesilla, where they established themselves. To increase the colony, the government of Mexico offered to give lands to other actual settlers, which offer induced large numbers of dissatisfied Mexicans living in New Mexico and in the small settlements along the Rio Grande, in Texas, to resettle there. More than half the population of Doña Ana resettled to La Mesilla within a year.[18]

Nuevo Mexicanos were particularly distressed by the colonial American practice known as "Texas head-rights." This refers to land grants under the Republic of Texas that granted lands to the heads of households,

the United States. See Daniels Taylor, *Mesilla, New Mexico*, 39; and Paul Neff Garber, *The Gadsden Treaty* (Philadelphia: The University of Pennsylvania Press, 1923), 159.

[18] Bartlett, *Personal Narrative of Explorations and Incidents*, I: 212–14; Baldwin, "A Short History of the Mesilla Valley," *New Mexico Historical Review* 13, (1938): 314–24. Located in "Border Heritage Center," El Paso Public Library (hereinafter BHC-EPPL).

usually to reward military veterans or promote settlement in regions that required some form of occupation or development. Bartlett continued:

> Immediately preceding, and after the war with Mexico, the Mexican population occupying the eastern bank of the Rio Grande in Texas and New Mexico were greatly annoyed by the encroachments of the Americans, and by their determined efforts to despoil them of their landed property. This was done by the latter either settling among them, or in some instances forcibly occupying their dwellings and cultivated spots; [which]...in most cases...was done by putting "Texas head-rights" on their property.... With these land certificates, or "head rights," many Americans flocked to the valley of the Rio Grande, and in repeated instances, located them on property which for a century had been in the quiet possession of the descendants of the old Spanish colonists. The latter, to avoid litigation, and sometimes in fear for their lives, abandoned their homes, and sought refuge on the Mexican side of the river.[19]

Dealing with the maze of complication involved in any legal system can be a daunting task for any citizen, particularly if said systems are foreign and in a different language and social tradition. But as Bartlett indicates, local Mexicans struggling to retain their land holdings faced the additional burden of dealing with the legal morass of an entirely new national system of government, and many chose to avoid it altogether. More telling is that twenty years after the signing of the treaty, "[T]he Mexican government presented few, if any, claims for property losses suffered by Mexican Americans in violation of the Treaty of Guadalupe Hidalgo in the claims settlement of 1868."[20]

As we have seen, the Mexican government did offer the enticement of land rights across the border for those wishing to remain Mexican citizens as opposed to those content to live under the new scheme of things. This consideration, coupled with American squatting and legal hurdles served to drive many south across the border. Such promises were met by many with suspicion, with the cold logic of survival, and in the interest of self preservation.

---

[19] Bartlett, *Personal Narrative of Explorations and Incidents*, I: 212–13.
[20] Rodolfo O. De La Garza and Karl Schmitt, "Texas Land Grants and Chicano-Mexican Relations: A Case Study," *Latin American Research Review* 21(2) (1986): 123–38.

The Event that Would Split La Mesilla

In 1944 a local writer conducting interviews for a story on the bells of the Old Mesilla Church happened upon the retelling of an event which had occurred nearly seventy years prior, and for which the church stood as a perennial reminder.[21] "The Riot of La Mesilla of 1871" stands out as perhaps the bloodiest event in the history of La Mesilla, New Mexico. This event is described as an election riot because it occurred during a very important congressional race involving two candidates from the New Mexico Territory. The consequence of this episode of electoral violence distinguishes itself from previous repatriation cases in that an election riot lay at the motivation to return to Mexico in the 1870s. Not long after the event, the so-called Republican losers chose to leave for Chihuahua rather than accept the victory of their Democrat opponents.

The following analysis differs significantly from most treatments of this frequently discussed event by following a faction of Mesilleros south to their newfound homes in La Ascensión, Chihuahua. I begin by examining the event as it occurred in New Mexico and then continue with an analysis of repatriate settlement in Chihuahua. Eruptions of violence of the magnitude of the Riot of La Mesilla, in which approximately eight to nine individuals lost their lives and dozens were wounded, can often be traced to forces brewing under the surface. In this case the hostilities were incubated through suspicions of election fraud in the previous elections for delegate and coupled by past instances of using illegal Mexican voters, a common accusation of the period.[22]

In the election of 1871 the Democrats were represented by José Manuel Gallegos, an ordained priest considered at the time sympathetic to the United States. The Republicans nominated as their candidate José Francisco Chávez. Although they differed to a large degree in their ideologies and perhaps in their education as well, the one thing that the two contestants had in common was their participation in,

[21] Margaret Page Hood, "Bells of Old Mesilla," *New Mexico Magazine,* (December 1944): 15.
[22] See United States Congress, House of Representatives, *Contested Election – New Mexico. February 24, 1854, Memorial of William Carr Lane, Contesting the Right of José Manuel Gallegos,* 33rd Congress, 1st Session, Report No. 121; also U.S. Congress, House of Representatives, *Contested Election – New Mexico. Memorial of Miguel A. Otero Contesting the Seat of Hon. José Manuel Gallegos, as Delegate from the Territory of New Mexico, 14 February 1856,* 34th Congress, 1st Session, Miscellaneous Document No. 5.

and sensitivity to, electoral fraud.[23] Gallegos was accused of using illegal Mexican voters in his bid to become a delegate in 1854 and again in 1856.[24] Chávez accused his then opponent, Charles P. Cleaver, of using the same tactic in the election of 1868.[25] By 1871, the two would meet to challenge each other for a seat as a territorial delegate for the U.S. Congress – one of the most influential and powerful positions in the New Mexico Territory at that time.

Despite public awareness of the tensions between Democratic and Republican sympathizers, the decision was made, unwisely in retrospect, to conduct election related political rallies on the same day in La Mesilla on August 27, 1871. Both candidates as I've alluded to, were familiar with allegations of fraud and electoral violence, at least if we are to believe the many published reports emanating from the U.S. Congress. But, cognizant of past problems at the electoral booth, local officials did make efforts to avoid clashes in the days leading up to the election. For instance, political rallies were planned on opposite sides of the small town. According to a *New York Times* article on the riot:

> The Republican and Democratic parties had each selected today as the most suitable time for a grand demonstration of the campaigns, and at an early hour this morning both parties commenced their preparations. The leaders were evidently desirous of avoiding disturbances, and the respective parties formed in procession and passed each other's place of meeting without an outbreak.[26]

The previously agreed upon arrangements called for the Republicans to hold their rally in front of the home of the Hon. John Lemmon,

---

[23] For Chávez see United States Congress, House of Representatives, *Chávez VS. Cleaver. Additional Papers in the Case of J. Francisco Chávez Against Charles P. Cleaver, of New Mexico*, 25 July 1868, 40 Congress, 3 Session, Miscellaneous Document No. 14.

[24] See U.S. Congress, House of Representatives, *Contested Election – New Mexico. February 24, 1854, Memorial of William Carr Lane, Contesting the Right of José Manuel Gallegos*, 33rd Congress, 1st Session, Report No. 121; also U.S. Congress, House of Representatives, *Contested Election – New Mexico. Memorial of Miguel A. Otero Contesting the Seat of Hon. José Manuel Gallegos, as Delegate from the Territory of New Mexico*, 14 February 1856, 34th Congress, 1st Session, Miscellaneous Document No. 5.

[25] United States Congress, House of Representatives, *Chávez VS. Cleaver. Papers in the Case of J. Francisco Chávez vs. Charles P. Cleaver, of New Mexico*, 24 June 1868, 40 Congress, 2 Session, Miscellaneous Document No. 154.

[26] "The Riot in New Mexico," 26 September 1871 *New York Times*, 2.

a Republican candidate for probate judge. The opposing party was to set up their grandstand in front of the Griggs & Reynolds Store. The Democrats' rally was led by I. N. Kelly, a prominent Democrat and a printer on the staff of *The Borderer/El Fronterizo.*

The processions marched to the rallying sounds of town brass bands. Brass bands are the source of local pride in pueblos across Mexico, but in this case there was not one, but two bands, and each was highly partisan. Playing for the Democrats was the well-known Gamboa Band while the Thomas Bull Band took the side of the Republicans. As the quote just cited indicated, the processions marched past each other's primary meeting places without incident. But tensions escalated when the Democrats decided to start parading around the main plaza of La Mesilla.[27]

The Republican procession decided to follow suit. Town plazas across Mexico follow the colonial urban planning set up by the Spanish, and they constitute the central space for the political, economic, religious, and sociocultural life of towns. Occupying the plaza was a highly symbolic gesture of staking a claim for the party's legitimacy. As the two bands began marching toward one another, both groups kept up a constant stream of partisan shouts and taunts. The Gamboa Band (Democrat) began circling around the plaza playing a tune with the lyrics: "They are leaving, they are leaving, the Republicans, to La Ascensión, because the Democrats won the *elección* (election)."[28]

The Republican band, not to be outdone, played their own partisan tunes. At this point "epithets were traded," and the candidates and other leaders of the opposing parties tried to defuse the tension. In one relatively cordial exchange, "I. N. Kelly...told John Lemmon that the interruptions in the Democratic rally by the Republicans were unnecessary."[29] All of these relatively cordial exchanges and suggestions by the political leaders were in vain as the two bands started circling one another in opposite directions, in the form of circling combatants.

At this point the mêlée between the Republicans and the Democrats erupted. According to an eyewitness: "suddenly in front of the Church, the Republicans and Democrats came face to face. How could they pass each other, for nobody wanted to be the first to step aside.... Then

[27] Frietze, *A History of La Mesilla and Her Mesilleros,* 89.
[28] Ibid., 89.
[29] Taylor, *Mesilla, New Mexico,* 158.

a shot!"[30] According to reports, the individual who fired the shot was
Apolonio Barela. Barela was part of the main contingent of Mesilleros
who migrated southward to Chihuahua after the riot; he later became
one of the main founders of La Ascensión.[31]

The details of what occurred next are confusing but it appears that
I. N. Kelly struck Lemmon with a pickaxe handle or club, knocking
him unconscious. Reporter Margaret Page Hood, the aforementioned
local reporter doing research on the church bells in 1944, interviewed
Teresa Garcia some seventy years after the riot. Garcia, a young girl at
the time, recalled being present when the trouble started:

> I was swinging by the Church doors listening to the music of
> my father's band...when suddenly in front of the Church, the
> Republicans and Democrats came face to face. How could they
> pass each other, for nobody wanted to be the first to step aside....
> Then a shot! Apolonio Barela had fired a pistol. Señor Kelly,
> a Democrat, got excited and hit Señor Lemmon, a Republican,
> with a pick handle, killing him. Felicito Arroyas y Lueras drew
> his pistol and killed Kelly. There were many, many shots. As I
> still swung on the Church doors I saw men falling down in the
> dust.[32]

The accuracy of Garcia's memory of the event is corroborated by primary and secondary sources published before and after this particular
interview. In 1871, the *New York Times* reported that "many women
and children hurried to their houses, but the fight was kept up from
windows and housetops, the dead and wounded falling on all sides....
The balance of the killed and wounded are mostly Mexicans."[33] The
sizeable military forces enlisted to quell the unrest were drawn from
both La Mesilla and Las Cruces. Troops arrived from Fort Selden later
in the evening and "order was quickly restored and the firing stopped,"
according to one report.[34] Several sources agree that six to nine people

---

[30] Margaret Page Hood, "Bells of Old Mesilla," *New Mexico Magazine*, (December 1944): 15.

[31] Ramón Ramírez Tafoya, "Fundación de La Ascensión, Chihuahua," (Unpublished Essay, 22 June 2004), passim; see especially the new book *De la Mesilla a La Ascensión* (Ascensión, Chihuahua, ICHICULT, 2009), 15–27.

[32] Margaret Page Hood, "Bells of Old Mesilla," *New Mexico Magazine*, (December 1944): 15.

[33] "The Riot in New Mexico," 26 September 1871, *New York Times*, 2.

[34] Taylor, *Mesilla, New Mexico*, 162.

lost their lives that day and dozens more were wounded.[35] The *New York Times* reporter estimated around thirty wounded, but as Taylor mentions, "several of the wounded had been spirited home" and their fates were not recorded.[36]

CONCLUSION

It is notable that no direct eyewitness reports were ever filed and no attempts were made to prosecute the perpetrators of this violence. Could it be that the psychological wounds were so pronounced that people refrained from official accounts? Or could there have been a conscious effort made by the "winning" Democrats to erase the resistance from the historical record? Could the remaining Republican sympathizers have felt too intimidated to speak up about casualties and concerns? Pscyhoanalysts León and Rebeca Grinberg note in their study of exiles that: "To face their complex problems they may use as a defense the denial of the present, which then becomes imprisoned between a past mythologized life (converted into the 'only thing worthwhile') and the future, represented by the illusion of being able to return home: an illusion all the more nourished the greater the impossibility of acting upon it."[37] A complete answer is difficult to discern, but it seems that the opportunity to head south deeper into Chihuahua provided an effective outlet for the disgruntled. And perhaps it provided an avenue for historical silencing, something common to the experience of dissenters forced into a migratory and refugee status.

Today a yearly celebration is held in La Mesilla, New Mexico and La Ascensión, Chihuahua commemorating the migration southward, and both places use the occasion to publicly recognize the importance of this historical event.[38] The event has in part been regenerated by the work of local historians who have historical roots in these towns, and a few have written well-researched monographs that capture

[35] For a list of the dead see "The Riot in New Mexico, Some Particulars of the Bloody Encounter Between Republicans and Democrats in Las Cruces, New Mexico – The Killed and Wounded," 26 September 1871, *New York Times*, 2.

[36] "The Riot in New Mexico," 26 September 1871, *New York Times*, 2; Taylor, *Mesilla, New Mexico*, 162.

[37] León Gringberg, M.D. and Rebeca Grinberg, M.D., *Psychoanalytic Perspectives on Migration and Exile* (New Have: Yale University Press, 1989), 158.

[38] Marjorie Lilly, "A Tale of Two Cities: La Mesilla, NM and Ascensión, Mexico," *Desert Winds Magazine* 16 (4): 10, 17.

these early experiences.[39] And recently, one of the local chroniclers of La Ascensión, Chihuahua has written about this shared history.[40] The following chapter will complement and contribute to these local histories, beginning with the trek of the Mesilleros southward toward Chihuahua and the subsequent founding of La Ascensión, Chihuahua the following year.

[39] Ramón Ramírez Tafoya, *De la Mesilla a La Ascensión*, (Ciudad Chihuahua: Instituto Chihuahuense de Cultura, 2009); Joe Frietze, *A History of La Mesilla and Her Mesilleros, Written and Compiled by a Native Mesillero*, (La Mesilla, NM: privately printed, 1995); Mary Daniels Taylor, *Mesilla, New Mexico*.

[40] See Ramón Ramírez Tafoya, *De la Mesilla a La Ascensión*, (Ciudad Chihuahua: Instituto Chihuahuense de Cultura, 2009). I was honored to write the prologue on behalf of my good friend and colleague Ramón.

The Government is conscious of its duty to make an effort to attract all those *countrymen* that are located on foreign soil, and today we are presented with a very favorable occasion to fulfill that duty, taking advantage of the good will that encourages them to return to their country, all the more convenient the [corresponding] increase in population, inasmuch as this [repatriation] adds the advantage of covering the borders with nationals specifically in that part of the Republic that finds itself so near to the United States, and to reinforce the element of destroying the savages that still inhabit that region of the state of Chihuahua.

Engineer Barrios to the Ministry
of Foreign Relations, March 12, 1885

CHAPTER SIX

COLONIZING LA ASCENSIÓN,

CHIHUAHUA

THE PREHISTORY OF REVOLT

INTRODUCTION

The repatriation of the Mexican populace, as we have read in previous chapters, occurred largely from the 1830s to the 1850s, but by the 1870s the federal government had seemingly forgotten how to foment a viable colonization program. Once the earlier projects of the postwar period were implemented and executed, the Mexican government, according to the state officials searching for federal laws to grant lands, did not continue applying the postwar lessons of a colonization law that addressed the particularities of Mexican American colonization, at least not until the period from 1875 to 1883.[1] The case of La Ascensión may serve as a microcosm into the inner workings of how Mexico went about settling colonies along the northern frontier during the 1870s.

Letters requesting repatriation to Mexico are few and far between during the period between 1855 and 1875, due primarily to the ongoing wars against the Indios Bárbaros and, according to government officials,

---

[1] Major legislation regarding colonization and immigration appeared in 1863, at least according to Jan de Vos, but it was the laws of 1875 and especially 1883 that signaled a shift in this policy. See Jan de Vos, "Una legislación de graves consecuencias: el acarpamiento de tierras baldías en México con el pretexto de colonización, 1821–1910," *Historia Mexicana* 34(1), (Julio-Septiembre 1984): 76–113; For the Land and Colonization Law of 1883 see "Ley de 15 de Diciembre de 1883," in De la Maza, *Código de colonización*, 936–45; After La Ascensión, other colonies were eventually settled along the northern frontier such as Tecate, El Boleo in Baja California, and Inominada and Las Palomas, Chihuahua, to name only a few. See also Holden, *Mexico and the Survey of Public Lands*, 7. He too remarks on this watershed period in terms of the transfer of these public lands.

"administrative disorder."[2] Not until the Porfirian period do we see an increase in repatriation requests, perhaps influenced in large measure by the case of La Ascensión, including an increase in advertisement of the law proper. Moreover, the case of La Ascensión influences the foundation of the 1883 Land and Colonization Law that established the first modern colonization program outlining preferential treatment for the Mexican American population residing outside of the country. La Ascensión was a watershed in terms of actually implementing and administering a repatriation policy, and ultimately forced the government to pass legislation concerning the colonization process.

This chapter begins where we left off in the previous chapter on the 1871 riot, and outlines the repatriation of the Mesilleros to La Ascensión by discussing the social history of land displacement, early trials and tribulations, populations that left, and the subsequent growth of the repatriate population throughout the nineteenth century. I will end the chapter by discussing various cases of fraudulent surveys, most notably the very government official charged with overseeing this particular repatriate colony. Tensions between new repatriates to the area and those of the original settlers will also be described and analyzed. Let us now turn to a brief history of how Mesilleros arrived in La Ascensión, Chihuahua the year after the election riot of 1871.

THE 1872 REPATRIATION OF MESILLEROS
TO LA ASCENSIÓN, CHIHUAHUA

A few short years after the Mexican American War (1846–1848) and the first repatriation experience of colonists from the La Mesilla valley,

---

[2]   Or if we follow the argument made by Carlos Pacheco in 1883, then in charge of the Departamento de Fomento, when he stated, "Constant civil war, accompanied by its inseparable retinue of public insecurity, industrial and commercial paralysis, administrative imbalance and scarcity in the treasury reduced with each passing day the hope of establishing a system of colonies. Even when the different governments, which have succeeded each other since the Independence epoch, were able to command sufficient pecuniary resources to undertake the great task of colonizing the country, European colonists avoided settling in Mexican territory due to the lack of security that reigned in it. Peace is the greatest attraction to colonization, and unfortunately that has been lacking in the Republic for a long time." See México, Secretaría de Fomento, *Memoria Presentada al Congreso de la Unión por el Secretario de Estado y del Despacho de Fomento, Colonización, Industria y Comercio de la República Mexicana. General Carlos Pacheco Corresponde á los años Trascurridos de Diciembre de 1877 á Diciembre de 1882*, 3 vols. (México: Oficina Tipográfica de la Secretaría de Fomento, 1885), 1, 3–4.

Colonel Emilio Langberg reported the availability of wood, water, and forage near El Ojo de La Ascensión during an inspection of the area.[3] The boundary commission sent by Mexico City took a strong interest in an area with great potential for serving as a colony, repatriate destination, and buffer between the United States and Mexico.[4] What later became the colony of La Ascensión, Chihuahua, in other words, had been identified as a potential site for repatriation as early as the 1850s. The colony, though, would not see substantial growth until 1872 when it was colonized by the Mesilleros who chose to leave La Mesilla after the violence of the electoral riot.

After the election revolt that we discussed in the last chapter, roughly ninety-six families left in an initial trek southward, but these numbers would increase very rapidly. By the middle of May 1872, upward of 150 families composed the new colony of La Ascensión. Four years later, the colony increased to around 500 inhabitants. By 1892, the population would swell to 1,200 inhabitants from all parts of New Mexico and Chihuahua.

In a matter of only a few decades, land holding patterns in the repatriate colony shifted as the increase in population created a competitive environment for land and land titles.[5] Not content to return to Mexico as field hands on large haciendas, the migrants to La Ascensión asserted their right to formally hold deeds in their new destination. In this regard, and as held true for most return migrants throughout the world, historian Mark Wyman reminds us that: "On land rested status; from land came dignity." Citing a number of cases of return migrants from Finland, Wyman concludes that "land was a major goal of return migration," and so it only makes sense that a primary concern of the Mesilleros would be the question of land.[6] A letter written describing the changing landscape in 1875 to the president of Mexico begins with a characterization of the repatriation to La Ascensión in the following (nationalist) manner:

> [T]he location ... we chose to establish ourselves as Colonists in the beautiful Mexican soil/land, seeking the shelter and protection of the flag [to which] we once belonged, but due to political upheavals, we had to belong to the United States of the

[3] Bartlett, *Personal Narrative*; also Baldwin, "History of the Mesilla Valley," 314–24, in BHC-EPPL.

[4] Taylor, *Mesilla, New Mexico*, 167–8.

[5] "Luis Terrazas acompaña original de una estancia de los colonos pobladores de La Laguna de La Ascensión. Los colonos piden se les adjudiquen los terrenos destinados a la colonia," 1872–1887, in AHTN, 1.361 (06), Leg. 10, Exp. 339.

[6] Wyman, *Round Trip to America*, 129, 132.

North, and not in agreement with this change, we made efforts to come and reside in the land that corresponds to Our Supreme Government of the Mexican Republic.[7]

A simple overview of such correspondence could be read as an indication of patriotic nostalgia. However, the main purpose of the letter is revealed thereafter as a request for land, specifically for five "Sitios de Ganado Mayor," or the equivalent of about 21,690 acres.[8]

As soon as the Mesilleros arrived in La Ascensión in the fall of 1872, the search for the basics of survival, namely, land, wood, and water, became the primary concern for these settler colonists. The accommodations and concessions to these needs made by the Mexican government may have lulled repatriates into the territory, but the haphazard and surreptitious manner in which they were executed would eventually contribute to the conditions for rebellion two decades later.

The problems that arose when the Mesilleros first arrived in La Ascensión had to do with finding the bare necessities: land for dwelling and cultivation, water for drinking and irrigation, and wood for fuel and construction. According to some reports, it may have taken up to three expeditions to the area prior to finding a suitable location. Initially ten men made the trek south, and these were followed by an apostolic twelve who pinpointed the area of future settlement.[9] The actual trip south took a few months since dozens of families were required to travel closely together amid a flurry of Apache attacks on their person and property.[10] As they turned to the fundamental question of resolving the partition of arable lands from which to grow crops and build homes, the Mesilleros petitioned the government about this matter.

The Mesilleros were subsequently granted property *en arrendamiento* (rented or leased out) until the Mexican congress returned to session

[7] "Carta de los Emigrados de la Mesilla al C. Presidente de la República de los Estados Unidos Mexicanos, 1875," AHTN, 1.361, (06), Leg. 10, Exp. 339. Original: "el punto que escogimos para establecernos como Colonos en el hermoso suelo Mejicano, buscando el amparo y protección de la bandera que pertenecíamos y que por los trastornos políticos, tuvimos que pertenecer a la de los Estados Unidos del Norte y no conformes con este cambio, hicimos esfuerzos porvenir a residir en el suelo que corresponde a Nuestro Supremo Gobierno de la Republica Mejicana."
[8] One *sitio* equals one square league or 4,338 acres.
[9] Ramírez Tafoya, *De la Mesilla a La Ascensión*, 21.
[10] Jesús Ramírez Caloca, "Ascensión," *Boletín de la Sociedad Chihuahuense de Estudios Históricos* 5, número 6 (20 Agosto 1944): 245–60.

to officially approve the land grant of five *sitios*. Thus in La Ascensión, as in other parts of the borderlands, land settlement preceded specific legal entitlement, and so were sown the seeds for competition, corruption, entrepreneurship, and social upheaval. The process of living in *arrendamiento* was quite problematic for those entering into such an arrangement, particularly after a generation of dubious land claims under U.S. governance.[11] When a people does not own or share in the future possibility to own the land they inhabit, there may be a tendency to disregard it. When land is rented out, the same care may not go into its cultivation and long-term preparation. Without the security of land titles, houses may be built reluctantly and shabbily. As late as 1885, thirteen years after the first settlers arrived in the colony, the colony's overseer, Colonel Ángel Bouquet, alluded to this problem when he wrote "but the insecurity due to the absence of property titles was such that the constructed houses are very simple, and they did not build their Church as they wanted."[12] However, once houses are constructed; lands cultivated; and families settled; the real estate gains value and attention, especially in a climate of increased migration and land subdivision. The defense of such lands can subsequently become quite violent.[13]

The final granting of land and the issuing of land titles for these first repatriates would not come for another decade in 1883; and even then, the land issues would be far from settled. Regarding all of the letters and correspondence from the colonists asking to settle land or water claims, the government moved at a snail's pace in granting what reasonably would be called prerequisites for repatriation. It seems the Mexican government was caught unprepared to deal with the new challenges of these repatriate colonies or they were simply indifferent in the face of perpetually depleted treasuries.

Why did this happen? One could consider the situation's novelty to provide part of the answer. As we have seen, an apparatus was put in place

---

[11] Cases of land displacement had become common during this period and perhaps figured into the multiple anxieties over land. For examples of land displacement in New Mexico, a succinct overview is provided in Juan Gómez-Quiñones, *Roots of Chicano Politics, 1600–1940* (Albuquerque: University of New Mexico Press, 1994), 257–62.

[12] "Carta de Ángel Bouquet a Secretario de Fomento," 12 Septiembre 1885, AHTN, 1.361, (06), Leg. 10, Exp. 339, Documentos 53–7.

[13] Andrés Villarreal, "The Social Ecology of Rural Violence: Land Scarcity, the Organization of Agricultural Production, and the Presence of the State," *American Journal of Sociology 110*, number 2, (September 2004): 313–48.

for repatriation after the Mexican American War, but, such as it was, it did not survive into the early 1870s. Yet the Mexican government undoubtedly desired to integrate this generation of borderlanders into its colonial plans, even if it meant allowing them to essentially "squat" on tenuously held national territory along the northern periphery of the republic.

Statements by Luis Terrazas, governor of the state of Chihuahua, reflect government concerns on this issue. In May 1872, he commented on the possibility of repatriates colonizing the frontiers of the Chihuahuan desert in the following manner:

> [W]ith regard to the irregularity with which the aforementioned colonists proceeded to occupy the terrain in which they have established themselves, this can be rectified by arranging now for such an award, whether the lands in question are *baldíos* (vacant government lands), or can be purchased from their owners, if they come from private property, in order to yield them to those that solicit them....[14]

The Mexican government was willing to make accommodations to repatriate requests in the hope that they could continue to occupy the frontier and ward off Apache attacks.[15] In advocating for the repatriate petitions for land, Governor Terrazas assumes the colonial rhetoric that attributes resident demands to national fidelity and unity:

> [As] part of the colonization of extensive deserts that surround those along its western Frontier, in my opinion, and as an obligation of justice, it is necessary to give consideration to petitioning Colonists, who, surely segregated from the Republic because of the treaty of La Mesilla, want to return to form part of the

14 "Carta de Luis Terrazas a Ministro de Fomento, Colonización, Industria y Comercio, 7 Mayo 1872," AHTN, 1.361 (06), Leg. 10, Exp. 339, "Luis Terrazas acompaña original de una estancia de los colonos pobladores de La Laguna de La Ascensión. Los colonos piden se les adjudiquen los terrenos destinados a la colonia," 1872–1887; Original: "... y solo añadiré, por tanto, a cerca de la irregularidad con que se ha procedido por los mencionados colonos a ocupar el terreno en que se han establecido, antes de que les sea adjudicado con los requisitos legales necesarios, que esto puede subsanarse disponiéndose ahora tal adjudicación, y en el caso de ser baldíos los propios terrenos o que se compren a sus dueños, si fuesen de propiedad particular, para cederlos a los que los solicitan...."

15 Barrick and Taylor, "The Mesilla Guard, 1851–1861," passim; For problems arising among Mesilleros and Apaches see "Asesinato del Jefe Apache 'Cuentas Azules,' Cometido por mexicanos los que huyeron a la Mesilla; Lista de los prisioneros en el fuerte Webster, Nuevo México, 1853," AHSRE, Exp. 30–16–58.

Mexican family.... It would insult the patriotism and well-known intelligence of the Supreme National Government to elucidate the convenient reasons that speak in favor of this petition....[16]

This particular colonization was understood to be so practical as to be almost unworthy of debate.[17] Chihuahua's foremost Indian fighter, Governor Terrazas represented the common belief about the benefits of repatriate colonization: settling repatriates along the extensive deserts would achieve a number of mutually beneficial goals for all concerned parties, particularly the state of Chihuahua where the social context between the state and its military colonists was the key to civilizing the frontiers against the Indios Bárbaros.[18]

As soon as the colonists arrived in the area, the supply of water became an issue requiring immediate resolution. The situation provides yet another opportunity to gauge what truly mattered to the Mexican government, its local representatives, and the repatriates themselves in the context of repatriation and the colonization of the northern frontier. A letter written to the president of Mexico by settlers soon after

[16] "Carta de Luis Terrazas a Ministro de Fomento, Colonización, Industria y Comercio, 7 Mayo 1872," AHTN, 1.361 (06), Leg. 10, Exp. 339, "Luis Terrazas acompaña original de una estancia de los colonos pobladores de La Laguna de La Ascensión. Los colonos piden se les adjudiquen los terrenos destinados a la colonia," 1872–1887: Original: "... la colonización de los extensos desiertos que circundan a aquel en su Frontera occidental hay que considerar a mi juicio, como un deber de justicia a los Colonos peticionarios, supuesto que segregados de la Republica por el tratado de la Mesilla quieren volver a formar parte de la familia mejicana."

[17] In 1883 there was little debate when discussing the pros and cons of repatriating the Mexican-origin population in the United States, at least not in comparison to nineteenth-century essays surrounding Asians, Africans, or Europeans. The Mexican-origin population, in fact, plays the role of "El Mexico Olvidado" in the sense that opponents of European immigration argue against this particular immigration by discussing the more promising, not to mention practical, advantages of repatriating this particular population. See *México, Diario de los Debates de la Cámara de Diputados, undécima legislatura constitucional de la unión. Tomo III. Correspondiente á las sesiones ordinarias y extraordinarias durante el primer periodo del segundo año*, (México: Imprenta de G. Horcasitas, 1883): III; 393–410. Located at *Dirección General de Bibliotecas, Cámara de Diputados, Honorable Congreso de la Unión, México City*.

[18] See Jane-Dale Lloyd, *Cinco ensayos sobre cultura material de rancheros y medieros del noroeste de Chihuahua, 1886–1910* (México: Universidad Iberoamericana, 2001) also *El proceso de modernización capitalista en el noroeste de Chihuahua, 1880–1910*, (México: Universidad Iberoamericana, 1987); Katz, *The Life and Times of Pancho Villa*; Alonso, *Thread of Blood*; Nugent, *Spent Cartridges of Revolution*.

their arrival illustrates their difficulties with respect to securing water in this place called Ojo de La Ascensión:

> After constructing some crude shacks for the sheltering of our families we undertook the task of digging a well for the common use and for cultivation of the lands; but due to our bad luck, after opening a great canal of more than a league we were disappointed to find that the waters of the Ojo de La Ascensión could not reach the population nor the arable lands, in these circumstances and although without elements but forced by need we undertook to dig a new well from the Rio de Janos and Corralitos, and when we had two leagues of canal that reached to the lands that we should be cultivating, the River was cut and as a consequence we have been unable to do any sowing with the circumstances being that our families lack that which is most indispensable for survival....[19]

To review the conditions in La Ascensión, the Mexican government sent an engineer by the name of Ingeniero Barrios, who sympathized with the appeals of the repatriates on this matter.

But what is most interesting is the grounds upon which that sympathy was based. First, a secure water supply was needed because the colony clearly held promise for meeting the goals of populating the region, according to the engineer sent to assess and survey the colony: "[W]ithout a doubt the Colony of La Ascensión will not be limited to the number of its founding families, since there exists many (families) of Mexican origin in New Mexico that desire to be repatriated, and having looked preferably upon the Colony of La Ascensión for their

[19] "Carta de Cesarío Duran y Julián Apodaca al Presidente de la Republica, 4 Mayo 1872," AHTN, 1.361 (06), Leg. 10, Exp. 339, "Luis Terrazas acompaña original de una estancia de los colonos pobladores de La Laguna de La Ascensión. Los colonos piden se les adjudiquen los terrenos destinados a la colonia," 1872–1887: Original: "... y después de formar unos malos jacales para habitación de nuestras familias emprendimos el trabajo de sacar una toma de agua para el uso común y para cultivo de las tierras; pero por nuestra desgracia después de abrir una gran acequia de más de una legua tuvimos el desengaño de que el agua de ojo de la Ascensión no podía llegar a la población ni a los terrenos cultivables, en estas circunstancias aunque sin elementos pero estrechada por la necesidad emprendimos sacara una nueva toma de agua del Río de Janos y Corralitos y cuando ya teníamos dos leguas de acequia que llego hasta los terrenos que debíamos cultivar, el Río se corto y en consecuencia no hemos podido hacer ninguna siembra en circunstancias en que nuestras familias carecen de los más indispensable para la vida y aun de herramientas para nuestros trabajos."

establishment, they only wait to have the titles of those lands expedited; and that the question of water is finally fixed, in order to negotiate their repatriation and income to the referred colony."[20] Similarly, repatriate requests should be addressed, according to Ingeniero Barrios, "because they are based on the impulse that needs to be given to that rising town, so that it progresses in the forecast that should be had regarding the difficulties with which it might falter in the future, and in the precautions that should be taken to avoid them."[21] Once titles, water, and other concessions were made and put into practice, the town could conceivably serve as a model that would encourage others to repatriate.[22]

As was often the case in such correspondences, the initial tone of the engineer's written appeal was couched in terms of nationalist ideology and moral consciousness attributed to both state and citizen. Note here the words of the engineer: "The Government is conscious of its duty to make an effort to attract all those *countrymen* that are located on foreign soil, and today we are presented with a very favorable occasion to fulfill that duty, taking advantage of the good will that encourages them to return to their country." However, he then proceeds to outline the many practical benefits that the government could take advantage of with this particular colonization of repatriates: "all the more convenient the [corresponding] increase in population, inasmuch as this [repatriation] adds the advantage of covering the borders with nationals specifically in that part of the Republic that finds itself so near to the United States, and to reinforce the element of destroying the savages that still inhabit that region of the state of Chihuahua."[23] Almost four decades after the founding of La Mesilla, the use of repatriates to pacify and "destroy" various Indios Bárbaros continued to be the understood government policy.

Repatriate colonization would not only populate the frontiers and serve as a buffer zone against the United States, but the war against "the savages" would be reinforced with their settlement of the area. Note the laundry list of advantages laid out by the engineer in the final paragraphs of his report:

... but before the considerations of the general good regarding the importance in exercising a manner to repatriate so many Mexicans

[20] "Carta al Señor Ministro, 12 Marzo 1885," AHTN, 1.361 (06), Legajo 10, Exp. 341, Documento 10, "Los colonos de La Ascensión, Chihuahua piden se les asegure la propiedad de las aguas de La Palotada y Rancho Esparseño, 1887."
[21] Ibid.
[22] Ibid.
[23] Ibid.

that reside on foreign soil, to enlarge the number of arms, to create new settlements, to cover our borders, and to impede the invasion of the savages, private interests should be silenced. . . .[24]

Interesting, he argued that private interests should yield to the "general good" of the "nation," that is, to the colonial and modernizing designs of the state. The private interests in this case are landowners whose properties intersect the colony's route to this important water source. Although it was understood that private owners should be compensated, the general idea in this case was to favor the repatriates over individual landowners. Concessions were required in order to not delay the progress of La Ascensión.

Further appeals (including an appeal signed by all of the inhabitants of La Ascensión) requesting access to watering holes, whether privately held or not, would follow. Though not very expeditiously, many of these appeals were eventually approved, thus providing vital natural resources for the burgeoning colony.

These practical concerns and the recognition of the benefits of Mexican American colonization did little to affect the government's earlier concern over supplying these colonies with adequate and arable land, sufficient water, and a well-defined contract that outlined each and every provision. Later repatriations dealt more efficiently with these very basic questions around settlement.[25] But in the case of La Ascensión, these early struggles and battles to clear up titles, provide access to wood, and obtain fresh water for crops were dealt with at a slow pace with La Ascensión playing the role of a test case.

Similarly, requests for other bare necessities were generally accommodated, though they were spread out over the dozen or so years that would pass before formal institutional logistical support would come in the mid-1880s with the 1883 Land and Colonization Law.[26] If we consider La Ascensión as a test case for establishing a successful repatriate colony, its population growth and degree of accommodation might on the surface suggest that it functioned as an exemplary model. It is worth

[24] Ibid.
[25] See, for instance, some of the irrigation projects under President Lazaro Cardenas in Balderrama and Rodríguez, *Decade of Betrayal*, 220–1.
[26] Subsequent requests for repatriation in the 1880s usually invoked the 1883 Land and Colonization Law. See, for example, "Carta de Comisionados Antonio José Valdez, José Anaya, y Marcelino Trujillo a la Secretaría de Estado y del Despacho de Relaciones Exteriores y Colonización, 22 Junio 1889," in *Protección Consular a Mexicanos*, 169–70.

recalling here that even Porfirio Díaz, the longtime dictator of Mexico, argued that La Ascensión "would become one of the most important towns in the north."[27] However, a closer look at the practice of granting lands en arrendamiento is merited to illustrate how, in retrospect, instabilities were in fact incubated in the La Ascensión experiment.

DUBIOUS SURVEYING DIVIDES LA ASCENSIÓN

When the Mexican congress finally awarded La Ascensión 21,690 acres and passed the 1883 Land and Colonization Law, Colonel Angel Bouquet was assigned to the colony to oversee its administration and distribute land titles. The constant stream of letters requesting land titles compelled the Departamento de Fomento to send engineer Emilio Ordóñez to provide key survey information regarding the properties awarded to colonists. His lack of written specification about the entire colony, however, left the door open for land grabbing by Bouquet, and also, it was rumored, his associate Rafael Ancheta, a minor government official who would become municipal president on two separate occasions. A scientific survey confirmed local suspicions, but it was conducted only after a riot in 1892 that was partly associated with the questionable purchasing of several properties by Bouquet. A final report corroborated the side of the colonists.

A few years after the founding of La Ascensión, the Departamento de Fomento donated land to establish the colony and had the area surveyed by two engineers, first by engineer Juan Zuloaga in 1880, and later by engineer Emilio Ordóñez. The colony was divided by Zuloaga into three sections: a common central town square, a large tract to the west, and another large tract to the east. Ordóñez, following Zuloaga, scientifically surveyed and granted title to the western side of the colony and the center, but he left the eastern side of the colony's properties in question; over two sitios de ganado mayor (constituting close to ten thousand acres) were assigned only en palabra, that is, by giving one's word rather than abiding by documented scientific measurement.[28]

In other words, by the time of the second survey, only around forty percent of the colony had been surveyed, and most residents lived on parcels of land that had been surveyed only in word. The absence of a complete scientific survey for the area was known only to a handful of

[27] González Navarro, La colonización en México, 121.
[28] "Informe de Hijar y Haro a Fomento, 10 Abril 1893," AHTN, (1.361) (06), Legajo 10, Exp. 345.

government officials, including Bouquet, who would later exploit this knowledge for his own benefit. Over eighty properties, accounting for 1,404 hectares, in the colony itself had yet to be counted in the new survey. It was at this point that Angel Bouquet arrived on the scene in such unwelcome circumstances.

The initial surveying performed by Zuloaga and Ordóñez temporarily satisfied the needs of the first generation of colonists to La Ascensión, but new generations of migrants were drawn to the region by promises of land and opportunity. By the time Bouquet arrived in the colony in the mid-1880s, hundreds of families had already migrated to the area, and these demanded a clearer picture of which lands they were entitled to. The earlier Mesilleros, known pejoratively as "the sellouts of Santa Anna," clashed with settlers and repatriates who arrived at a later date.[29] Benefiting from open choice, the earlier group of colonists occupied the best lands and were adamant about respecting the earlier surveying done by Zuloaga and Ordóñez. By contrast, the newer colonists wanted an official government tally – a tension that Bouquet would exploit.

The stakes for acquiring land rose as the price of real estate increased along with the population. Colonists continued to pour in from New Mexico and Texas and occupied those lands yet to be settled, which in most cases involved the properties on the eastern side of the colony surveyed only in word. When colonists first settled in the area, land prices averaged about .75 cents per hectare. By the end of the century, the price jumped to four pesos a hectare.[30] Colonists commonly demanded specification and rectification of land boundaries, water rights, and other questions arising from land titles.

After Bouquet started his work in April 1885, many residents lobbied to reenlist Zuloaga to the task of title granting and distribution in place of Bouquet. In effect, several groups formed around each of the surveys, with two factions favoring the first two surveys while a new group formed around Bouquet's survey, including Ancheta, who appears quick to always spot an opportunity to make money. The differences were articulated in the following manner by a report sent to the president of the republic himself:

A determined group of colonists, because of private interests, asked the Secretary to award the commission of [land title] distribution

[29] They were called "Los Vendidos de Santa Anna" because they resided in the strip of land that Santa Anna would later sell to the U.S. government for $15 million. See Ramírez Tafoya, *De la Mesilla a La Ascensión*, passim.
[30] Ibid.

to Mr. Juan Zuloaga, something which the Secretary did not agree with, and therefore the division was verified by the informing one [Bouquet], distributing lots to the interested in conformity with the arrangement by the Secretary and in accordance with the authorities.[31]

At least for the time being, Bouquet held on to his assignment.

The orders given to Bouquet when he was first assigned to the colony appeared simple enough: to distribute land titles to colonists who were surveyed and within the parameters of the grant and to withhold those titles from colonists who resided outside of the aforementioned boundaries. Dozens of colonists had deliberately (or not) extended the boundaries of their own properties over the course of only a few years, and so any survey was bound to upset the repatriate settlers. Those that happened to reside outside of the predetermined parameters would be allowed to enter the colony with stipulations like a fee or a minor charge.

Problems arose when Bouquet's survey resulted in an "excess," in other words, areas settled by colonists that lay outside the boundaries of what had been donated by the government. According to Agustín Sangines, the military officer sent to report on the conditions that gave rise to this rebellion in 1892:

> Up to this point things went perfectly well; but Bouquet was put in charge of the demarcation of the land before delivering the titles, and he executed it; resulting in excess, according to him, of five *sitios* of land. In the new survey, many plots of land that were already distributed were left outside [of the parameter].[32]

[31] "Informe sobre asunto Bastidos," AHTN, (1.361) (06), Legajo 10, Exp. 342, Documento 19–21, "Ángel Bouquet queja que los vecinos de la colonia La Ascensión elevan contra el, 1887–1892." Original: "un grupo determinado de colonos, por miras particulares, pido a la Secretaria se diera la comisión del reparto al Sr. Juan Zuloaga, algo cual no accedió la Secretaria, y por lo tanto el fraccionamiento fue verificado por el informante, repartiendo sus lotes a los interesados de conformidad con lo dispuesto por la Secretaria y de acuerdo con las autoridades del lugar."

[32] "Carta de Sangines a Díaz, 26 Febrero 1892," in *Colección Porfirio Díaz*, Correspondencia, Doc, #4694–4697. "Hasta aquí las cosas marchaban perfectamente bien; pero a Bouquet se le puso practicar el apeo del terreno antes de entregar los títulos, y lo practicó; resultando excedidos, según él, los cinco sitios de terreno. En el nuevo amojonamiento, quedaron fuera muchos lotes que ya estaban repartidos, y con el fin de evitar los grandes perjuicios que resultaban a los dueños de estos lotes, ocurrieron los colonos al Gobierno, por conducto del mismo Bouquet, pidiéndole la donación del exceso; pero la resolución les fue desfavorable." [Hereafter cited as CPD].

As one would expect, this was met with alarm by the individuals affected and "in order to avoid the resulting great damage to the owners of those plots, the colonists petitioned the Government, with the same Bouquet, asking for a donation of the excess; but the resolution was unfavorable."[33] In sum, Bouquet knowingly and deliberately purchased the excess of lands from the government in order to resell them to current and potential repatriates for a profit. Like Ancheta, Bouquet was out to make a profit.

Bouquet at this point did not act to retitle excess lands, but instead told the colonists they had to move their plots to areas within the proper perimeters of the colony. Adding insult to injury, as the post-riot scientific assessment by engineer Hijar y Haro would reveal, "instead of having received [the titles] from those colonists, he [Bouquet] returned them to this Secretary to then be able to despoil them of their plots and to take possession of them."[34]

In his own defense, Bouquet called attention to encroachment by residents onto land beyond the perimeters of the town proper. The overseer, in other words, was not the only party with questionable motives. For instance, in some cases repatriate colonists manipulated property markers in order to amplify their own plots of land. As they encroached upon the lands of others, a domino effect caused other properties to overlap or intercept. As he went about surveying the properties, at least according to Bouquet:

> The first boundary was found accurate, but not so for the second, for which the measurement was repeated, observing that the line established was found defiled, therefore all the boundaries were established at a greater distance than the ones that corresponded to them, although located with every regularity. The fact that those boundaries covered a greater extension than that of the five sitios belonging to the Colony remain verified and explained, why in spite of my having distributed more than three sitios there nevertheless remained another four. That failure or abuse was excused, attributing it to the work of the authorities when the measurement was done to set the boundaries, ordering that they be placed at a later date. The agents, due either to a mistake,

33   Ibid.
34   "Carta al Ministro de Fomento, 11 Mayo 1893," AHTN, (1.361) (06), Legajo 10, Exp. 345.

or because they did not find the old signs well marked, wrongly placed them....[35]

Despite this point, Bouquet's purchase of land that he earlier claimed was outside of the perimeter shatters his credibility.[36]

The analysis by Hijar y Haro revealed more details about how this sleight of hand came about. According to the engineer, Bouquet sought to diminish landholdings by deliberately manipulating each of the lots by about one-third of their prescribed size and employing a different unit of measurement. In the scientific survey finalized in mid-1893, the engineer discovered that Bouquet only provided eight of the twelve hectares awarded to each colonist when "the true surface measurements for each rectangular lot in the northern series of the parallelogram is that of twelve hectares, eighty-seven aras, and 94 centiaras."[37] This excess of four hectares, Bouquet thought, could be accumulated into a larger piece of land of which he could obtain "legal" possession. In a three-step process, Bouquet first reclassified plots of land he claimed were outside of the perimeter and then informed the former owners of this reclassified land; they could either move to plots within legal boundaries or purchase the outlying parcels. At the final stage he could "legally" request from the Mexican government possession of reclassified and unpurchased land. Bouquet thus placed himself in a position to

---

[35] "Carta de Ángel Bouquet a Srio de Fomento, 27 Enero 1891," AHTN, (1.361) (06), Legajo 10, Exp. 342, Doc. #22–32. My italics.; original: "La primera mojonera se encontró bien, pero no así la segunda por lo que se repitió la medida, observándose que la línea establecida se hallaba viciada, pues *todas las mojoneras estaban establecidas a mayor distancia de la que les correspondía*, aunque si colocadas con toda regularidad. El hecho de que con aquellas mojoneras abarcaba mayor extensión que la de los cinco sitios que le pertenecían a la Colonia, quedo comprobado y explicado él porque, a pesar de haber repartido yo más de tres sitios sobraban sin embargo otros cuatro. Se disculpo aquella falla o abuso atribuyéndolo a que por la misión de las autoridades cuando se hizo la mensura para fijar las mojoneras, al mandarse más tarde que se pusieran, los comisionados, ya por error o por no haber encontrado bien marcadas las antiguas señales, las colocaron mal según se veía...."

[36] See "Escala de La Colonia de La Ascensión hecha por el Ingeniero Enrique Hijar y Haro, Marzo 1893" in "Informe de Hijar y Haro a Fomento, 10 Abril 1893," AHTN, (1.361) (06), Legajo 10, Exp. 345.

[37] "Informe de Ing. Hijar y Haro a Secretaria de Fomento, 10 Abril 1893," AHTN, (1.361) (06), Legajo 10, Exp. 345, "Copia autorizada de las diligencias de identificación de las mojoneras reconocidas por el Ing. E. Hijar y Haro en la colonia de La Ascensión, 1893."

resell "excess" parcels at a profit to colonists who already sacrificed time and worked the land, or he could sell them to the new incoming colonists from the United States, Mexico, or elsewhere.

A number of coincidences and maneuvers by Bouquet lend credence to the claims of colonists against him. The lands Bouquet alleged were outside of the perimeter happened to be some of the oldest and most productive in the colony. He charged colonists seven pesos to rectify and regularize their titles. He also began to favor colonists willing to sell him their lands at discounted prices. Carefully timing his actions, Bouquet appears to have held on to knowledge about valid irregularities in surveying and to have silently watched residents work land upon which he had designs until he could actually execute his plan to swindle landowners.

Bouquet's original scheme went according to plan until others were affected by the domino effect of his faulty surveying. He probably believed that his skimming off the top would go unnoticed, particularly when dozens of the colonists were owners not only of their own lots, but in some cases claimed several properties because of the stipulations laid out in the 1883 Land and Colonization Law.[38] According to several dozen colonists, more than forty plots lay partially outside the parameter, representing about 702 hectares of land.[39] In the end Bouquet accumulated several thousand hectares of land.

MOUNTING WRITTEN COMPLAINTS
AGAINST BOUQUET

A set of letters in protest against Bouquet's surveying methods surfaced in the first months of 1890 and eventually sparked a government response. This correspondence lends a human face to circumstances colonists encountered and provides more detail about the inner workings of settlement era competition and corruption after the implementation of the 1883 Land and Colonization Law.[40]

The first complaint that appears in the archival record is a letter written directly to the Departamento de Fomento by resident Lázaro

[38] Copy of the 1883 Land Law is located in *Memoria, Secretaría de Fomento,* 1883–1885.

[39] See "Carta de los Suscritos de La Ascensión a Secretaria de Fomento, 15 Octubre 1891," AHTN, (1.361) (06), Legajo 10, Exp. 342, Documento 19–21, "Ángel Bouquet queja que los vecinos de la colonia La Ascensión elevan contra el, 1887–1892."

[40] Holden, *Mexico and the Survey of Public Lands,* 3–24.

Padilla in 1890. Padilla, like most other colonists Bouquet targeted, was not from the elite sector of the populace, but was a humble rancher like those mentioned in other studies of this area.[41] Padilla describes his personal investment in the property:

> I was given as a member of the colony a lot of land for sowing, which I have procured by way of my own personal work, to put it into a state of production to then be able to subsist with my family, because it is the only resource that I can count on to live.[42]

Padilla argued that, after working and clearing land for sowing, Bouquet told him that his property, along with several other colonists, was outside of the parameter granted by the Mexican congress in 1883. How could he leave a plot that he had toiled on for so long and that "with sacrifice, I have managed to achieve some advantage to the land," according to Padilla's letter.

"But now," he went on to say, "that someone has seen how much I've worked, and now that the land is cleared and ready to sow they tell me that it does not belong to me; that part of it is outside of the measurements of the town and that for such reason it belongs to Bouquet." Padilla maintained that "this circumstance, as you must understand, damages me greatly and I believe Sir that I am not to blame whatsoever that the first measurements turned out to be mistaken.... It is not fair that Mr. Bouquet left me to work my land and then came to me at the last minute declaring that it belongs to him by a purchase he made from the Government."[43] Bouquet not only told Padilla that he had to move his land inside the parameters given by the government, but that the ground that he had broken belonged to the same government official that sought to "rectify" previous surveys.

A second letter, written by Miguel Bastidos to the Departamento de Fomento in May 1891, was probably dictated in response to an allegation that his property also remained outside of the original five *sitios* granted by congress to the repatriates of La Ascensión in 1883. Bastido immediately paid a visit to Mr. Ordóñez (the previous surveyor) in a neighboring municipality to corroborate the claim. During the encounter, Ordóñez told

---

[41]   See Lloyd's, *Cinco ensayos sobre cultura material de rancheros y medieros del noroeste de Chihuahua*; Katz, *The Life and Times of Pancho Villa*; Alonso, *Thread of Blood*; Nugent, *Spent Cartridges of Revolution*.

[42]   "Carta de Lázaro Padilla a Sria de Fomento, 28 Julio 1890," AHTN (1.361) (06), Legajo 10, Exp. 339.

[43]   Ibid.

Bastido that his property was in fact outside of the parameter; however, it was possible this circumstance could result from the use of an alternate surveying method, which would come with an alternate method of measuring. According to Bastido, "Mister Ordóñez informed me that [my plot] was found [outside of the parameter], but that it could be made to appear as such if instead of employing metric measurements for the survey one employed the Mexican *vara*; that he [Bouquet] had employed as the first and only legal one for this effect."[44] Bouquet was able to do what he did by simply changing the standard of measurement for his own devices, which appeared to be the Mexican *vara* instead of the agreed upon metric system. One meter would be the equivalent of around 1.20 Mexican *varas*, thus providing the conditions for an excess of property if employing the latter rather than the former unit of measurement.

This charge would be followed by a series of allegations from several dozen colonists, many of whose names reappeared during the 1892 revolt. For these colonists, Bouquet was a man who "lacks dignity and a manipulator of the confidence that the Supreme Government has placed in him." The person sent to presumably take charge and rectify the problem of land titles actually served to displace them by employing dubious survey methods. As Sangines noted, "since Bouquet later became the owner of the excess lands mentioned, the colonists believed themselves mocked by him, and *here is the germ of discord*."[45] Díaz's own godson put it plainly, "To my thinking, nobody had greater right to the land in question than the colonists, for having been in possession of it."[46]

BOUQUET'S QUESTIONABLE DEFENSE

Bouquet replied to the charges against him in the form of an extended and verbose letter. Posing the problems as mere misunderstandings of the law, Bouquet, citing current laws and adopting a highly legalistic

[44] "Carta de Miguel Bastidos a Secretaria de Fomento, 26 Mayo 1891," AHTN, (1.361) (06), Legajo 10, Exp. 342, Documento 19–21; original: "El Señor Ordóñez me informo que se encontraba, pero que podía hacer que apareciera así si en lugar de emplear medidas métricas para la mensura se empleaba la vara mexicana; que él [Bouquet] había empleado la primera como única legal para el efecto."

[45] "Carta de Sangines a Díaz, 26 Febrero 1892," CPD, Correspondencia, Doc. #4694–4697. In his investigation of the colony and his report to Díaz, Sangines officially becomes the first "historian" explaining the many variables that led to the Revolt of La Ascensión of 1892.

[46] Ibid.

writing style, penned responses to each and every issue brought up by
the colonists during several months of correspondence. He (at least for
a while) was able to make his case against the colonists of La Ascensión.
His confident language defending his charge as a person looking over
the best interest of the federal government was so well constructed that
for a few months the Porfirian apparatus repeated his wording almost
verbatim in their exchanges with the aggrieved colonists. For example, the first *Informe* circulated among federal government officials on
Bastidos's charges against Bouquet focused on what was portrayed as an
abundant distribution of land to colonists:

> As can be seen, Bastidos has completely failed in truth and thus
> remains proven...because though it is certain that although some
> alone had received one title, the majority would receive for the
> same gratification 3, 4, and even 5 titles, being Bastidos one of the
> latter as is evident in relation to the first distribution.[47]

In other words, why was the repatriate complaining when so many
owned several plots of land?

Though in many cases colonists did own more than one plot of land,
the assignment of plots must be considered in relation to the typical
composition and requirements of a working farmstead. Each head of
household, including unmarried young men, were usually given two
plots of land: one for living (a *solar* with a small garden) and one for
cultivating (a larger *lote de siembra*). It is easy to see how one head
of household would have in his or her possession upward of five plots
of land. Land, however, was not equivalent to a liquid asset in late-
nineteenth-century Chihuahua, nor did it guarantee credit to the property owners. An impoverished farmer or *ranchero* could hold title to
three to five plots of land and live in a relatively wretched state.

At first the secretary of Fomento accepted Bouquet's case that the
properties in question remained outside of the parameter. The government saw no contradiction in his purchasing said properties from the
colonists and then reselling them thereafter. But when several other colonists joined in to further challenge Bouquet and to reinforce Bastido's
earlier allegations, the secretary began to sing a different tune. Yet it
would take many more letters and an all-out revolt before the government would ultimately make concessions to the colonists' demands. For

[47] "Informe sobre asunto Bastidos," AHTN, (1.361) (06), Legajo 10, Exp. 342,
Documento 19–21.

many of the colonists, it appeared as though the government not only sided with Bouquet, but also with Ancheta, thereby perpetuating a longer series of abuses of power. In the end it was ultimately the relationship between Bouquet and Ancheta that led the colonists to rebel against local authorities that they perceived as collaborating with one another.

According to much of the primary and secondary documentation available, the cozy relationship between Ancheta and Bouquet was one of convenience and of collusion. Ramírez Caloca points out that "he [Ancheta] struck up an intimate friendship with Colonel Bouquet, helping him in his [survey] work and supporting him with his influence in order to effect the displacements."[48] Governor Carrillo of Chihuahua shared in this characterization of Ancheta's enlistment of Bouquet in a similar fashion when he noted: "Ancheta situated his party in the federal representatives found in the referred Pueblo, in Bouquet, and we could say in the most enlightened people of the region."[49] When Ancheta was elected municipal president in late 1891, the colonists had finally reached the limit of their tolerance. Ancheta, although a repatriate himself and someone who had been a colonist for some time, was not an original settler, that is, he was one of the "sell-outs of Santa Anna," something that did not work in his favor.

When the supporters of the independent candidate arrived at the offices of the municipal presidency in November 1891 – together with colonists aggrieved by Bouquet's faulty survey – in order to assure that no fraud would be committed, their requests were denied and they were forced to leave the building under the threat of assault from the local police and outgoing municipal president Teodoro Rueda. Because Ancheta had taken the presidency against the will of the people, according to the historian of Chihuahua, Francisco Almada, more than 100 men came together to question his authority in early January of the following year.[50]

CONCLUSION

This chapter examined the repatriation of Mesilleros to La Ascensión in 1872 and the initial problems with land, water, wood, and Indios

---

[48] Ramírez Caloca, "Ascensión," 251.
[49] "Carta de Lauro Carrillo a Porfirio Díaz, 18 Enero 1892," CPD, Correspondencia, Doc. #271–276.
[50] Francisco Almada, La revolución en el estado de Chihuahua, 2 vols. (Chihuahua: Patronato del Instituto Nacional Estudios Históricos de la Revolución Mexicana, 1964–1965), I; 93–106.

Bárbaros as they sought to settle this colony.[51] Compounding their problems after their arrival in Mexican territory was the appointment of an overseer who sought to defraud them of their land through dubious survey methods, thus sowing the seeds of discord and revolt.

After years of requesting title to their lands and after numerous complaints against Colonel Angel Bouquet, a number of the repatriates lodged a series of complaints against the overseer, setting the stage for the rebellion of 1892. When one of the main collaborators of Bouquet took the most important political office of the colony the following year, the colonists rebelled in protest. Bouquet's corrupt practices resurfaced time and again until the end of the century as an example of governmental apathy, inaction, incompetence, and abuse.

On a broader scale, the general climate was one of growth and competition. The sale of lands promised monetary value for all concerned, including colonists able to obtain title to more than one plot, allowing them to legally sell any unused portions of land. The administrator of the customs house in La Ascensión noted that the repatriation of Mexicans from the United States had "awoken a furor to acquire federal lands, not to work them, but in order to sell them to the Americans."[52] The rebellion of residents of La Ascensión, therefore, was not merely a case of poor timing or mishandling in the midst of novel circumstances. The response by colonists did not involve a spontaneous conversion of a populous from passive acceptance of authority to violent challenger. It was, rather, the active reassertion of residents' right of competition free from graft, and it was consistent with similar assertions expressed many times previously in Mexican history. The details of their rebellion are elaborated as the prime focus of the following chapter.

---

[51] Remigio Saenz, who would later be involved in the revolt of 1892 and whose mill was fortified against the "addicts of the government" wrote a letter only a few months after promises from the state government. Aside from the repeated request to give title to their lands, Saenz made mention of the many problems faced in this colonization without much logistical support from any authorities, particularly as it related to Indian raids. Saenz noted, for example, that "lo más costoso y punible para nosotros es la persecución de los indios bárbaros que a cada instante vienen a destrozar nuestros intereses y la fecha tenemos un hijo llevado, 56 bestias caballares y bastantes reses robadas por ellos, cuyos intereses nos eran de mucha utilidad para nuestro progreso y para la persecución de dichos bárbaros." See AHTN (1.361) (06), Legajo 10, Exp. 339.

[52] "Secretaria de Hacienda a Secretaria de Fomento, 28 Agosto 1884," AHTN (1.21) (06), Exp. 733.

To end, this man was a bad Mexican, the kind that are raised in the United States who then return talking negatively about their country.

Carta de Miguel Ahumada
a President Porfirio Díaz, 10 Enero 1892

Anatomy of the 1892 Revolt of La Ascensión, or the Public Lynching of Rafael Ancheta

The *Linchamiento* of Rafael Ancheta

At five o'clock on the afternoon of January 6, 1892, 100 armed men gathered behind the Church of La Ascensión to confront the newly elected municipal president, Rafael Ancheta of the regional ruling party.[1] Angry, intoxicated, and armed, the residents of this repatriate colony on the Chihuahua–New Mexico border questioned the legitimacy of Rafael Ancheta's election victory over the preferred, and more popular, independent candidate José León Urrutía. Warned of the discontent and the brewing rebellion, Ancheta went behind the church with several men, also armed, to inquire about the gathering. There Ancheta was met by locals who claimed that he should not be the municipal president and that they had gathered to "un-recognize his authority."[2]

[1] My use of the term *linchamiento* is taken from contemporary usage of the term, which does not always entail a lynching per se, with a rope or some other device with which the victim is hung from a tree, telephone, telegraph pole, and so forth. *Linchamientos* in Mexico today involve not just public lynchings, put public beatings and killings that involve various forms of violence and death. This particular revolt and the rebels involved, as can be seen from the archival record, produced the following descriptions: *Motín, Tumulto, Revuelta, Sedición, Malos Mexicanos, Revoltosos, Rebelion, Tumultuosos, Sediciosos, Bandidos, Criminales Comunes, Asotea, Asoteo, Borrachera,* and *Asonada.* One can see how a similar event carries numerous names and labels over time. Hence my historicizing of the term is important, if at times ironic. Today, these killings average about twenty-five per year. See Carlos M. Vilas, "(In) justicia por mano propia: linchamientos en México contemporáneo," *Revista Mexicana de Sociología,* LXIII, numero 1, (2001): 131–60.

[2] "Declaración de Policía Miguel Zapata," *Archivo Municipal de Ciudad Juárez, Biblioteca Arturo Tolentino* (hereafter cited as AMCJ), Caja 1892, "Expediente

In the argument that ensued between Ancheta and the rebels, Atilano Baca, past municipal president and one of the main leaders of the opposition, accused Ancheta of being "nothing more than an infamous ingrate that wants to be an authority by force." Ancheta maintained that he was the legally elected president of the municipality.[3] At some point during this heated exchange, which had fueled an already angry crowd, someone knocked Ancheta unconscious with a rifle butt to the head and then dragged him by a rope to a mill owned by Remigio Saenz situated just outside the colony.[4] One of the police accompanying Ancheta, José Ávalos Salazar, was gravely wounded in the rioting, barely escaping the mob to reach the home of postmaster Marcos Sifuentes, where he died later that evening.[5] On the way to the Saenz mill, people kicked and beat Ancheta, and once in the mill he suffered further torture, gunshots, beatings, and humiliations until a blow to his head from a pickaxe killed him three days later. Back in the colony, local prisoners, some of whom were related to the rebellious repatriates, were released from the jail without resistance from the guards.[6] With such a well-fortified position in the mill, the number of *revoltosos* grew to well over 130 men.

When the "addicts of the government," as Ancheta's Porfirian-backed supporters were referred to by the rebels, were warned of the "tumult" in La Ascensión, they immediately sent word to local and state officials, who relayed the news to President Porfirio Díaz.[7] But while Díaz was organizing a pro-government federal force to send to La Ascensión, a local militia consisting of roughly thirty-nine men from Janos and fifty more from Corralitos and Colonia Díaz was already on its way.[8]

The following morning, the group, under the leadership of Postmaster Sifuentes, charged the fortified mill. The *revoltosos* defended

que contiene todos los documentos relativos á los motines ocurridos en La Ascensión en los días 6 y 7 del presente año," Doc. 196–205.

3   "Declaración del Policía Miguel Zapata," AMCJ, Caja 1892, Doc. 32–6. A municipal president can be compared to the contemporary role that a town mayor undertakes.

4   Acalia Pozo Marrero, "Dos Movimientos Populares en el Noroeste de Chihuahua: Tomochic y La Ascensión, 1891–1892," (Universidad Iberoamericana, 1991), 105.

5   AMCJ, Caja 1892, Doc. 32.

6   "Sánchez Aldana to Jefe Político en Ciudad Juárez, 9 Enero de 1892," AMCJ, Caja 1892, Doc. 14.

7   "Rangel to Díaz, 9 Enero de 1892," CPD, Telegramos, Núm. #336.

8   "Barrios to Jefe Político del Distrito Bravos, 10 Enero de 1892," AMCJ, Caja 1892, Doc. 19–20.

their position from within the walls of the mill and repelled the attack. Sifuentes was killed in the first exchange of gunfire.

On the second day (January 7) the colony's overseer, Ángel Bouquet, from his fortified position in the customs house, sent a choppy telegram to the area's political chief requesting assistance: "[The *revoltosos*] continue re-concentrated in the mill and [it] appears to be under attack; I occupy [the] customs house and other houses; to avoid more inconveniences to the populace, aid is urgently needed; I don't understand object of riot ... expect to be attacked."[9]

Almost 100 hours later, federal forces arrived in La Ascensión at two in the morning on January 11, led by the president's godson, Agustín Sangines. Sangines promptly sent word to the "incited rebels" to surrender to the government, only to discover that there was no one at the mill.[10] He sent scouts out, and they arrested sixty men. Another forty men ran toward El Cerro de la Cal, and the remainder of the rebels, particularly the main conspirators, fled across the border to Las Cruces and La Mesilla, New Mexico; and they would later claim U.S. citizenship once the process of extradition began.

The reaction and response of the Mexican government to this rebellion was quick, calculated, and ultimately effective. Mired in numerous confrontations throughout the republic, the government handled "La Revuelta de La Ascensión" in a diplomatic manner that took into account the nature, context, and ultimate outcome of the revolt.[11] Even as Sangines made his way to the colony and pondered the possibility of visiting violence upon the rebellious repatriates, he was compelled to consider the possible consequences of his actions and the grist he could offer to the enemies of the Mexican government.[12] He knew that any misstep on his part might engender other rebellions or encourage those enemies of the state already in open revolt.

Historian Friedrich Katz has pointed out that it was during this three-year period (1891 to 1893) that "the greatest number of insurrections

9   "Bouquet a Jefe Político de Distrito Bravos, 7 Enero 1892, 4:00 pm," AMCJ, Caja 1892, Doc. 5–6.
10 "Carta de Sangines al Gobierno de Chihuahua, 12 Enero 1892," AMCJ, Caja 1892, Doc. 25–27.
11 See Friedrich Katz and Jane-Dale Lloyd, et al., *Porfirio Díaz frente al descontento popular regional, 1891–1893: antología documental* (México: Universidad Iberoamericana, 1986), 11.
12 "Carta de Sangines al Gobierno de Chihuahua, 12 Enero 1892," AMCJ, Caja 1892, Doc. 25–7.

happened during the Porfirian dictatorship prior to the Revolution of 1910. In many cases, like in the center of Mexico and in the mountainous zones of western Chihuahua, the revolutions happened in the same regions and places where twenty years earlier the first buds of the Revolution would take place."[13] The Revolt of La Ascensión certainly shares a number of the characteristics of the 1891–3 insurrections in the state of Chihuahua that were unfolding at the very same time, but one that ultimately has a unique history conditioned by a diverging set of circumstances. In the end, of the dozens of participants involved in the revolt, only four would be sentenced to death; the others were pardoned.[14] But why another election rebellion almost twenty years after a similar incident prompted their repatriation to Mexico in the first place?

I suggest that the public beating of Rafael Ancheta was the culmination of a series of frustrations that had at its root fights over land and ambiguous titles. As a result of this confrontation between the local inhabitants of La Ascensión and the representatives of local and federal power, the Díaz government undertook to rectify the myriad complaints of citizens regarding problems associated with land surveys, displacement at the hands of federal officials appointed to these districts, water rights, and titles to their properties. Like similar cases examined by sociologist Andrés Villarreal in contemporary Mexico, "conflict over land may result not only from scarcity, but also when property rights over plots are not clear, are not well enforced, or are contingent."[15] These were the same principal concerns the inhabitants of La Ascensión had outlined in their missives to the federal government in the years prior to the *linchamiento* (public lynching) of Rafael Ancheta in 1892.

ANCHETA'S PAST AND DEATH DESCRIBED

Unlike the impetus for other local rebellions, the election victory of Ancheta was not truly a "Porfirian imposition" per se, even though

---

[13] Katz and Lloyd, *Porfirio Díaz frente al descontento popular regional*, 11.

[14] "Copia autorizada de las diligencias de identificación de las mojoneras reconocidas por el Ing. E. Hijar y Haro en la colonia de La Ascensión, 1893," AHTN, 1.361 (06), Legajo 10, Exp. 345.

[15] Andrés Villarreal, "The Social Ecology of Rural Violence: Land Scarcity, the Organization of Agricultural Production, and the Presence of the State," *American Journal of Sociology*, 110;2, (September 2004): 313–48.

Ancheta was – as one telegram described him – one of their own and
therefore part of the Porfirian apparatus.[16] Although not an original
settler, Ancheta was well-known in La Ascensión and had run for
office in the past, even holding the post of municipal president on at
least one other occasion. Some Porfirian authorities commented that
during his past tenure as president, Ancheta abused his authority on
more than one occasion. According to Miguel Ahumada's knowledge
of the "people of the frontier," the highest ranking military official of
the region believed that the motive behind the La Ascensión rebellion "was the ill will [the people] felt toward Ancheta." He was "a man
of bad antecedents," according to Ahumada, who, as municipal president, had "harassed the employees of the frontier customs house who
resided there, making it difficult to effectively administer the frontier
outpost." In his past, he engendered discord and resentment among his
fellow colonists.[17]

It was not only his neighbors who felt harassed by Ancheta, according to some local officials, who noted his involvement in the selling of fictitious land titles to Mr. Thompson, an American rancher
who later accumulated a substantial amount of property in northern
Chihuahua.[18] But while Ancheta's past transgressions and participation in suspicious activities contributed to the violence he met in
early January 1892, the catalyst for the revolt was his collaboration
with Bouquet and their dubious surveying and acquisition of the colony's lands. It was this dispute that set the stage for Ancheta's murder.
His election victory was simply the proverbial straw that broke the
burro's back.

[16] "Sangines a Díaz, 9 Enero 1892," CPD, Telegramos, Doc. #342; In this telegram
to Díaz just two days after the revolt began, Sangines incorrectly pointed out
that "Han muerto cinco de los nuestros," a number that would later be reduced
to three government officials. What is interesting to note, as the chapter will
illustrate, is that although Ancheta and the others are described as *nuestros* in
the aftermath, and although the colony is described in glowing terms in the
initial phases of settlement, the language describing this colony will shift negatively thereafter.

[17] "Carta de Ahumada a Díaz, 10 Enero 1892"; CPD, Correspondencia, Doc. #132.

[18] "Secretaria de Hacienda a Secretaria de Fomento, 28 Agosto 1884," in AHTN
1.21 (06), Exp. 733, "Colonia de La Ascensión. El gobernador del Estado remite
una solicitud de los pobladores del Valle de la Ascensión quienes piden terrenos
para formar una Colonia."

Eyewitness Accounts of the Killings

The details surrounding the humiliation, beating, and death of Rafael Ancheta are revealed through eyewitness accounts of participants in the revolt. As historian Shahid Amin said, "the speech of humble folk is not normally recorded for posterity, it is wrenched from them in courtrooms and inquisitorial trials."[19] These testimonies recovered and recorded in La Ascensión just weeks after the event tell us much about local feelings toward Ancheta and enrich earlier accounts and histories that overlooked these regional particulars.[20]

Unlike public executions in which the person on trial is relieved of his position with a quick death, Ancheta was not simply shot, or merely lynched, or banished from the community. They "beat him in an atrocious manner," according to one eyewitness. Each of these acts of brutality and violence involved a conscious act imbued with meaning and conveying a particular message. As sociologist Carlos M. Vilas has argued with respect to violence and lynchings, "Beating makes the individual an undifferentiated participant in the crowd and even endows him/her with certain anonymity, as his/her action reinforces a collective dimension which, in the image of the lynchers, favors the idea that it is 'the community,' 'the people,' 'the villages' (los pueblos) who does the lynching, at the same time that it hides the individual involvement."[21] The written record bears repeating when officials describe the killings as the "most treacherous and cowardly [of] assassinations" at the hands of the rebels of La Ascensión.[22]

Even though the death was brutal and "atrocious," the killing and the manner in which Ancheta was killed illustrate a level of calculated violence that requires some analysis. My intention is neither to glorify violence nor to shock; rather, I attempt to demonstrate that this rebellion was not a spontaneous and disorganized event but a

---

[19] See Shahid Amin, *Event, Metaphor, Memory: Chauri Chaura, 1922–1992,* (Berkeley: University of California Press, 1995), 1–6.

[20] Pozo Marrero, "Dos Movimientos Populares"; Almada, *La revolución en el estado de Chihuahua*; and Jesús Ramírez Caloca, "Ascensión," *Boletín de la Sociedad Chihuahuense de Estudios Históricos* 5, número 6 (20 Agosto 1944): 245–60.

[21] Carlos M. Vilas, "By their Own Hands: Mass Lynchings in Contemporary Mexico," *Southwestern Journal of Law and Trade in the Americas,* (2001/2002).

[22] "Letter Addressed to Miguel Ahumada, 8 Enero 1892," CPD, Correspondencia, Doc. #133; the term *asesinatos mas cobardes alevosos* taken from "Carrillo a Díaz, 10 Enero 1892," CPD, Telegramos, Doc. #364.

calculated and conscious demonstration with intended consequences. And the manner in which he was killed is subject to the same examination as the act of resistance itself: hence, violence is a form of communication.

According Dr. Montero's sworn testimony after examining the bodies, Ávalos Salazar died as a result of a bullet wound fired from a .44 caliber pistol, or perhaps a rifle.[23] Sifuentes, the other government official killed in the events, was also shot by "a bullet in the chest that deprived him of life, passing through the left lung."[24] By contrast, the killing of Ancheta was not so simple or merciful.

In his coroner's report describing the deaths of these three government officials, Dr. Montero noted that Sifuentes and Ávalos were shot once. From this, it would appear that the intent was to kill them quickly (even if that was not the result in the case of the latter). The report states that Ancheta was tortured before he was killed. Clearly the intent was to prolong his suffering. He was shot three times and beaten to the point where the physician could not make out where one bruise ended and another began. His left leg and foot had been dislocated. His neck and wrists were scarred from the thick rope used to drag him to the mill of Remigio Saenz.

Unlike the single-gunshot deaths of Sifuentes and Ávalos Salazar, Ancheta's death reveals a much more systematic, calculated, and organized public execution, one intended to send a message and to voice public outrage over an issue that had been manipulated, coerced, and ultimately (as perceived by the people of La Ascensión) legitimized politically by the Mexican government when Ancheta was "elected" municipal president in late 1891. The three gunshot wounds did not kill him; they only served to cause him more pain. One of the bullets entered his chest on the left side and exited on the right (just under the collarbone), while another bullet entered his abdominal area on the left side and exited on the right. The third bullet wound was to his left leg, just above the knee – which was already dislocated. There was a large lesion on the right side of his face, and his eyes, lip, and face were very swollen and heavily bruised.[25] And although the doctor believed the wound on the right side of his face to be the result of gunshot flesh

[23] "Reconocimiento del herido Ávalos Salazar por el Dr. Montero," AMCJ, Caja 1892, Núm. 5395.
[24] Ibid.
[25] "Juzgado Menor de La Ascensión." In AMCJ, Caja 1892, Núm. 5395.

wound, eyewitness reports tell us that it was most likely from an axe wielded by one of the land claimants, Julián Pérez.[26]

The individuals who witnessed the death of Ancheta also provided the testimony that this narrative is built on. It should be noted that many of those involved would eventually renounce their participation in the rebellion when they pleaded with the state governor for leniency in the days following the killing. Indeed, once federal forces arrived to quell the uprising, a number of the inhabitants and rioters were willing to provide testimony to the military officials taking note of the revolt.[27] But, significantly, some did, and one of the most descriptive testimonies was from Canuto Montano, whose testimony corroborated other regional, federal, and "insiders," accounts, as well as historical memory.

Montano was forty-five years old, a married laborer, and a neighbor of the municipality. When interrogators asked where he was between January 6 and January 9, Montano responded that he witnessed people heading toward the mill, some of them mounted on horses. Joining the gathering crowd, Montano recognized Sifuentes, who was later shot. He could also see a wounded Ancheta lying in the vicinity of the mill and then watched as Juan Mestas, Bernardo Duran, Decidero Chávez, Félix Lara, Francisco Sainz, and Julián Pérez "took him outside and shot at him." According to Montano, Ancheta pleaded with his captors to bring over his only daughter, requesting that "they take over his daughter in order to give her a blessing." Decidero Chávez, according to the testimony, then pulled out his "member" and told Ancheta "here is your daughter" and proceeded to urinate on him. Thereafter Julián Pérez hit Ancheta against the side of his head with a pickaxe. The other *revoltosos* then threw the body in the aqueduct and continued with their efforts to fortify the mill and prepare for the government response they knew would soon arrive.[28]

The aforementioned description by this witness is worth analyzing. For one, the disrespect paid to this government official just before his death was clearly intended to relay a message. When Ancheta asked his captors to bring his daughter in order that he might give her a blessing, and perhaps that she might bless him as well, he is told by

[26] Pérez will eventually be sentenced to capital punishment for his involvement in this revolt.

[27] An example of these recantations can be seen in Paul Vanderwood, *The Power of God Against the Guns of Government: Religious Upheaval in Mexico at the Turn of the Nineteenth Century*, (Stanford: Stanford University Press, 1998).

[28] "Indagatorio de Canuto Montano," AMCJ, Caja 1892, Núm. 5395.

a rebel, "here is your daughter" as he displays his penis. Chávez's sexual insinuation that the daughter will surely also be given her own "blessing" as soon as Ancheta is dead turns to mocking when he then urinates on him. With this humiliation, even the last vestiges of an honorable death are reduced to insults intended to further antagonize and torture Ancheta.

These actions are not only reminiscent of the violence described in the historiography of the colonial period, but also recounted in a recent sociological survey of 103 contemporary lynchings in Mexico from 1987–98.[29] Carlos M. Vila's extensive sociological study concludes that "In all cases the lynchings appear as a response to actions actually or presumably committed by the lynched that strongly offend the lynchers. In lynchings committed by eye-witnesses the reaction is immediate to the action that triggers them, and in several cases they were conducted by the same people hurt by the actions of the offenders. In these situations lynchings imply a mechanical appeal to the principle of 'an eye for an eye,' which is not confined however to this specific type of lynching."[30] Violence, hence, is intended to relay a particular kind of communication that in this case is carried out by those defrauded of their lands. Those that tortured and later killed the municipal president were to a certain degree communicating the kind of treatment they felt they had received from Ancheta.

The various types of wounds – bruises, lacerations, gunshots – are also telling in this case, since they suggest that the death of Ancheta was intended to be painful and degrading. As Vila argues with respect to this sort of action, "In contrast to the cold or distant character of a gunshot, and to the comparatively easy identification of who pulled the trigger, the beating, the hanging, the fire, increase the feeling of direct personal involvement in the commission of the act, without anyone being able to be held responsible individually, or feel individually responsible for the final, additive outcome."[31] The other two victims,

---

[29] For the colonial period in Mexico, please consult William B. Taylor, who examines 142 cases of judicial investigations between 1680–1811 in *Drinking, Homicide and Rebellion in Colonial Mexican Villages* (Stanford: Stanford University Press, 1979).

[30] Carlos M. Vilas, "Linchamiento: Venganza, Castigo e Injusticia en Escenarios de Inseguridad," *El Cotidiano 20; 131*, (Universidad Autónoma Metropolitana-Azcapotzalco: Mayo/Junio 2005): 20–6.

[31] Carlos M. Vilas, "(In) justicia por mano propia: linchamientos en México contemporáneo," *Revista Mexicana de Sociología, LXIII, numero 1*, (2001): 131–60.

Sifuentes and Ávalos, died from gunshot wounds to their bodies, not their faces, so their bodies could be displayed in an open casket before and during the funeral, the practice of the day. By contrast, Ancheta's body was dragged, beaten, and severely maimed, thus preventing the display of his body prior to burial. The repeated attacks upon Ancheta's person suggest an anger and furor satiated only with the final blow of the pickaxe to the head.

The Quelling of the Revoltosos

Attempts to forestall revolt began weeks prior to the actual event. It seemed as though Ancheta could tell the future and foresee the death that awaited when, on the morning of January 6, he wrote to the *jefe político* (political chief) of Ciudad Juárez about the social and tumultuous conditions of La Ascensión. He described how past crimes in the colony remained unsolved due to the lack of a police presence in that area. He asserted that the need for a substantial police force would not only assist in the investigation and enforcement of the laws but would also serve as a deterrent for those "malefactors" who saw the proximity of the border as a license to live out their "bad lives" along the Chihuahuan frontier. Ancheta proposed a detachment of twenty-five men to provide local authorities with an effective means to enforce the law.[32] His request was justified, he maintained, because of the number of crimes committed in the colony in recent memory. In a sad coincidence, the letter was sent on the very day that this municipal president met his death by the very individuals he believed mocked the law and then migrated north across the border in search of refuge.

Ancheta cited an incident in which an armed assault on an elderly man named Arcadio Carvajal went unpunished because of the lack of an organized policing body to persecute malefactors who, in only a few hours, "trespass the frontiers of the country." Not long after that there was an assassination attempt on one Cecilio Guigon, whose left arm was "torn to pieces" by a bullet fired into his home but that penetrated his door. The wound, in Ancheta's words, caused grave injury, and the crime remained unsolved because of the same reason: There was no police unit to persecute the criminals that carried out these crimes.[33] He

[32] "Carta de Ancheta a Jefe Político, Distrito Bravos," 6 Enero 1892; AMCJ, Caja 1892, Núm. 5395.
[33] "Ancheta al Jefe Político, Distrito Bravos," 6 Enero 1892; AMCJ, Caja 1892, Núm. 5395.

mentioned twice the proximity of the border to La Ascensión and the relative ease of escaping to the other side without reprisals from U.S. or Mexican authorities.

Being in a "settlement that was isolated in a desert and next to the American frontier makes this place more purposeful for those people of bad living to commit crimes that almost always remain enveloped in a most irritating impunity," Ancheta wrote in his letter.[34] The relative isolation of this new settlement along the northern frontier also lent the colony an air of "impunity," whereby the vast and open terrain surrounding it provided a distance, and therefore freedom, from centralized authorities in the United States and Mexico.

Ancheta's purpose in writing the letter to the political chief of Ciudad Juárez was threefold: to request a detachment of a twenty-five-man police force; to highlight the crimes committed in the past and therefore justify his request; and finally, to illustrate how the isolation of the town, coupled with the close proximity of the U.S. border, facilitated and encouraged crime among those who enjoyed "bad living."

But, in one of those moments of historical irony, the detachment of twenty-five men arrived only after the fatal axe blow to his head. The response from the Porfirian administration, although swift and effective, came too late to save Ancheta's life. Telegrams sent immediately after the outbreak of the rebellion in La Ascensión illustrate the gravity of the situation as Díaz wasted little time in orchestrating the response to quell the uprising in the borderlands. The response to this particular situation can be broken down into a few simple processes intended to squelch this rebellion and quell the contagion of revolt to neighboring colonies, towns, and malcontents in the area. The first step was the efficient communication between the border and the periphery, beginning with Lechuga's first report to the *jefe politico* and followed by the military orchestration from the neighboring garrisons and the extradition of the rebels from abroad.

Controlling and containing the revolt entailed military and rhetorical moves intended to silence any and all opposition to the regime, whether from within or from without. The military quelling of the rebels was followed by complementary moves employed in the aftermath of the revolt when the escaped rebels sought immunity across the border and claimed U.S. citizenship. The migration of repatriates

34 Ibid.

to New Mexico produces yet another set of questions that have to do with examining a population that has not only been resettled three times within a generation, but one whose members transgress an international boundary with such impunity. This fluidity has been overlooked in all of the past literature that attempts to explain the rebellion and the colonization of the northern frontiers of the republic during the nineteenth century.

Although described as a "regional occurrence," the 1892 Revolt of La Ascensión shares a historiography that is emplotted as one of rebellion and nationalism.[35] It continues to be a source of interest to historians, even as various government officials during the period questioned the very "transnationality" of this *motín* by arguing that the revolt of La Ascensión was of a local nature. Or following the words telegraphed to President Díaz by way of Chihuahuan governor Lauro Carrillo's description of the "riot" immediately after it surfaced in 1892: "in reality the incident of La Ascensión has no other character than that of a vile revenge exercised against the President, and two most cowardly and treacherous murders; but because of the rest, there is no political cause nor revolutionary goals, nor have these men been in combination with any outside elements."[36] This observation is understandable given the source of the citation; however, given the other factors discussed, historical analysis cannot afford to take these observations as all encompassing.

Recasting the Repatriates: From Repatriating Modernity to Repatriating Revolt

Influenced by the anthropological fieldwork done by Ana María Alonso in her historical ethnography of Namiquipa, I would also suggest that the Ascensiónenses were cast by the Porfirian regime as ingrates and drunkards after the rebellion, whereas beforehand these repatriates were imagined as "agents of modernization," colonists who would populate

---

[35] Pozo Marrero, "Dos Movimientos Populares en el Noroeste de Chihuahua; Almada, *La revolución en Chihuahua*, I; 93–106; Ramírez Caloca, "Ascensión," 245–60.

[36] "Lauro Carrillo a Porfirio Díaz, 10 Enero 1892," CPD, Telegramos #364; Original: "En realidad el incidente de La Ascensión no tiene otro carácter que el de una venganza ruin ejercida contra el Presidente, y dos asesinatos mas cobardes alevosos; pero por lo demás, no hay ninguna causa política ni miras revolucionarias, ni han estado estos hombres en combinación con elemento alguno de fuera."

the frontier regions and ward off the "Apache menace" – the symbol
of "barbarity" during that period. Or, to use Alonso's apt description
of the Namiquipans: the "one-time agents of 'civilization'…subse-
quently became redefined by the state and elites as obstacles to 'order'
and 'progress.'"[37] In much the same vein, the people of La Ascensión
were framed by Porfirian military and political figures in negative terms
whereas in the previous generation these repatriates were imagined as
modern stalwarts of progress and civilization, and their repatriation, it
was believed, would help modernize Mexico and populate the northern
regions.

This framing needs to be considered in the context of the frontier rebellions and insurrections of the time. Not only was Díaz bom-
barded by nationwide revolts, but his regime was dealing with tensions
involving the border, particularly the openness of the frontier and the
access to arms.[38] Also, revolutionary journalists and politically minded
Mexican Americans across the border served as a refuge for political
prisoners, and neighboring Mexican-origin communities had long ago
become safe havens for many a revolutionary looking to overthrow the
Díaz regime.[39]

So when the colonists first arrived in this area in the early 1870s
the Mexican government saw their colonization in terms of *realpolitik*
coupled with a healthy dose of nationalist rhetoric. The granting of
water, wood, and land rights to the colony was done at the expense
of two minor landowners in the area, who were told quite matter of
factly of the importance of repatriating so many Mexicans that reside in foreign territory, because their presence would serve to "augment the number of arms, of creating new settlements, of populating
our borders, and of impeding the invasions of the savages."[40] Early

---

[37] Alonso, *Thread of Blood: Colonialism*, 7; also Nugent, *Spent Cartridges of
      Revolution*, passim.
[38] For rebellions and uprisings along the border see David Dorado Romo, *Ringside
      Seat to a Revolution: An Underground Cultural History of El Paso and Juarez,
      1893–1923*, (El Paso: Cinco Puntos Press, 2005); Vanderwood, *The Power of God*;
      Katz and Lloyd, *Porfirio Díaz frente al descontento popular*, passim; Almada, *La
      revolución en Chihuahua*, I; 93–106.
[39] See Romo, *Ringside Seat to a Revolution*, 15–75.
[40] "Carta al Señor Ministro, 12 Marzo 1885," AHTN, (1.361) (06), Legajo 10,
      Exp. 341, Documento 10, "Los colonos de La Ascensión, Chihuahua piden se les
      asegure la propiedad de las aguas de 'La Palotada' y 'Rancho Esparseño', 1887."
      My italics.

on, the repatriate colony of La Ascención was described as one of the "successes" of the Departamento de Fomento, prompting Díaz to state that it "would become one of the most important towns in the north."[41]

These expectations were dashed once news surfaced that the people of La Ascensión were in open revolt against regional authorities. When Miguel Ahumada testified about the events that unfolded in La Ascensión on January 6, 1892, he explained that the rebellion was caused "by a bad Mexican, the kind that are raised in the United States who then returns talking negatively about their country."[42] Whereas previous government discourse lauded the potential to "repatriate modernity" in order to "civilize the frontiers," those in open revolt were now repatriating bad ideas from the United States that speak negatively of the *patria*. The revolt was portrayed in a less temperate tone by the governor when he noted that "the uprising of La Ascensión was originated by drunkenness and probably some advice from the independent candidate, Lic. Urrutia, without the intention that things would reach the proportions of a crime."[43] Sangines chimed in with his own observation of the events and the inhabitants of the area generalizing *in toto* that "the major part of the incited rebels pertains to that class of people that go wherever life takes them."[44] In other words, those Ascensionenses who partook in the rebellion of 1892 were uncontrollable drunken vagabonds that simply took bad advice, according to Sangines.

To further marginalize and reframe this group as a "class of people that go wherever life takes them," Sangines sought to historicize the event almost two months after the revolt in an extended letter to his godfather, President Díaz. "It has been about twenty years that there was a riot in La Mesilla, because of some elections, which resulted in some deaths," he wrote. "This caused a considerable number of individuals that partook in the aforementioned riot to emigrate from the neighboring Republic and come to our country; these individuals

[41] González Navarro, *La colonización en México*, 121.
[42] "Carta de Ahumada a Díaz, 10 Enero 1892," CPD, Correspondencia, Doc. #132; Original: "un mal mexicano de esos que se crían en los Estados Unidos y regresan expresándose mal de su país."
[43] "Carta de Carrillo a Díaz, 18 Enero 1892," CPD, Correspondencia, Doc. #271–276; "Carta de Sangines a Díaz, 11 Enero 1892," Doc. #1321.
[44] "Carta de Sangines a Díaz, 11 Enero 1892," CPD; Correspondencia, Doc. #1320.

were established in what is today La Ascensión, in an extension of five sites of land that was donated to them by the Government."[45] Here he collapses the 1892 revolt into that of 1871, thus suggesting that there was something endemic about this "rebellious repatriate colony" and making them appear as criminals before any crime is committed.

The governor of the state of Chihuahua added to this trope of pathological rebelliousness, saying, "I have knowledge that that same colony when they came to Mexico, did so fleeing 'Las Cruces' due to an identical event that they executed with the local judge."[46] With such rhetoric, the founding of the colony was no longer lauded as a benefit to the nation but blamed for being part of a rebellious pathology shared by those "bad Mexican(s), the kind that are raised in the United States who then return talking negatively about their country."[47]

This is an illustration of how a once promising repatriate colony is quickly demonized and marginalized by those in power once its usefulness has been exhausted, or until the behavior of its members is considered threatening. The subsequent flight of the leaders of this revolt led the Porfirian administration into the messy diplomatic arena of extradition politics, and the continued condemnation of the repatriates served to expedite the re-re-repatriation (or extradition) of these colonists. Articulations of national belonging, by both the colonizer and the colonized, also shift as conditions on the ground change.

THE FLIGHT TO LA MESILLA AND RECTIFICATION OF SURVEYS

When Sangines arrived in the colony almost five days after the insurrection had begun, the rebels fled in all directions north and south of La Ascensión. Between thirty-five and forty of the men fled to El Cerro de la Cal. Fifty-five to sixty of the men were later arrested, tried, and exonerated of their role in the events of January 6, 1892. Several others fled across the border into New Mexico and claimed U.S. citizenship

---

45 "Carta de Sangines a Díaz, 26 Febrero 1892," CPD; Correspondencia, Doc. #4694.
46 "Carta de Lauro Carrillo a Díaz, 25 Febrero 1892," CPD, Correspondencia, #3470.
47 "Carta de Ahumada a Díaz, 10 Enero 1892," CPD, Correspondencia, Doc. #132.

as a way to try and avoid extradition to Mexico. Among those who
fled across the border, most of them were later caught and held in
the jailhouse in Las Cruces, New Mexico. E. Provencio, the political
chief of Ciudad Juárez, traveled directly to where a number of these
rebels were jailed in Las Cruces and wrote directly to the governor of
Chihuahua regarding the possibility that these outlaws might claim
U.S. citizenship.

When Provencio arrived in Las Cruces to claim the rebels and return
them to Ciudad Juárez for processing, he was told that he would have
to wait until it was proven that they were indeed Mexican citizens and
not U.S. citizens as they claimed. Even so, the governor of New Mexico
assured him that they would be handed over irrespective of their citizenship status, particularly given the nature of the documentation of
events presented. According to Provencio, "After we spoke, [the gov-
ernor] assured me that in light of the documents that the imprisoned
would be delivered, but that we had to hear them because they had
appealed to Washington alleging to be American citizens."[48] Given the
location of this colony, it was further suggested that an outfit of soldiers
be stationed at the border to prevent any more flights, since those that
managed to get across dragged the Mexican government into the messy
arena of extradition politics.[49]

The political connections that Remigio Saenz enjoyed when he
was a resident of La Mesilla twenty years earlier apparently resurfaced
once more in 1892. Seen as the most important of the escapees, Saenz
had wealth "with which to pay," according to Chihuahua's governor,
Lauro Carrillo. Either because of his money or his political connections,
Saenz succeeded in claiming U.S. citizenship while all the others were
eventually extradited to Chihuahua, where they faced several charges,
including capital murder.[50]

But it was not merely a case of the rebels claiming U.S. citizenship; they also included requests for amnesty in their petitions.
Amnesty was later denied to all but Saenz, who continued to hold
on to it throughout the yearlong extradition process. According to

[48] "Carta de E. Provencio a Lauro Carrillo, 6 Febrero 1892," CPD, Correspondencia,
Doc. #1842.

[49] "Telégramo de Sangines a Díaz, 22 Enero 1892," CPD, Telegramos, #608.

[50] "Carta de Lauro Carrillo a Díaz, 23 Febrero 1892," CPD, Correspondencia, Doc.
#3471; documentation exists that also paints Atilano Baca as the leader of this
particular revolt. See "Nacionalidad Mexicana a los Colonos, 1892," AHSRE,
3742–6.

Carrillo, he was able to prove the Mexican citizenship of each of the rebels, including Saenz's long list of citizenship qualifications, which included land ownership, voting records in La Ascensión, and past political offices held there. But the U.S. judge continued to grant the well-connected Saenz opportunities to prove otherwise. According to Carrillo, the judge, "in his eagerness to help...Saenz...opened avenues so that [Saenz] could present evidence, and declared that his detention was not prosecuted because he was not implicated in the assassinations of La Ascensión."[51] Eventually Saenz returned to La Ascensión on his own where he was later arrested by local authorities as a Mexican citizen.

This episode illustrates yet another problem with the process of repatriation during this period, and this has to do with the continued ambiguity about citizenship for colonists. Because the state did not issue documents conferring Mexican citizenship in practice, a number of these colonists had retained U.S. citizenship.[52] This episode, argued the Mexican consulate in Deming, New Mexico, proved that "even when the colonization laws say that all individuals that enter the country do so as Mexican citizens, I think it necessary that documents are expedited to them in order to make valid the citizenship that our constitution requires."[53] Much like the faulty surveying of Bouquet and the problems surrounding appropriate title to lands, the state appears to have overlooked the question of Mexican citizenship for the Ascensionenses.

---

[51] Ibid.

[52] Mexico's 1883 Land and Colonization Law did in fact confer Mexican citizenship for those entering as colonists. As such, the colony of La Ascensión fell under this particular set of laws and agreements. See Artículo 13. "Los colonos serán considerados con todos los derechos y obligaciones que a los mexicanos y a los extranjeros en su caso, concede e impone la Constitución Federal, gozando de las exenciones temporales que les otorga la presente ley; pero en todas las cuestiones que se susciten, sean de la clase que fueren, quedarán sujetos a las decisiones de los tribunales de la República con absoluta exclusión de toda intervención extraña." A copy of the 1883 Land Law is located in *Memoria, Secretaría de Fomento*, 1883–5.

[53] "Carta del Consul en Deming, NM a la Secretaría de Relaciones Exteriores, 14 Mayo 1892" in AHSRE, 3742–6, "Nacionalidad Mexicana a los Colonos, 1892." Original: "aun cuando las leyes de colonización dice que todo individuo que entre al pais como cuidadanos Mexicanos, creo necesario que se les expidan los documentos que para ser valida la cuidadania que exije nuestra constitución."

The extradition cases of the rest of the rebels caught the attention of many border Mexicans. Although research is needed to more fully examine the sentiments of the region and the sort of publicity this case generated in southern New Mexico and west Texas, from observations provided by agents returning with the extradited men, there is evidence to suggest borderlanders were aggravated by this case. According to Sangines's telegram to Díaz suggesting the reinforcement of the border region, "the extradition of the criminals of La Ascensión has exalted the spirit of the Mexicans residing along the border on the American side, and this causes some armed groups to marauder throughout on the side indicated."[54] The presence of such groups, at the very least, provides ample evidence that local communities were aware of the rebellion and the causes that may have contributed to the death of three government officials. Mexicans residing along the borderlands clearly sided with the rebels and showed their dissatisfaction by "marauding" the frontier in their "exalted spirit." With this background in mind, one could surmise, federal officials sought to correct the grievances of the past by moving quickly to rectify the past mistakes involving land surveys.

RECTIFICATION OF SURVEYS AND THE DISAPPEARANCE OF BOUQUET'S SURVEY

When a commission was eventually sent to the colony of La Ascensión, engineer Enrique Hijar y Haro made sure that the measurements were scientifically and arithmetically accurate. By the end of the year, in December 1892, the engineer awaited orders and his surveying instruments in order to proceed with the rectification of the lands in question.

When Hijar y Haro requested the plans and methods that Bouquet employed when surveying the lands, and which gave rise to the bloody revolt earlier that year, he was told by the judge of Ciudad Juárez that the surveys were not available. According to Hijar y Haro, when he ordered Bouquet to deliver his plan of the division of land, he "declared that he had no plan, for that reason complicating the location of plots and solares." Thus, in the titles he'd sent off for registration, there is no data of orientation. Also, many colonists who held

---

[54] "Telegramo de Sangines a Díaz, 26 Febrero 1892," CPD, Telegramos, #1442.

titles did not know the exact place where their lands were situated.[55] It seems that much like Saenz had enjoyed the legal protection of authorities in Las Cruces, Bouquet would also capitalize on his superior connections in Ciudad Juárez and successfully appeal to his own ignorance of surveying when the lawsuit by the colonists was subsequently prosecuted.

But the "disappearance" of Bouquet's original surveying did not interfere or weaken the resolve of Hijar y Haro as he proceeded to take his own measurements of the colony. After he completed the task, he illustrated for the federal government the erroneous survey that Bouquet undertook and why so many colonists were left out of the original plot granted by the government. According to the engineer only a week after his arrival in the colony, "I believe it prudent to evidence this error that seems due to an arithmetic mistake committed by the former overseer of this colony."[56]

However, this evidence of "arithmetic mistakes" by Bouquet, although compelling and "scientifically" conclusive by the surveyor's more accurate survey of the colony, was for naught. The lawsuit filed by the colonists of La Ascensión, although detailing the many abuses committed by Bouquet, was dismissed on a legal technicality: Bouquet was not qualified to survey the lands in question and could therefore not be held totally accountable for these "arithmetic mistakes."[57]

CONCLUSION

The revolt that surfaced in La Ascensión in early 1892 culminated with the public lynching of Rafael Ancheta – the face of state power. I maintain that this was a conscious and calculated reaction to repeated

55 "Carta de Enrique Haro a Secretaria de Fomento, 1 Marzo 1893," AHTN, (1.361), (06), Legajo 10, Exp. 344, "Se Comunica al Ing. Enrique Hijar y Haro para que se practique unas diligencias de rectificación en los terrenos de la Colonia La Ascensión, Chihuahua, 1892–3.
56 "Haro a Secretaria de Fomento, 8 Marzo 1893," AHTN, (1.361), (06), Legajo 10, Exp. 344, "Se Comunica al Ing. Enrique Hijar y Haro para que se practique unas diligencias de rectificación en los terrenos de la Colonia La Ascensión, Chihuahua, 1892–3.
57 "Informe de Ing. Hijar y Haro a Secretaria de Fomento, 10 Abril 1893," AHTN, (1.361) (06), Legajo 10, Exp. 345.

and unaddressed grievances against government officials. Given the recovery of heretofore unexamined eyewitness reports uncovered in various depositories throughout the United States and Mexico, the evidence provides enough rich material to describe in great detail the manner in which this calculated violence was exacted upon these government officials. Although barbaric in its communication, the violence that visited Ancheta in early January of 1892 should not be interpreted as prepolitical but as a form of communication intended to illustrate the frustration and anger over material interests. Or, as Vila has put it, "the brutality and cruelty present in many lynchings can be considered illustrations of the effect of perverse pedagogy…of the exercise of power by the ruling classes or state agencies."[58]

In the case of La Ascensión, Chihuahua, the problems with land titling and surveys were compounded by more aggressive land laws intended to free up more land for foreign investors and local power holders. Thus, although the Ascensionenses eventually resolved a number of the issues that sparked the 1892 rebellion, other problems would soon emerge to further undercut their claims to the land. For instance, by the time of the rebellion, Mormon and American settlers had already started colonizing these same areas and subsequently accrued substantial fortunes at the expense of their surrounding neighbors.[59] It was while amassing thousands of hectares of land that the people of La Ascensión decided to rebel against Ancheta that one New Year's Day. The same 1883 law that provided repatriates with preferential treatment when returning to the "homeland" became the primary vehicle for the sale of millions of acres of *terrenos baldíos* to U.S. and foreign interests, but primarily Mexican interests.[60]

Unlike a large body of literature that suggests that the Porfirian regime was cold to cases of displacement and dispossession, the fact that federal authorities would immediately rectify land claims in the months following this revolt raises a series of questions. How did the

---

[58] Vilas, "(In) justicia por mano propia, 131–60.

[59] The effects of these laws, Katz points out, "had a catastrophic impact on the free villagers of Chihuahua… making many of them landless laborers, forced to work outside their villages in order to survive." See Katz, *Pancho Villa*, 28–9.

[60] De Vos, "Una legislación de graves consecuencias, 76–113. He states on page 84, for instance, "En Chihuahua fueron tres familias a quienes se les concedieron 14,208,458 ha, es decir, más de la mitad de la superficie total del estado."

Ascensionenses interpret this response from the government? Did their revolt reveal to them that violence works? Or is rebellion the only way to get your grievances heard? Was this just standard operating procedure for the administration? Was the quick quelling of the rebellion precisely because the Porfirian administration saw the colony as a valuable representation for potential repatriates? We return to one of the concerns guiding this book: What does this rebellion tell us about how repatriates fared once living under a Mexican system of governance?

I have proudly affirmed that the Mexican nation extends beyond the territory enclosed by its borders...and Mexican immigrants are an important, a very important, part of that.

President Ernesto Zedillo to the
National Council of La Raza, 1997

Conclusion

REPATRIATING MODERNITY?

Throughout the nineteenth century, private, collective, and government-sponsored repatriations and their subsequent settlements took place in Mexico. For four decades following the Mexican American War, it is estimated that upward of twenty-five percent of ethnic Mexicans in California, Texas, and New Mexico may have returned to Mexico proper. These first repatriations were facilitated by an ongoing military tradition that frequently requested the settlement of this region with colonists from the northern frontiers. After implementation of the 1883 Land and Colonization Law that stood in as official immigration policy, and up to the time of the Mexican Revolution in 1910, sixty colonies would be established: Sixteen by the Díaz administration and forty-four by private companies. Mexicans and Mexican Americans populated eight of the sixteen colonies established by the government, or fifty percent. In the colonies founded by private companies, Mexicans repatriated from the United States composed almost twenty-five percent of the settlements during this thirty-five-year period.[1] These are the official numbers that we have, however, a more comprehensive study of this period might reveal a larger pattern that includes private and collective repatriations not mentioned in the final government tally.[2]

The repatriation of colonists from the United States to Mexican territory after the Mexican American War accomplished a number of objectives guided by the Mexican government's desire to consolidate

---

[1] Enrique Cortés, "Mexican Colonies During the Porfiriato." *Aztlán: International Journal of Chicano Studies Research* 10 (Fall 1979), 3–12.

[2] There were several requests for repatriation that I located at various archives and which were not recorded in the *Memorias* from *El Departamento de Fomento*.

the northern frontiers. Although the government deserves credit for
authoring laws encouraging the settlement of the northern frontiers
with new colonies such as El Remolino, La Mesilla, Guadalupe, Piedras
Negras, Nuevo Laredo, San Ignacio, and La Ascensión, these towns came
into existence largely out of the efforts of the settlers themselves. State
organization and financing of repatriation after the Mexican American
War was limited at best. Given the situation after the end of hostilities,
this is somewhat understandable. At the same time this assessment is
not in tune with more contemporary historiographical accounts that
described repatriation as a nationalist endeavor "in defense of la Raza"
or as one bent on "protecting Mexico de Afuera." Although laws and
decrees, as stated earlier, can be read as a nation's collective imagining
of itself, it is important to analyze the limits of such legislation, not to
mention the political uses and abuses of such discourse in the past, present, and future.[3]

The historiography on Mexican repatriation has not adequately
considered that practicality guided Mexican colonization policy. These
repatriate resettlements occurred in tandem with the quelling of Indios
Bárbaros along the northern frontiers of the republic. Moreover, Mexican
colonization and immigration policies were developed at a moment in
history that witnessed the migration of millions of Europeans to the
Western Hemisphere. Evidence for nationalist motivations notwithstanding, the overriding concern of the state was not so much the protection of citizens who continued to migrate toward the United States
as it was *realpolitik*, national security, and territorial integrity. In other
words, Mexico's nineteenth-century colonization policies were "determined by practical, rather than moral or ideological considerations."[4]
This practicality dictated addressing the challenges and opportunities
presented by the distinct populations and competing interests that came
together at the colonial frontier.

Though appearing on the surface as a nationalist project, repatriation
was designed to address preoccupations with ongoing Indian raids, northward Mexican migration, threats of more territorial losses, secessionist
movements that raised the specter of the Texan rebellion, and finally
the need to settle (modernize) the north with loyal citizens. Each of

---

[3] The phrase "Use and Abuse of History" is in reference to Friedrich Nietzsche's
    The Use and Abuse of History (1878), translated by Adrian Collins (New York:
    Macmillan Publishing, 1957).
[4] See *Oxford English Dictionary Online* (Oxford: Oxford University Press, 2007).

these concerns underscored deeper structural factors beyond nationalist sentiment.[5] As we have seen, the repatriation of Mexicans from the United States after the Mexican American War did not always have the intended consequence of simply settling the north. At times, and as has often been the case along a nation's frontiers, settlers returning from the United States (and borderlanders in general) had various worlds to compare and often did so to the detriment of both governments.

We can conclude that the repatriation of the migrants from the United States during the nineteenth century did not repatriate the modernity, progress, or the entrepreneurship that Vicente Fox Quesada alluded to as mentioned in the opening sentences of this book. Interesting, a lack of historical memory on the part of both Mexico and the diaspora persists amid the continued discourse of "returning to the homeland." During a presentation for the "International Day of the Migrant" in Tijuana, Baja California, President Felipe Calderón continued this trope of modernity alongside return migrants as he announced a new program, "Repatriación Humana." Here, President Calderón noted a pilot program in Baja California that could serve as a model for the country when he noted:

> With this effort, we ensure that our compatriots receive food and shelter when they require it, to count on medical attention in cases of emergency, that they can *formally validate knowledge acquired through their work experience in the United States*, that they have access to offers of temporary work and, of course, that they can communicate with their loved ones.[6]

---

5   Nationalism has its uses, and Claudio Lomnitz provides a more nuanced way of approaching the topic, I believe. For him, "the power of nationalism lies not so much in its hold on the souls of individuals (though this is not insignificant) as in the fact that it provides interactive frames in which the relationship between state institutions and various and diverse social relationships (family relationships, the organization of work, the definition of forms of property, and the regulation of public space) can be negotiated." See *Deep Mexico, Silent Mexico*, 13–14.

6   *El Presidente Calderón en el Día Internacional del Migrante*, 17 de Diciembre 2007; Discurso en Tijuana, Baja California. Original: "Con este esfuerzo nos aseguramos que nuestros compatriotas reciban comida y cobijo cuando así lo requieran, que cuenten con atención médica en casos de emergencia, que puedan validar formalmente los conocimientos adquiridos mediante su experiencia laboral en Estados Unidos, que tengan acceso a ofertas de trabajo temporal y, desde luego, que puedan comunicarse con sus seres queridos." My italics.

Almost four years after the announcement of "Repatriación Humana," today we continue to read headlines like "Tijuana no quiere repatriados" and dozens of accounts of repatriates returning to a more impoverished existence than the one they left in the first place.[7] The program, much like other projects that purport to protect the diaspora abroad, has become an instrument of corruption, extortion, and a species of modern day "administrative disorder."[8] Calderón seems destined to continue the policies of the past. A recent article by journalist Sandra Rodriguez Nieto lends credence to the idea that this recognizable contemporary return to the discourse of "protecting Mexico de Afuera" has not translated into an effective and cogent repatriation policy that addresses contemporary deportations.[9]

In all fairness to President Calderón, it is not only politicians that continue with this discourse of "returning to the homeland" more "modern" than those that have never left, but the intelligentsia as well. For instance, in a recent book, Jorge G. Castañeda, the Global Distinguished Professor of Politics and Latin American Studies at New York University, takes this running theme to its extreme when he posits the question in his latest book:

> [W]e will try to ascertain whether Mexicans in the United States, when placed in a different context, become different. There is almost a real-life, real-time experiment under way, involving millions of Mexicans about whom we know a great deal and can discover much more, who have decided, or been forced to decide, to transport themselves into an environment that is even more contradictory to their national character than the country they left behind ... can Mexicans acquire the

[7] Nohemi Barraza, "Deportados llegan sin un peso...y cada vez les dan menos apoyo," *El Diario de Juarez*, 9 Agosto 2011; Gastón Monge, "Mexicanos deportados de EU son 'carne de cañón' para el crimen organizado," *Linea Directa*, 19 Julio 2011; Krystel Gómez Sevilla, "Tijuana no quiere repatriados: Alcide," *El Sol de Tijuana*, 11 Julio 2011; Rogelio Rodíguez Mendoza, "Generan deportaciones graves repercusiones," *El Diario de Ciudad Victoria*, 5 Junio 2011; "Deportaciones rebasan capacidad de Matamoros," *La Nota Roja de Mexico*, 17 Julio 2011.

[8] For an interesting and comparative analysis of contemporary programs for Mexicans abroad, see Natasha Iskander, *Creative State: Forty Years of Migration and Development Policy in Morocco and Mexico* (Ithaca and London: Cornell University Press, 2010), 274–304.

[9] Sandra Rodríguez Nieto, "Falla México en proteger a migrantes," *El Diario de Ciudad Juárez*, 01 Septiembre 2007.

traits of a new national character, one truly compatible with their double nationality and double new reality: at home and abroad?[10]

After an extensive analysis laid out in a series of varying chapters, Professor Castañeda concludes that "there is certainly a change in a couple of traits of the Mexican national character: saving and respect for the law."[11] Here there is no room to enter into the dense and dangerous territory of literature on *lo Mexicano*, but the overall conclusion that Professor Castañeda reaches is that Mexicans need to become less Mexican and more American, and migrants in the United States serve as a "real life" example of how such changes can take place. As concluded in González Navarro's analysis of the supposed success of foreign versus Mexican colonies, Professor Castañeda seems to agree that success is measured by which individuals become more or less Mexicanized. In contrast to the disdain toward migrants and Mexicans in the United States à la Poniatowska and Paz that I noted in the introduction, here that idea is turned on its proverbial head. And this is not just my reading. According to a review by Richard Rodriguez, the well known writer and social commentator, Professor Castañeda's conclusions are "unprecedented…an acknowledgement of the notorious pocho as the best hope for Mexico…."[12]

The discourse of Mexico's "expanding boundaries" similarly falls short of going beyond nationalist rhetoric. Calderón Hinojosa provides another example: "I have said that Mexico does not stop at its border, that wherever there is a Mexican, there is Mexico."[13] Here he echoes an idea President Ernesto Zedillo expressed fifteen years earlier to a Latino rights organization. In that 1997 speech to the National Council of La Raza, the largest Latino rights organization in the United States, the president stated, "I have proudly affirmed that the Mexican nation extends beyond the territory enclosed by its borders … and Mexican immigrants are an important, a very

[10] Jorge G. Castañeda, *Mañana Forever? Mexico and the Mexicans*, (New York: Alfred A. Knopf, 2011), xvi.

[11] Ibid., 248.

[12] Richard Rodriguez, Book Review of *Mañana Forever? Mexico and the Mexicans* by Jorge G. Castañeda, Special to the *San Francisco Chronicle*, 28 May 2011, GF-2.

[13] James C. McKinley Jr., "Mexican President Assails US Measures on Migrants," *New York Times*, 3 September 2007.

important part of that."[14] The ideas here could not be made clearer, but practice leaves much to be desired.

Yet little evidence shows that "México de Afuera" enjoys the genuine protection of the Mexican government. In the Mexican presidential election of 2006 (whose legitimacy continues to be in question to this very day), Mexican migrants in the United States faced significant obstacles to obtain the right to vote in the presidential elections. They were thwarted by bureaucratic requirements that were unrealistic in relation to the lives of these Mexican migrants in the United States

Governments of Mexico, irrespective of party affiliation, have shown more interest in remittances than in the welfare of those expatriates who, according to Mexican news sources, have reduced the poverty level of Mexico by fifteen percent. Although remittances have reached a record high of between $16 billion and $20 billion, the government of Mexico only allocates $36 million (0.002 percent) in assistance to its migrants.[15] Additionally, of that $36 million, approximately seventy percent goes to the salaries of employees and functionaries of those immigrant programs, according to a 2005 article.[16]

The discourse of expanded Mexican boundaries may be an attempt to mend postwar trauma over the "loss" of Mexican territories over 150 years ago. In practice, however, the idea of a diasporic Mexican citizenry is intended for local consumption and has more to do with the very real economic viability of the emigrant community primarily situated with the territorial confines of the United States.[17]

By articulating this brief study on nineteenth-century colonization, the arguments laid out in this monograph have sought to historicize the relationship between the state of Mexico and the populations of Mexican origin residing north of the new border from 1848 until the close of the century. Even before the pivotal moment of the war between Mexico and the United States, movements of Mexican born citizens, by

---

[14] S. Lynne Walker, "Zedillo visits Chicago with Message of Reform," *Copley News Service*, 24 July 1997; see also, "Mexico's Insidious Designs?" *Washington Times*, 23 January 2003.

[15] Remittances in 2010 were calculated at $21.27 billion and constituted the "second largest source of foreign currency for Mexico after oil sales." See EFE, "Remittances in Mexico up Marginally in 2010," 2 February 2011. http://latino.foxnews.com/latino/money/2011/02/02/remittances-mexico-marginally/.

[16] Patricia Torres, Gabriel Xantomila, Jorge Vega, y Diarios de OEM, "Regatea Mexico apoyo a migrantes," *El Sol de San Luis*, 27 Marzo 2005, 1B.

[17] In 2010 remittances exceeded $21 billion.

force or by choice, can be traced back and forth across that border, and those remaining north of the Rio Bravo have in some sense been considered lost to the nation. In time this diaspora also came to be largely forgotten. Today Mexican society is again reclaiming its once forgotten diaspora. Yet we must recognize – informed by the *longue durée* of colonization practices of the past – that nationalist politics based solely on sentimentality are not only incorrect, but historically inaccurate.

Although these findings complement and build upon previous studies situated in sociology, history, and political science, it is important to point out more recent articulations of these questions for our contemporary world. As I write these final sentences, for instance, both governments today are unwilling to address the millions of undocumented Mexican migrants who reside in the United States, and the millions deported to Mexico are arriving more impoverished than when they left. I am reminded of Professor De La Garza's conclusions that "neither government has a history of being concerned about Chicanos [here, read migrants historicized], and there is no reason to expect that either will change its policies for altruistic reasons."[18] Whether because of local and regional politics, or due perhaps to the longest and most drawn out economic crisis since the Great Depression of 1929, neither the United States or Mexico have come to practical and pragmatic accord about how to accommodate the millions already in the United States or the millions who have already returned to Mexico. My hope is that this analysis of Mexican American colonization during the nineteenth century may contribute to providing a more nuanced and historical understanding of this process. Perhaps it may serve to generate a more modern and effective policy to accommodate today's "México de Afuera."

---

[18] De La Garza, "Chicanos and US Foreign Policy," 582. The term *Chicanos*, or *Chicamos*, was a term of derision before it was appropriated in the 1960s during the Chicana/o Movement. Manuel Gamio remarked on the use of the term when he mentioned that the "American-Mexicans" referred to recent Mexican migrants as "*cholos* or *chicamos*." See *Mexican Immigration to the United* States, 129.

Bibliography

ARCHIVES & LIBRARIES

THE UNITED STATES OF MEXICO

Estado de Chihuahua

Archivo Municipal de Ciudad Juárez, Biblioteca Arturo Tolentino

Archivo Municipal de La Ascensión, Archivo Histórico

Mediateca Municipal, Archivo Histórico del Honorable Ayuntamiento de Chihuahua

Mexico City

Archivo Colección Porfirio Díaz, Universidad Iberoamericana
    Ramo Correspondencia
    Ramo Telegramos

Archivo del Senado

Archivo Histórico Genaro Estrada, Secretaría de Relaciones Exteriores
    Archivo de Concentraciones
    Archivo de la Embajada de Mexico en los Estados Unidos de América

Archivo Histórico de Terrenos Nacionales, Secretaría de la Reforma Agraria
    Ramo del Estado de Chihuahua (06)
        Serie Baldíos (1.21)
        Serie Colonias (1.361)
        Serie Diversos (1.29)
    Ramo del Estado de Sonora (22)
    Ramo de la Republica (32)
        Serie Baldíos (1.21)
        Serie Diversos (1.29)

Archivo Histórico Militar Mexicano, Secretaría de la Defensa Nacional

Bibliotecas

Biblioteca, Archivo General de la Nación

Biblioteca Arturo Tolentino, Ciudad Juárez, Chihuahua

Biblioteca Francisco Xavier Clavijero, Universidad Iberoamericana

Biblioteca José María Lafragua, Secretaría de Relaciones Exteriores

Biblioteca Miguel Lerdo de Tejada, Secretaría de Hacienda

Biblioteca Nacional, Universidad Nacional Autónoma de México Fondo Reservado

Dirección General de Bibliotecas, Cámara de Diputados, Honorable Congreso de la Unión

The United States of America

AMHERST, MASSACHUSETTS

W.E.B. Dubois Library, University of Massachusetts-Amherst

AUSTIN, TEXAS

Center for American History, University of Texas at Austin
  Archivo Histórico del Estado de Saltillo
Nettie Lee Benson Latin American Collection, University of Texas at Austin

CHICAGO, ILLINOIS

Harold Washington Public Library
John T. Richardson Library, DePaul University
Joseph M. Regenstein Library, The University of Chicago

EL PASO, TEXAS

El Paso Public Library, Border Heritage Center
University Library, University of Texas at El Paso
  Department of Archives and Special Collections

HOUSTON, TEXAS

Houston Central Public Library
M.D. Anderson Library, The University of Houston

LAS CRUCES, NEW MEXICO

Department of Archives and Special Collections, New Mexico State University

SAN ANTONIO, TEXAS

Elizabeth Huth Coates Library, Trinity University
John Peace Library, University of Texas at San Antonio
San Antonio College Library
San Antonio Public Library

NEWSPAPERS CONSULTED

Christian Science Monitor
Copley News Service
Desert Winds Magazine
El Clamor Público
El Diario de Ciudad Juárez
El Diario de Ciudad Victoria
El Sol de San Luis
El Sol de Tijuana
La Jornada
La Nota Roja de Mexico
Linea Directa
New Mexico Magazine
Pacific News Service
San Francisco Chronicle
The Arizona Daily Star
The New York Times
The Washington Times
Washington Informer

PRIMARY PUBLISHED SOURCES

Alcaraz, Ramón, et al. *Apuntes para la historia de la guerra entre México y los Estados Unidos* (México: Tipografía de Manuel Payno, 1848).

Almonte, Juan N. *Proyectos de Leyes Sobre Colonización* (México: Ignacio Cumplido, 26 Enero 1852).

Azcarate, Juan Francisco de. *Dictamen Presentado a la Soberana Junta Gubernativa del Imperio Mexicano por la Comisión de Relaciones Exteriores en 29 de Diciembre de 1821, Primero de Independencia* (México: Publicaciones de la Secretaria de Relaciones Exteriores, 1932).

Bartlett, John Russell. *Personal Narrative of Explorations and Incidents in Texas, New Mexico, California, Sonora, and Chihuahua, Connected with the United States and Mexican Boundary Commission, During the Years 1850, 1851, 1852, and 1853*, 2 vols. (New York: D. Appleton & Company, 1854; republished in facsimile by Rio Grande Press: Chicago, 1965).

Bautista Alberdi, Juan. *Bases y puntos de partida para la organización política de la República Argentina* (Buenos Aires, 1852).

Bustamante, Carlos María de. *México durante su guerra con los Estados Unidos.* In Genaro García, *Documentos inéditos o muy raros para la historia de México* (México: N.P., 1905).

Calderón Hinojosa, Felipe. *Intervención del Presidente de la Republica, Felipe Calderón Hinojosa, durante la visita de supervisión del Programa Paisano* (Nogales: Sonora, 20 Diciembre 2006). http://www.presidencia.gob. mx/2006/12/diversas-intervenciones-durante-la-visita-de-supervision-al-programa-paisano-que-encabezo-el-presidente-de-los-estados-unidos-mexicanos-lic-felipe-calderon/

Carroll, H. Bailey and J. Villasana Haggard. *Three New Mexico Chronicles: The Exposición of Don Pedro Bautista Pino, 1812; the Ojeada of Lic. Antonio Barreiro, 1832; and the additions of Don José Agustín de Escudero, 1849* (Albuquerque: The Quivira Society, 1942).

Chávez Orozco, Luis. *Colección de documentos para la historia del comercio exterior de México, segunda serie II* (México: Publicaciones del Banco Nacional de Comercio Exterior, 1966).

Cortés, José. *Memorias sobre las provincias del norte de nueva España por D. José Cortés, Teniente del cuerpo real de yngenieros* (1799).

Views from the Apache Frontier: Report on the Northern Province of New Spain, edited by Elizabeth A. H. John and translated by John Wheat (Norman: University of Oklahoma Press, 1989).

De la Maza, Francisco F. *Código de Colonización y Terrenos Baldíos de la República Mexicana, formado por Francisco F. De La Maza y Publicado Según el Acuerdo del Presidente de la República, Por Conducta de la Secretaría de Estado y del Despacho de Fomento, Años de 1451 a 1892* (México: Oficina Tipográfica de la Secretaria de Fomento, 1893).

Dublán, Manuel y José María Lozano. *Legislación Mexicana o Colección Completa de las Disposiciones Legislativas Expedidas desde la Independencia de la Republica, Ordenada por los Licenciados Manuel Dublán y José María Lozano, Edición Oficial* (México: Imprenta de Comercio, a Carga de Dublán y Lozano, hijos, 1876).

Gadsden, James, Manuel Diez de Bonilla, José Salazar Ylabegui, and J. Mariano Monterde. *Gadsden Purchase Treaty*, December 30, 1853.

Herrera, José Joaquín de. *Colonias militares, proyectos para su establecimiento en las fronteras del oriente y occidente de la república* (México, 1848).

Inconvenientes de una colonización indiscreta, o sea la impugnación al establecimiento de la libertad de cultos en la Republica Mexicana por F.F.C. (Oaxaca: Impreso por Ignacio Rincón, México, 1848).

Islas, Jesús. *Situación de los habitantes Ispano-Americanos en el Estado de Alta California, 26 Junio 1855* (Puerto de Mazatlán: Imprenta de Rafael Carreon, 1855).

Jenkins, John S. *History of the War between the United States and Mexico* (New York, 1850).

Law Olmsted, Frederick. *A Journey Through Texas, or, a Saddle-Trip on the Southwestern Frontier; with a Statistical Appendix* (New York: Dix, Edwards & Co., 1857).

Llanos y Alcaráz, Adolfo. *No vengáis á América; libro dedicado al pueblo Europeo* (México: Imprenta de la "Colonia Española" de Adolfo Llanos, 1876).

Madero, Francisco I. *La sucesión presidencial en 1910. El partido nacional democrático* (San Pedro, Coahuila, 1908).

México. *Junta Provisional Gubernativa, Comisión de Relaciones Exteriores. Dictámenes Números 1 y 2. Naciones Bárbaras de las Indias. Anglo-Americanos. Dictamen Presentado a la Soberana Junta Gubernativa del Imperio Mexicano por la Comisión de Relaciones Exteriores en 29 de Diciembre de 1821, Primero de Independencia* (México: Biblioteca Aportación Histórica, reprinted 1944).

Proyectos de Colonización presentados por la junta directiva del ramo, al Ministerio de Relaciones de la Republica Mexicana en 5 de Julio de 1848 (México: Imprenta de Vicente García Torres, 1848).

Memoria del Ministro de Relaciones Interiores y Esteriores, D. Luis G. Cuevas, leída en la Cámara de Diputados el 5 y en la de Senadores el 8 de Enero de 1849 (México: Imprenta de Vicente García Torres, Ex-Convento del Espíritu Santo, 1849).

Memoria del Ministro de Relaciones Interiores y Esteriores, leída al Congreso General en Enero de 1850 (México: Imprenta de Vicente García Torres, 1850).

Memoria del Ministro de Relaciones Interiores y Esteriores Leída en las Cámaras en 1851 (México: Imprenta de Vicente García Torres, 1851).

Memoria del Secretaría del Estado y del Despacho de Guerra y Marina Leída en la Cámara de Diputados el 3, y en la de Senadores el 4 de Enero de 1851 (México: Imprenta de Vicente García Torres, 1851).

Memoria del Secretaría del Estado y del Despacho de Guerra y Marina Leída en la Cámara de Diputados el 30 y 31 de Enero y en la de Senadores el 13 de Febrero (México: Imprenta de Vicente García Torres, 1852).

Diario de los Debates de la Cámara de Diputados, undécima legislatura constitucional de la unión. Tomo III. Correspondiente á las sesiones ordinarias y extraordinarias durante el primer periodo del segundo año (México: Imprenta de G. Horcasitas, 1883).

Memoria Presentada al Congreso de la Unión por el Secretario de Estado y del Despacho de Fomento, Colonización, Industria y Comercio de la República Mexicana. General Carlos Pacheco Corresponde á los años Trascurridos de Diciembre de 1877 á Diciembre de 1882, 3 vols. (México: Oficina Tipográfica de la Secretaría de Fomento, 1885).

Memoria Presentada al Congreso de la Unión por el Secretario de Estado y del Despacho de Fomento, Colonización, Industria y Comercio de la República

Mexicana. *General Carlos Pacheco Corresponde á los años Trascurridos de Enero de 1883 á Junio de 1885*, 5 vols (México: Oficina Tipográfica de la Secretaría de Fomento, 1887).

Diario de los Debates de la Cámara de Senadores Decimocuarto Congreso Constitucional, Primero y Segundo Periodos (México: Imprenta de Gobierno Federal, en el ex-Arzobispado, 1889).

Mier y Terán, Maneul. *Texas by Terán: The Diary Kept by General Manuel Mier y Terán on his 1828 Inspection of Texas*, edited by Jack Jackson and translated by John Wheat (Austin: University of Texas Press, 2000).

Moyano Pahissa, Ángela. *Protección Consular a Mexicanos en los Estados Unidos, 1849–1900* (México: Archivo Histórico Diplomático Mexicano, Secretaria de Relaciones Exteriores, 1989).

Ortiz de Ayala, Simón Tadeo. *Resumen de la estadística del imperio mexicano, 1822: estudio preliminar, revisión de texto, notas y anexos de Tarsicio García Díaz* (México: Biblioteca Nacional, Universidad Autónoma de México, Reimprimido 1968).

Paredes, Mariano. *Proyectos de leyes sobre colonización y comercio en el estado de Sonora, presentados a la Cámara de Diputados por el representante de aquel estado, en la sesión de extraordinaria de día 16 de Agosto de 1850* (México, DF: Ignacio Cumplido, 1850).

Peña y Reyes, Antonio, ed. *Algunos documentos sobre el tratado de Guadalupe y la situación de México durante la invasión Americana* (México, 1930).

Pimentel, Francisco. *Memoria sobre las causas que han originado la situación actual de la raza indígena de México, y medios de remediarla, por Don Francisco Pimentel, A S.M.I. Maximiliano Primero, Emperador de Mexico, en prueba de amor y respeto* (México: Imprenta de Andrade y Escalante, 1864).

Ramírez, José Fernando. *El nuevo Bernal Díaz del Castillo o sea historia de la invasión de los Anglo-Americanos en México*, 2 vols. (México, DF: Imprente de Vicente García Torres, 1847).

Romero, Matías. *Mexico and the United States: A Study of Subjects affecting their Political, Commercial, and Social Relations, Made with a View to Their Promotion*, 2 vols. (New York: The Knickerbocker Press, 1898).

Secretaría de Gobernación y Gobierno del Estado de Chihuahua. *Los Municipios de Chihuahua.* (México: Secretaría de Gobernación y Gobierno del Estado de Chihuahua, 1988).

United States Congress, House of Representatives. *Contested Election – New Mexico. February 24, 1854, Memorial of William Carr Lane, Contesting the Right of José Manuel Gallegos*, 33rd Congress, 1st Session, Report No. 121.

Contested Election – New Mexico. Memorial of Miguel A. Otero Contesting the Seat of Hon. José Manuel Gallegos, as Delegate from the Territory of New Mexico, 14 February 1856, 34th Congress, 1st Session, Miscellaneous Document No. 5.

Chávez VS. Cleaver. Papers in the Case of J. Francisco Chávez vs. Charles P. Cleaver, of New Mexico, 24 June 1868, 40th Congress, 2nd Session, Miscellaneous Document No. 154.

Chávez VS. Cleaver. Additional Papers in the Case of J. Francisco Chávez Against Charles P. Cleaver, of New Mexico, 25 July 1868, 40th Congress, 3rd Session, Miscellaneous Document No. 14.

Wallace, Ernest, David M. Vigness, and George B. Ward. *Documents of Texas History, 2nd Ed.* (Austin, TX: State House Press, 1994).

UNPUBLISHED DISSERTATIONS, THESES, AND PAPERS

Aguila, Jaime R. *Protecting "México de Afuera": Mexican Emigration Policy, 1876–1928* (Ph.D. Dissertation, Department of History, Arizona State University, 2000).

Alanis Encino, Fernando Saúl. *El gobierno de México y la repatriación de mexicanos en Estados Unidos, 1934–1940* (Ph.D. Dissertation, El Colegio de México, 2000).

Berninger, George Dieter. *Mexican Attitudes Towards Immigration, 1821–1857,* (Ph.D. Dissertation, Department of History, University of Wisconsin, 1972).

Burden, David K. *La idea salvadora: Immigration and Colonization Politics in México, 1821–1857* (Ph.D. Dissertation, Department of History, University of California, Santa Barbara, 2005).

Gamio, Manuel. "The Influence of Migrations in Mexican Life" (unpublished paper, circa 1931).

Hernández, José Angel. *El México Perdido, El México Olvidado, y El México de Afuera: A History of Mexican American Colonization, 1836–1892* (Ph.D. Dissertation, Department of History, The University of Chicago, 2008).

Martinez, Patricia. *'Noble' Tlaxcalans: Race and Ethnicity in Northeastern New Spain, 1770–1810* (Ph.D. Dissertation, The University of Texas at Austin, 2004).

Morton Ganaway, Loomis. "New Mexico and the Sectional Controversy, 1846–1861," PhD Dissertation republished in *The Historical Society of New Mexico XII* (March 1944).

Pozo Marrero, Acalia. "Dos Movimientos Populares en el Noroeste de Chihuahua: Tomochic y La Ascensión, 1891–1892" (Tesis de Maestría, Universidad Iberoamericana, 1991).

Ramírez Tafoya, Ramón. "La Tenencia de la Tierra en La Ascensión." (unpublished essay, 2003–5).

"Fundación de La Ascensión, Chihuahua." (unpublished essay, June 22, 2004).

Reynolds McKay, Robert. *"Texas Mexican Repatriation during the Great Depression,"* (Ph.D. Dissertation, University of Oklahoma, 1982).

Sisneros, Samuel E. *Los Emigrantes Nuevomexicanos: The 1849 Repatriation to Guadalupe and San Ignacio, Chihuahua, Mexico* (M.A. Thesis, Department of History, University of Texas, El Paso, 2001).

Watkins, Lucy Rebecca. *Mexican Colonization on the United States Border, 1848–1858* (M.L. Thesis, University of California, Berkeley, 1912).

SECONDARY SOURCES

Aboites Aguilar, Luis. *Norte precario: poblamiento y colonización en México, 1760–1940* (México: El Colegio de México, Centro de Estudios Históricos: Centro de Investigaciones y Estudios Superiores en Antropología Social, 1995).

Acuña, Rodolfo. *Occupied America: A History of Chicanos*, 4th Ed. (New York: Longman, 2000).

Alanís Enciso, Fernando S. "Los extranjeros en México, la inmigración y el gobierno: ¿Tolerancia o intolerancia religiosa? 1821–1830," *Historia Mexicana XLV*: 3 (1996): 539–66.

Alanís Enciso, Fernando S.. "No cuenten conmigo: La pólitica de repatriación del gobierno mexicano y sus nacionales en Estados Unidos, 1910–1928," *Mexican Studies/Estudios Mexicanos 19;2* (Summer 2003): 401–61.

Almada, Francisco. *La revolución en el estado de Chihuahua, 2 vols.* (Chihuahua: Patronato del Instituto Nacional Estudios Históricos de la Revolución Mexicana, 1964–1965).

Almaguer, Tomás. *Racial Fault-Lines: The Historical Origins of White Supremacy in California* (Berkeley: University of California Press, 1994).

Alonso, Ana María. *Thread of Blood: Colonialism, Revolution, and Gender on Mexico's Northern Frontier* (Tucson: University of Arizona Press, 1995).

Alonzo, Armando. *Tejano Legacy: Rancheros and Settlers in South Texas, 1734–1900* (Albuquerque: University of New Mexico Press, 1998).

Amin, Shahid. *Event, Metaphor, Memory: Chauri Chaura, 1922–1992* (Berkeley: University of California Press, 1995).

Andrews, George Reid. *Blacks and Whites in São Paolo, Brazil, 1888–1988* (Madison: The University of Wisconsin Press, 1991).

Appadurai, Arjun. *Fear of Small Numbers: An Essay on the Geography of Anger* (Durham: Duke University Press, 2006).

Augusto dos Santos, Sales. "The Historical Roots of the Whitening of Brazil," *Latin American Perspectives 29*(1) (January 2002): 61–82.

Balderrama, Francisco E. *In Defense of La Raza: The Los Angeles Consulate and the Mexican Community, 1929–1936* (Tucson: University of Arizona Press, 1982).

Balderrama Francisco E. and Raymond Rodríguez. *Decade of Betrayal: Mexican Repatriation in the 1930s* (Albuquerque: University of New Mexico Press, 2006).

Baldwin, Percy M. "A Short History of the Mesilla Valley," *New Mexico Historical Review* 13 (1938): 314–24.

Barker, Eugene C. *Handbook of Texas Online*, "National Colonization Law," http://www.tshaonline.org/handbook/online/articles/ugmo1

Barker, Nancy N. "The French Colony in México, 1821–1861," *French Historical Studies* 9(4) (Fall 1976): 596–618.

Barrera, Mario. *Race and Class in the Southwest: A Theory of Racial Inequality* (Notre Dame: The University of Notre Dame Press, 1979).

Bartra, Roger. *Blood, Ink, and Culture: Miseries and Splendors of the Post-Mexican Condition* (Durham: Duke University Press, 2002).

Behdad, Ali. *A Forgetful Nation: On Immigration and Cultural Identity in the United States* (Durham: Duke University Press, 2005).

Benjamin, Thomas. "Recent Historiography of the Origins of the Mexican War," *New Mexico Historical Review* 54(3) (1979): 169–81.

Berninger, George Dieter. "Immigration and Religious Toleration: A Mexican Dilemma, 1821–1860," *The Americas* 32(4) (April 1976): 549–65.

Bishop, Curtis. *Handbook of Texas Online*, "The Law of April 6, 1830," http://www.tshaonline.org/handbook/online/articles/LL/ngl1.html

Buchanan, Patrick J. *The Death of the West: How Dying Populations and Immigrant Invasions Imperil Our Country and Civilization* (New York: St. Martin's Press, 2002).

Bucheneau, Jürgen. "Small Numbers, Great Impact: Mexico and Its Immigrants, 1821–1973," *Journal of American Ethnic History* (Spring 2001): 23–49.

Bulmer-Thomas, Victor. *The Economic History of Latin America Since Independence*, 2nd Edition (Cambridge: Cambridge University Press, 2003).

Burkholder, Mark A. and Lyman L. Johnson. *Colonial Latin America*, 5th Ed. (New York: Oxford University Press, 2004).

Cajen Frietze, Lionel. *History of La Mesilla and Her Mesilleros*, Written and Compiled by a Native Mesillero, aka Joe Lee Frietze, 2nd Ed. (El Paso, TX: Book Publishers of El Paso, 2004).

Cárdenas, Enrique. "A Macroeconomic Interpretation of Nineteenth Century Mexico," in *How Latin America Fell Behind*, edited by Stephen Haber (Stanford: Stanford University Press, 1997): 65–92.

Carreras de Velasco, Mercedes. *Los mexicanos que devolvió la crisis, 1929–1932* (Tlatelolco, México: Secretaría de Relaciones Exteriores, 1974).

Carrigan, William D. *The Making of a Lynching Culture: Violence and Vigilantism in Central Texas, 1836–1916* (Urbana: University of Illinois Press, 2004).

Castillo Crimm, Ana Carolina. *De León: A Tejano Family History* (Austin: The University of Texas Press, 2003).

Ceballos Ramírez, Manuel. "Consecuencias de la guerra entre México y Estado Unidos: la traslación de mexicanos y la fundación de Nuevo Laredo," en *Nuestra Frontera Norte*, compiladora Patricia Galeana (México: Archivo General de la Nación, 1997): 39–59.

Chakrabarty, Dipesh. *Provincializing Europe: Postcolonial Thought and Historical Difference* (Princeton: Princeton University Press, 2000).

Chávez Chávez, Jorge. "Retrato del Indio Bárbaro. Proceso de Justificación de la Barbarie de los Indios del Septentrión Mexicano y Formación de la Cultura Norteña," *New México Historical Review* 73(4) (Octubre 1998): 389–424.

Los indios en la formación de la identidad nacional (Ciudad Juárez: Universidad Autónoma de Ciudad Juárez, 2003).

Clayton Anderson, Gary. *The Conquest of Texas: Ethnic Cleansing in the Promised Land, 1820–1875* (Norman: University of Oklahoma Press, 2005).

Cockcroft, James D. *Outlaws in the Promised Land: Mexican Immigrant Workers and America's Future* (New York: Grove Press, 1986).

Cortés, Enrique. "Mexican Colonies During the Porfiriato." *Aztlán: International Journal of Chicano Studies Research* 10 (Fall 1979): 1–14.

Corwin, Arthur. "Early Mexican Labor Migration: A Frontier Sketch, 1848–1900," chapter 2 in *Immigrants—and Immigrants: Perspectives on Mexican Labor Migration to the United States*, edited by Arthur F. Corwin (Westport: Greenwood Press, 1978): 25–37.

Cotner, Thomas Ewing. *The Military and Political Career of Jose Joaquin de Herrera, 1792–1854* (Austin: University of Texas Press, 1949).

Craib, Raymond. *Cartographic Mexico: A History of State Fixations and Fugitive Landscapes* (Durham: Duke University Press, 2004).

Craig, Ann L. *The First Agraristas: An Oral History of a Mexican Reform Movement* (Berkeley: University of California Press, 1983).

Crosby, Alfred W. *Ecological Imperialism: The Biological Expansion of Europe, 900–1900* (Cambridge: Cambridge University Press, 1986).

Germs, Seeds and Animals: Studies in Ecological History (Armonk, NY: M.E. Sharpe, 1994).

Cue Cánovas, Agustin. *Los Estados Unidos y el México olvidado* (México City: B. Costa-Amic, 1970).

Dawson, Alexander S. "From Models for the Nation to Model Citizens: Indigenismo and the 'Revindication' of the Mexican Indian, 1920–40," *Journal of Latin American Studies* 30;2 (May 1998): 279–308.

De La Garza, Rodolfo O. "Chicanos and U.S. Foreign Policy: The Future of Chicano-Mexican Relations," *The Western Political Quarterly* 33(4) (December 1980): 571–82.

De La Garza, Rodolfo O.. "Demythologizing Chicano-Mexican Relations," *Proceedings of the Academy of Political Science* 34(1) "Mexico-United States Relations" (1980): 88–96.

"Texas Land Grants and Chicano-Mexican Relations: A Case Study," *Latin American Research Review* 21(1) (1986): 123–38.

Mexican Immigrants and Mexican Americans: An Evolving Relation (Austin: CMAS Publications, Center for Mexican American Studies, University of Texas at Austin, 1986).

Mexico, Mexicans, and Mexican-Americans in U.S.-Mexican Relations (Austin: Institute of Latin American Studies, University of Texas at Austin, 1989).

Bridging the Border: Transforming Mexico-U.S. Relations (New York: Rowman & Littlefield Publishers, 1997).

"Interests Not Passions: Mexican-American Attitudes toward Mexico, Immigration from Mexico, and Other Issues Shaping U.S.-Mexico Relations," *International Migration Review* 32(2) (Summer 1998): 401–22.

Latinos and U.S. Foreign Policy: Representing the "Homeland"? (Lanham: Rowman & Littlefield Publishers, 2000).

Looking Backward Moving Forward: Mexican Organizations in the U.S. as Agents of Incorporation and Dissociation (Claremont, CA: Tomas Rivera Policy Institute, 2003).

De León, Arnoldo. *The Tejano Community, 1836–1900* (Albuquerque.: University of New Mexico Press, 1982).

They Called them Greasers: Anglo Attitudes toward Mexicans in Texas, 1821–1900, (Austin: The University of Texas Press, 1983).

"Life for Mexicans in Texas After the 1836 Revolution." In *Major Problems in Mexican American History: Documents and Essays*, edited by Zaragosa Vargas (Boston and New York: Houghton Mifflin Company, 1999): 167–75.

De Vos, Jan. "Una legislación de graves consecuencias: el acarpamiento de tierras baldías en México con el pretexto de colonización, 1821–1910," *Historia Mexicana* 34(1) (Julio-Septiembre 1984): 76–113.

DeLay, Brian. "Independent Indians and the Mexican American War," *The American Historical Review* (February 2007) http://www.historycooperative.org/journals/ahr/112.1/delay.html

War of a Thousand Deserts: Indian Raids and the US-Mexican War (New Haven: Yale University Press, 2008).

Doremus, Anne. "Indigenism, Mestizaje, and National Identity in Mexico during the 1940s and the 1950s," *Mexican Studies/ Estudios Mexicanos* 17(2) (Summer 2001): 375–402.

Duara, Prasenjit. *Rescuing History from the Nation: Questioning Narratives of Modern China* (Chicago: The University of Chicago Press, 1995).

Durand, Jorge. "From Traitors to Heroes: 100 Years of Mexican Migration Policy," *Migration Policy Institute* (March 2004). http://www.migrationinformation.org/Feature/display.cfm?ID=203.

Faulk, Odie B. *Lancers for the King: A Study of the Frontier Military System of Northern New Spain*, With a Translation of the Royal Regulations of

1772, foreword by Kieran McCarty, OFM (Phoenix: Arizona Historical Foundation, 1965).

Faulk, Odie B.. "Projected Mexican Colonies in the Borderlands, 1852," *The Journal of Arizona History* 10 (Summer 1969): 115–28.

Faulk, Odie B. and Joseph A. Stout Jr. *The Mexican War, Changing Interpretations* (Chicago: Sage Books, 1973).

Flores Revuelta, Carlos and Álvaro Canales Santos. *Piedras Negras: Reseña Histórica, Protagonistas,* (Saltillo: Club del Libro Coahuilense, Editora el Dos, 2004).

Florescano, Enrique. "Colonización, ocupación del suelo y "frontera" en el norte de Nueva España, 1521–1750," in *Tierras: Expansión territorial y ocupación del suelo en América (siglos xvi–xix), Ponencias presentadas al IV Congreso Internacional de Historia Económica* (México: El Colegio de México, 1968): 43–76.

Gamio, Manuel. *Mexican Immigration to the United States: A Study of Human Migration and Adjustment,* with a new introduction by John H. Burma (New York: Dover Books, 1971).

Garber, Paul Neff. *The Gadsden Treaty* (Philadelphia: The University of Pennsylvania Press, 1923).

Garcia, Juan Ramon. *Operation Wetback: The Mass Deportation of Mexican Undocumented Workers in 1954* (Westport, Connecticut: Greenwood Press, 1980).

Gómez-Quiñones, Juan. "Mexican Immigration to the United States, 1848–1980: An Overview," chapter 4 in *Chicano Studies: A Multidisciplinary Approach,* edited by Eugene E. García, Francisco A. Lomelí, and Isidro D. Ortíz (New York: Teachers College Press, Columbia University, 1984): 56–78.

"Piedras Contra La Luna, México en Aztlán y Aztlán en México: Chicano-Mexican Relations and the Mexican Consulates, 1900–1920," chapter 26 in *Contemporary Mexico: Papers of the IV International Congress of Mexican History,* edited by James W. Wilkie, Michael C. Meyer, and Edna Monzón de Wilkie (Berkeley: The University of California Press, 1976): 494–527.

Roots of Chicano Politics, 1600–1940 (Albuquerque: University of New Mexico Press, 1994).

González, Gilbert G. and Raul A. Fernández. *A Century of Chicano History: Empire, Nations, and Migration* (New York: Routledge, 2003).

González, Manuel G. *Mexicanos: A History of Mexicans in the United States* (Bloomington: Indiana University Press, 1999).

González de la Vara, Martín. "El traslado de familias de Nuevo México al norte de Chihuahua y la conformación de una región fronteriza, 1848–1854," *Frontera Norte* 6(11) (Enero–Junio 1994): 9–21.

González Navarro, Moisés. *La Política Colonizadora del Porfiriato* (México: Separata de Estudios Históricos Americanos, 1953).

La colonización en México, 1877–1910 (México: 1960).

Los extranjeros en México y los mexicanos en el extranjero, 1821–1970, 3 Vols. (México: El Colegio de México, Centro de Estudios Históricos, 1993).

González-Polo y Acosta, Ignacio. "Ensayo de una bibliografía de la colonización en México durante el siglo XIX," *Boletín del Instituto de Investigaciones Bibliográficas 4* (1960): 179–91

"Colonización e inmigración extranjera durante las primeras décadas del Siglo XIX," *Boletín bibliográfico de la Secretaría de Hacienda y Crédito 412* (México: Departamento de Bibliotecas de la Secretaría de Hacienda y Crédito Público, 1954–1974): 4–7.

Gordillo, Gastón. "Indigenous Struggles and Contested Identities in Argentina: Histories of Invisibilization and Reemergence," *Journal of Latin American Anthropology 8*(3) (2003): 4–30.

Griggs, George. *History of Mesilla Valley or the Gadsden Purchase, Known in Mexico as the Treaty of Mesilla* (Mesilla, NM: Bronson Print Company, 1930).

Gringberg, León and Rebeca Grinberg, M.D. *Psychoanalytic Perspectives on Migration and Exile* (New Haven: Yale University Press, 1989).

Griswold del Castillo, Richard. *The Los Angeles Barrio: A Social History, 1850–1890* (Berkeley: University of California Press, 1979).

The Treaty of Guadalupe Hidalgo: A Legacy of Conflict (Norman: University of Oklahoma Press, 1990).

"The U.S. Mexican War: Contemporary Implications for Mexican American Civil Rights and International Rights," chapter in *Culture and Cultura: Consequences of the Mexican American War, 1846–1848* (Los Angeles: Autry Museum of Western Heritage Press, 1998): 76–85.

"Mexican Intellectuals' Perceptions of Mexican Americans and Chicanos, 1920–present," *Aztlán: A Journal of Chicano Studies 27;2* (Fall 2002): 33–74.

Guha, Ranajit. *Elementary Aspects of Peasant Insurgency in Colonial India* (New Delhi: Oxford University Press, 1983).

Guerin-Gonzales, Camille. *Mexican Workers and the American Dreams: Immigration, Repatriation, and California Farm Labor, 1900–1939* (New Jersey: Rutgers University Press, 1994).

Hammett, A. B. J. *The Empresario: Don Martín de León* (Waco: Texian Press, 1973).

Harstad, Peter T. and Richard W. Resh. "The Causes of the Mexican War: A Note on Changing Interpretations," *Arizona and the West 6*(4) (Winter 1964): 289–302.

Hart, John Mason. "The 1840s Southwestern Mexico Peasants' War: Conflict in Transnational Society," chapter 8 in *Riot, Rebellion, and Revolution: Rural Social Conflict in Mexico*, edited by Friedrich Katz (Princeton: Princeton University Press, 1988): 249–68.

Hatton, Timothy J. and Jeffrey Williamson, "Migration during 1820–1920, the First Global Century," *World Economic and Social Survey* (2004).

Hayworth, John D. *Whatever It Takes: Illegal Immigration, Border Security, and the War on Terror* (Washington, DC: Regnery Pub, 2006).

Hernández, José Angel. "From Conquest to Colonization: *Indios* and Colonization Policies after Mexican Independence," *Mexican Studies/ Estudios Mexicanos 26: 2* (Summer 2010): 285–315.

"Contemporary Deportation Raids and Historical Memory: Mexican Expulsions in the Nineteenth Century," *Aztlán: A Journal of Chicano Studies 52:2* (Fall 2010): 129–33.

Herrera, Carlos R. "New Mexico Resistance to U.S. Occupation during the Mexican American War of 1846–1848," chapter 1 in *The Contested Homeland: A Chicano History of New Mexico*, edited by David R. Maciel and Erlinda González-Berry (Albuquerque: University of New Mexico Press, 2000): 23–42.

Herring, Patricia. "A Plan for the Colonization of Sonora's Northern Frontier: The Paredes Proyectos of 1850," *Journal of Arizona History, 10(2)* (1969): 103–14.

Hinojosa, Federico Allen. *El Mexico de Afuera* (San Antonio: Artes Graficas, 1940).

Hoffman, Abraham. *Unwanted Mexican Americans in the Great Depression: Repatriation Pressures, 1929–1939* (Tucson: University of Arizona Press, 1974).

Holden, Robert. "Priorities of the State in the Survey of the Public Land in Mexico, 1876–1911, *Hispanic American Historical Review 70(4)* (1990): 579–608.

Mexico and the Survey of Public Lands: The Management of Modernization, 1876–1911 (DeKalb: Northern Illinois University Press, 1994).

Holloway, Tom. *Immigrants on the Land: Coffee and Society in São Paulo, 1886– 1934* (University of North Carolina Press, 1980).

Huntington, Samuel P. "The Hispanic Challenge," *Foreign Policy,* (March/ April 2004): 30–45.

Who Are We?: The Challenges to America's National Identity (New York: Simon & Schuster, 2004).

Iskander, Natasha. *Creative State: Forty Years of Migration and Development Policy in Morocco and Mexico* (Ithaca and London: Cornell University Press, 2010).

Joseph, Gilbert and Timothy J. Henderson eds, *The Mexico Reader: History, Culture, Politics,* (Durham: Duke University Press, 2002).

Kanstroom, Daniel. *Deportation Nation: Outsiders in American History* (Cambridge: Harvard University Press, 2007).

Katz, Friedrich. *The Secret War in Mexico: Europe, the United States, and the Mexican Revolution* (Chicago: The University of Chicago Press, 1981).

Riot, Rebellion, and Revolution: Rural Social Conflict in Mexico (Princeton: Princeton University Press, 1988).

The Life and Times of Pancho Villa (Stanford: Stanford University Press, 1998).

Katz, Friedrich and Jane-Dale Lloyd, et al. *Porfirio Díaz frente al descontento popular regional, 1891–1893: Antología documental* (México: Universidad Iberoamericana, 1986).

Kelly, Edith Louise and Mattie Austin Hatcher. "Tadeo Ortiz de Ayala and the Colonization of Texas, 1822–1833," *Southwestern Historical Quarterly* 32 (February–April 1929): 74–86.

Koreck, María Teresa. "Space and Revolution in Northeastern Chihuahua," in *Rural Revolt in Mexico: U.S. Intervention and the Domain of Subaltern Politics*, edited by Daniel Nugent (Durham: Duke University Press, 1998).

Kourí, Emilio. *A Pueblo Divided: Business, Property, and Community in Papantla, Mexico* (Stanford: Stanford University Press, 2004).

Landavazo, Marco Antonio. "De la razón moral a la razón de estado: violencia y poder en la insurgencia Mexicana," *Historia Mexicana* LIV (3) (2004): 833–65.

Lang, Aldon S. and Christopher Long. *Handbook of Texas Online*, "Land Grants," http://www.tshaonline.org/handbook/online/articles/LL/mpl1.html

Levinson, Irving W. *Wars within War: Mexican Guerrillas, Domestic Elites, and the United States of America, 1846–1848* (Fort Worth: Texas Christian University Press, 2005).

Lida, Clara E. *Una inmigración privilegiada: comerciantes, empresarios y profesionales españoles en México en los siglos XIX y XX*, compilación de Clara E. Lida (México: Alianza Editorial, 1994).

Lilly, Marjorie. "A Tale of Two Cities: La Mesilla, NM and Ascensión, Mexico," *Desert Winds Magazine* 16(4): 10–17.

Lomnitz, Claudio. *Exits from the Labyrinth: Culture and Ideology in the Mexican National Space* (Berkeley: University of California Press, 1992).

Deep Mexico, Silent Mexico: An Anthropology of Nationalism (Minneapolis: University of Minnesota Press, 2001).

Death and the Idea of Mexico (Cambridge: MIT Press, 2007).

Lloyd Daley, Jane-Dale. *El proceso de modernización capitalista en el noroeste de Chihuahua, 1880–1910* (México: Universidad Iberoamericana, 1987).

"Rancheros and Rebellion: The Case of Northwestern Chihuahua, 1905–1909." In *Rural Revolt in Mexico: U.S. Intervention and the Domain of Subaltern Politics*, edited by Daniel Nugent (Durham: Duke University Press, 1998).

Cinco ensayos sobre cultura material de rancheros y medieros del noroeste de Chihuahua, 1886–1910 (México: Universidad Iberoamericana, 2001).

Lynch, John. *The Spanish American Revolutions, 1808–1826* (New York: W.W. Norton & Company, 1973).

Maciel, David R. *El México olvidado: la historia del pueblo Chicano*, 2 tomos (Ciudad Juárez/El Paso: Universidad Autónoma de Ciudad Juárez and University of Texas at El Paso, 1996).

Maciel, David R. and Erlinda González-Berry. *The Contested Homeland: A Chicano History of New Mexico* (Albuquerque: University of New Mexico Press, 2000).

Martínez Montiel, Luz María. *Inmigración y diversidad cultural en México: una propuesta metodológica para su estudio* (México: Universidad Autónoma de México, 2005).

May, Robert E. *Manifest Destiny's Underworld: Filibustering in Antebellum America* (Chapel Hill: University of North Carolina Press, 2002).

McKay, Robert. "Mexican Americans and Repatriation," *The Handbook of Texas Online.* http://www.tshaonline.org/handbook/online/articles/MM/pqmyk.html

McKeown, Adam. "Global Migration, 1846–1940," *Journal of World History,* 15(2) (June 2004): 155–89.

McKinley Jr., James C. "Mexican President Assails U.S. Measures on Migrants," *New York Times,* September 3, 2007.

Medrano, Lourdes. "New President of Mexico Praises Accomplishments of Expatriates," *The Arizona Daily Star,* December 21, 2006, http://www.highbeam.com/doc/1P2-27043074.html

Miller Puckett, Fidelia. "Ramón Ortiz: Priest and Patriot," *New Mexico Historical Review* XXV (4) (October 1950): 265–95.

Milton Nance, Joseph. *Attack and Counter-Attack: The Texas-Mexican Frontier, 1842* (Austin: University of Texas Press, 1964).

Mindiola Jr., Tatcho and Max Martínez. *Chicano-Mexicano Relations* (Houston: Center for Mexican American Studies, The University of Houston Press, 1986, 1992).

Montejano, David. *Anglos and Mexicans in the Making of Texas, 1836–1986* (Austin: The University of Texas Press, 1987).

Montgomery, Charles. *The Spanish Redemption: Heritage, Power, and Loss on New Mexico's Upper Rio Grande* (Berkeley: University of California Press, 2002).

Moorehead, Max. *The Presidio: Bastion of the Spanish Borderlands,* with a foreword by David J. Weber (Norman: University of Oklahoma Press, 1975).

Mora-Torres, Juan. *The Making of the Mexican Border: The State, Capitalism, and Society in Nuevo León, 1848–1910* (Austin: University of Texas Press, 2001).

Mörner, Magnus. *Adventurers and Proletarians: The Story of Migrants in Latin America* (Pittsburgh: University of Pittsburgh Press and UNESCO, 1985).

Moya, José C. *Cousins and Strangers: Spanish Immigrants in Buenos Aires, 1850–1930* (Berkeley: University California Press, 1998).

"A Continent of Immigrants: Postcolonial Shifts in the Western Hemisphere," *Hispanic American Historical Review* 86(1) (February 2006): 1–28.

Nackman, Mark E. "Anglo American Migrants to the West: Men of Broken Fortunes? The Case of Texas, 1821–1846," *The Western Historical Quarterly* 5(4) (October 1974): 441–55.

Nazzari, Muriel. "Vanishing Indians: The Social Construction of Race in Colonial Sao Paulo," *The Americas* 57(4) (April 2001): 497–524.

Nieto-Phillips, John M. *The Language of Blood: The Making of Spanish-American Identity in New Mexico, 1880s-1930s* (Albuquerque: University of New Mexico Press, 2004).

Nietzsche, Friedrich. *The Use and Abuse of History (1878)*, translated by Adrian Collins (New York: Macmillan Publishing, 1957).

Novick, Peter. *The Holocaust in American Life* (Boston: Houghton Mifflin, 1999).

Nugent, Daniel. *Spent Cartridges of Revolution: An Anthropological History of Namiquipa, Chihuahua* (Chicago: The University of Chicago Press, 1993).

Nunn, Charles F. *Foreign Immigrants in Early Bourbon Mexico, 1700–1760* (Cambridge: Cambridge University Press, 1979).

Ocampo, Javier. "El entusiasmo, expresión espontánea ante el triunfo," capitulo I en *Las ideas de un día; el pueblo mexicano ante la consumación de su independencia* (México: Colegio de México, 1969), 13–45.

Ochoa, John A. *The Uses of Failure in Mexican Literature and Identity* (Austin: University of Texas Press, 2004).

Ong Hing, Bill. *Defining America through Immigration Policy* (Philadelphia: Temple University Press, 2004).

Page Hood, Margaret. "Bells of Old Mesilla," *New Mexico Magazine* (December 1944).

Paz, Octavio. *The Labyrinth of Solitude and Other Essays* (New York: Grove Press, 1985).

Perrigo, Lynn Irwin. *Hispanos: Historic Leaders in New Mexico* (Santa Fe, NM: Sunstone Press, 1985).

Pfaelzer, Jean. *Driven Out: The Forgotten War Against Chinese Americans* (New York: Random Books, 2007).

Portes, Alejandro and Rubén G. Rumbaut. *Legacies: The Story of the Immigrant Second Generation* (Berkeley: University of California Press and The Russell Sage Foundation, 2001).

Powell, T. G. "Mexican Intellectuals and the Indian Question, 1876–1911," *The Hispanic American Historical Review* 48, No. 1, (February 1968): 19–36.

Prieto, Guillermo. *Viaje á los Estados Unidos, 3 vols.* (México: Imprenta de Dublán y Chávez, 1877–1878).

Quiroz, Anthony. *Claiming Citizenship: Mexican Americans in Victoria, Texas* (College Station: Texas A&M University Press, 2005).

Ramírez Caloca, Jesús. "Ascensión," *Boletín de la Sociedad Chihuahuense de Estudios Históricos* 5(6) (20 Agosto 1944): 245–60.

Ramírez Tafoya, Ramón. *De la Mesilla a La Ascensión* (Ciudad Chihuahua: Instituto Chihuahuense de Cultura, 2009).

Ramos, Raúl. *Beyond the Alamo: Forging Mexican Ethnicity in San Antonio, 1821–1861* (Chapel Hill: University of North Carolina Press, 2008).

Rebert, Paula. *La Gran Linea: Mapping the United States-Mexico Boundary, 1849–1857* (Austin: University of Texas Press, 2005).

Reisler, Mark. *By the Sweat of Their Brow: Mexican Immigrant Labor in the United States, 1900–1940* (Westport, CT: Greenwood Press, 1976).

Reséndez, Andrés. "National Identity on a Shifting Border: Texas and New Mexico in the Age of Transition, 1821–1848," *The Journal of American History* 86(2) *Rethinking History and the Nation-State: Mexico and the United States as a Case Study: A Special Issue*: 668–88.

   Changing National Identities at the Frontier: Texas and New Mexico, 1800–1850 (Cambridge: Cambridge University Press, 2004).

Richmond, Douglas W. "Confrontation and Reconciliation: Mexicans and Spaniards During the Mexican Revolution, 1910–1920," *The Americas* 41(2) (October 1984): 215–28.

Ríos-Bustamante, Antonio José. *Regions of La Raza: Changing Interpretations of Mexican American Regional History and Culture* (Encino, CA: Floricanto Press, 1993).

Rodríguez, Richard. "Prodigal Father—Mexico's Change of Heart Towards Mexican Americans," *Pacific News Service*, December 6, 2000, http://news.newamericamedia.org/news/view_article.html?article_id=606b1f54 6a0082ae03a9b274acade552

Rodríguez Nieto, Sandra. "Falla México en proteger a migrantes," *El Diario de Ciudad Juárez*, 01 Septiembre 2007.

Rodríguez O., Jaime E., and Colin M. MacLachlan. *Forging of the Cosmic Race: A Reinterpretation of Colonial México, Expanded Edition* (Los Angeles: University of California Press, 1990).

Romo, David Dorado. *Ringside Seat to a Revolution: An Underground Cultural History of El Paso and Juarez, 1893–1923* (El Paso: Cinco Puntos Press, 2005).

Rush, Erik. *Annexing Mexico: Solving the Border Problem Through Annexation and Assimilation*, (Jamul, CA: Level 4 Press, 2007).

Ruiz, Ramón Eduardo, ed. *The Mexican War: Was it Manifest Destiny?* (Hinsdale, IL: The Dryden Press, 1963).

Ruiz de Gordejuela Urquijo, Jesús. *La expulsion de los españoles de México y su destino incierto, 1821–1836* (Sevilla: Consejo Superior de Investigaciones Científicas; Escuela de Estudios Hispano Americanos, 2006).

Salvucci, Richard J. *Politics, Markets, and Mexico's 'London Debt,' 1823–1887* (Cambridge: Cambridge University Press, 2009).

Sánchez, George J. *Becoming Mexican American: Ethnicity, Culture, and Identity in Chicano Los Angeles, 1900–1945* (New York: Oxford University Press, 1995).

Sánchez, Rosaura. *Chicano Discourse: Socio-Historical Perspectives* (Houston: Arte Público Press, University of Houston, 1994 co. 1983).

Santoni, Pedro. "A Fear of the People: The Civic Militia of Mexico in 1845," *The Hispanic American Historical Review*, 68(2) (May, 1988): 269–88.

Sayad, Abdelmalek. *The Suffering of the Immigrant* (Cambridge: Polity Press, 1999).

Schober, Otto. "Breve historia de Piedras Negras," http://www.piedrasnegras.gob.mx/contenido005/conoce-pn/historia/.

Schulman, Sam. "Juan Bautista Alberdi and his Influence on Immigration Policy in the Argentine Constitution of 1853," *The Americas* 5;1 (July 1948): 3–17.

Senkewicz S. J., Robert M. *Vigilantes in Gold Rush San Francisco* (Stanford: Stanford University Press, 1985).

Sewell, William H. *Logics of History: Social Theory and Social Transformation* (Chicago: The University of Chicago Press, 2005).

Solberg, Carl. *Immigration and Nationalism, Argentina and Chile, 1890–1914* (Austin: University of Texas Press, 1970).

Sims, Harold Dana. *Descolonizacion en Mexico: El conflicto entre mexicanos y españoles (1821–1831)* (México: Fondo de la Cultura Económica, 1982).

    The Expulsion of Mexico's Spaniards, 1821–1836 (Pittsburgh: University of Pittsburgh Press, 1990).

Skirius, John. "Vasconcelos and México de Afuera (1928)," *Aztlán: A Journal of Chicano Studies* 7(3) (Fall 1976): 479–97.

Stabb, Martin S. "Indigenism and Racism in Mexican Thought: 1857–1911," *Journal of Inter-American Studies* 1, No. 4, (October 1959): 405–23.

Standart, M. Colette. "The Sonoran Migration to California, 1848–1856: A Study in Prejudice," *Southern California Quarterly* LVIII (3) (Fall 1976): 333–57.

Steward, Luther N. "Spanish Journalism in Mexico, 1867–1879," *The Hispanic American Historical Review*, 45(3) (August 1965): 422–33.

Stout, Joseph. *The Liberators: Filibustering Expeditions into Mexico, 1848–1862 and the Last Thrust of Manifest Destiny* (Los Angeles: Westernlore Press, 1973).

    Schemers and Dreamers: Filibustering in Mexico, 1848–1912 (Fort Worth, TX: Texas Christian University Press, 2002).

Sweet Henson, Margaret. *Handbook of Texas Online*, "Anglo American Colonization," http://www.tshaonline.org/handbook/online/articles/AA/uma1.html.

Tancredo, Tom. *In Mortal Danger: The Battle for America's Border and Security* (Nashville: WND Books, 2006).

Taylor, Paul S. *An American-Mexican Frontier: Nueces County, Texas* (Chapel Hill: The University of North Carolina Press, 1934).

Taylor, William B. *Drinking, Homicide and Rebellion in Colonial Mexican Villages* (Stanford: Stanford University Press, 1976).

Taylor, Mary Daniels and Nona Barrick. "The Mesilla Guard, 1851–1861," *Southwestern Studies, Monograph No. 51* (El Paso, TX: Texas Western Press, 1976).

Taylor, Mary Daniels. *A Place as Wild as the West Ever Was: Mesilla, New Mexico, 1848–1872* (Las Cruces, New Mexico: New Mexico State University Museum Press, 2004).

Taylor Hansen, Lawrence Douglas. "La repatriación de Mexicanos de 1848 a 1980 y su papel en la colonización de la región fronteriza septentrional de México," *Relaciones 18, no. 69* (1997): 198–212.

Tijerina, Andrés. *Tejano Empire: Life on the South Texas Ranchos* (College Station: Texas A&M University Press, 1998).

Timmons, Wilbert H. "Tadeo Ortiz, Mexican Emissary Extraordinary," *The Hispanic American Historical Review* 51(3) 463–77.

Torres, Patricia, Gabriel Xantomila, Jorge Vega, y Diarios de OEM. "Regatea México apoyo a migrantes," *El Sol de San Luis*, 27 Marzo 2005.

Tucker, Aviezer. *Our Knowledge of the Past: A Philosophy of Historiography* (Cambridge: Cambridge University Press, 2004).

Tyler, Ronnie C. "Fugitive Slaves in Mexico," *The Journal of Negro History* 57(1) (January 1972): 1–12.

Van Young, Eric. *The Other Rebellion: Popular Violence, Ideology, and the Mexican Struggle for Independence, 1810–1821* (Stanford: Stanford University Press, 2001).

Vanderwood, Paul. *The Power of God Against the Guns of Government: Religious Upheaval in Mexico at the Turn of the Nineteenth Century* (Stanford: Stanford University Press, 1998).

Vilas, Carlos M. "(In)justicia por mano propia: linchamientos en México contemporáneo," *Revista Mexicana de Sociología LXIII*(1) (2001): 131–60.

"By their Own Hands: Mass Lynchings in Contemporary Mexico," *Southwestern Journal of Law and Trade in the Americas*, (2001/2002).

"Linchamiento: Venganza, Castigo e Injusticia en Escenarios de Inseguridad," *El Cotidiano* 20; 131, (Universidad Autónoma Metropolitana-Azcapotzalco: Mayo/Junio 2005): 20–6.

Villarreal, Andrés. "The Social Ecology of Rural Violence: Land Scarcity, the Organization of Agricultural Production, and the Presence of the State," *American Journal of Sociology* 110(2) (September 2004): 313–48.

Viñas, David. "The Foundation of the National State," in *The Argentina Reader: History, Culture, Politics*, edited by Gabriela Nouzeilles and Graciela Montaldo (Durham: Duke University Press, 2002): 161–9.

Viotti da Costa, Emilia. *The Brazilian Empire: Myths and Histories* (Chicago: The University of Chicago Press, 1985).

Von Humboldt, Alexander. *Political Essay on the Kingdom of New Spain*, translated by John Black (New York: I. Riley, 1811).

Wallace, Ernest and David M. Vigness, and George B. Ward. *Documents of Texas History, 2nd Edition* (Austin, TX: State House Press, 1994).

Weber, David J. *Foreigners in Their Native Land: Historical Roots of the Mexican Americans*, with a foreword by Ramón Eduardo Ruíz (Albuquerque, NM: University of New Mexico Press, 1973).

El México perdido: ensayos sobre el antiguo norte de México, 1540–1821 (México City: Secretaría de Educación Pública, 1976).

The Mexican Frontier, 1821–1846: The American Southwest Under Mexico (Albuquerque: University of New Mexico Press, 1982).

Bárbaros: Spaniards and Their Savages in the Age of Enlightenment (New Haven & London: Yale University Press, 2005).

Will de Chaparro, Martina. "From Body to Corpse: The Treatment of the Dead in Eighteenth-Century New Mexico," *New Mexico Historical Review* 79 (Winter 2004): 1–29.

Williams, Edward J. "Secularization, Integration and Rationalization: Some Perspectives from Latin American Thought," *Journal of Latin American Studies* 5(2) (November 1973): 199–216.

Wyman, Mark. *Round-Trip to America: The Immigrants Return to Europe, 1880–1930* (Ithaca and London: Cornell University Press, 1993).

Zeta Acosta, Oscar. *The Revolt of the Cockroach People* (San Francisco: Straight Arrow Books, 1973).

Zilli Mánica, José B. "Proyectos liberales de colonización en el siglo XIX." *La palabra y el hombre 52*, (Octubre–Diciembre 1984): 129–42.

Zolberg, Aristide R. *A Nation by Design: Immigration Policy in the Fashioning of America* (Cambridge: Harvard University Press, 2006).

Zorrilla, Luis G. *Historia de las relaciones entre Mexico y los Estados Unidos de América, 1800–1958* (México: Editorial Porrúa, 1977).

Index